CARING ABOUT HEALTH

Presenting a philosophical exploration of the ideas central to health care practice this book explores such concepts as caring, health, disease, suffering and pain from a phenomenological perspective. With deep philosophical insight this book draws out, not only the ethical demands that arise when one encounters these phenomena, but also the forms of ethical education that would help health care workers respond to those demands.

This is a book which explores the grounds for ethical living rather than enunciating ethical principles. Van Hooft argues that ethical responses arise from sensitive and insightful awareness of what is salient in clinical and other health care settings. This book draws upon thinkers from the classical canon, the Anglo-American tradition and from continental philosophical ideas.

ASHGATE STUDIES IN APPLIED ETHICS

Scandals in medical research and practice; physicians unsure how to manage new powers to postpone death and reshape life; business people operating in a world with few borders; damage to the environment; concern with animal welfare – all have prompted an international demand for ethical standards which go beyond matters of personal taste and opinion.

The *Ashgate Studies in Applied Ethics* series presents leading international research on the most topical areas of applied and professional ethics. Focusing on professional, business, environmental, medical and bio-ethics, the series draws from many diverse interdisciplinary perspectives including: philosophical, historical, legal, medical, environmental and sociological. Exploring the intersection of theory and practice, books in this series will prove of particular value to researchers, students, and practitioners worldwide.

Series Editors:

Ruth Chadwick, Director of ESRC Centre for Economic
and Social Aspects of Genomics (CESAGen) and Professor of Bioethics,
Lancaster University, UK
Dr David Lamb, Honorary Reader in Bioethics, University of Birmingham, UK
Professor Michael Davis, Center for the Study of Ethics in the Professions,
Illinois Institute of Technology, USA

Caring About Health

STAN VAN HOOFT
Deakin University, Australia

ASHGATE

Published by
Ashgate Publishing Limited
Gower House
Croft Road
Aldershot
Hants GU11 3HR
England

Ashgate Publishing Company
Suite 420
101 Cherry Street
Burlington
Vermont, 05401–4405
USA

Ashgate website: http://www.ashgate.com

British Library Cataloguing in Publication Data
Hooft, Stan van, 1945–
    Caring About Health. – (Ashgate Studies in Applied Ethics)
    1. Nursing ethics. 2. Caring. I. Title
    174.2

US Library of Congress Cataloging in Publication Data
Hooft, Stan van, 1945–
    Caring About Health / Stan van Hooft.
        p. cm. – (Ashgate Studies in Applied Ethics)
    Includes bibliographical references and index.
    1. Nursing ethics. 2. Caring. I. Title.
    RT85.H67 2005
    174.2–dc22   2005018590

ISBN 0 7546 5358 7

This book is printed on acid-free paper.

Printed and bound in Great Britain by
Antony Rowe Ltd, Chippenham, Wiltshire

Contents

In pain, sorrow, and suffering, we once again find, in a state of purity, the finality that constitutes the tragedy of solitude.[1]

---

[1]   Emmanuel Levinas, 'Time and the Other', in Seán Hand (ed.), *The Levinas Reader* (Oxford, 1989), p. 39.

Preface

The task of philosophy is to understand. Before the advent of modern science it might have thought its task was to explain, but today it seeks to place the central concepts of human life, such as knowledge, beauty, love, self-awareness, the nature of human existence, the demands of morality and the projections of spirituality, into the framework of accessibility which constitutes the world-view of a given culture. Of concepts such as these, philosophy asks what they mean and why they matter. If the answers to which it is driven are incomprehensible or in conflict with each other, it might urge revisions and offer critique, but it cannot question all at once the background assumptions which provide the context for understanding. These assumptions are the putative wisdom of a culture and of an age. They provide the barely articulated understanding upon which people base their lives. The task of philosophy is to articulate these assumptions, to urge their coherence and to critique departures from them.

It is often said that it is also a task of philosophy to prescribe how we should act. In particular, this is seen as the task of ethics or of moral philosophy. I think this claim is often overstated. The suggestion that philosophers are moral experts who have the ability or the right to tell us what is right or wrong disregards the importance of individual decision making. In a morally complex situation every individual has to evaluate the situation, discern what is ethically demanding in it, and act as he or she thinks best. While moral philosophy and moral theology may offer guidelines and principles which assist in this, they cannot usurp the responsibility that every individual has for their own actions and for their own insights into what is to be done. But these insights are an expression of the generally held assumptions and understandings which shape us all in our respective cultures. As such, they should be articulated and understood lest the guidance for action which they give us is incoherent or in conflict with our other values. It is here that philosophy has its role in guiding action: not in prescribing norms, but in helping us understand what is at stake.

The related fields of health care ethics, nursing ethics, bioethics and medical ethics have been largely caught up in a prescriptive paradigm. They often see their task in solving the ethical dilemmas which arise in health care and from advances in medical science so as to mandate or permit particular courses of action. My stance is that before any such guidance can be offered, the issues have to be understood. This book gathers together a number of essays that I have written over some fifteen years. They begin with discussions of the aims of, and values inherent in, nursing, and move to exploring the goals of medicine. They explore the nature of caring as a professional stance in health care and how such a stance might be inculcated, and then move on to a discussion of the lived experience of the human body and of the pains and sufferings to which it is subject. At all times the aim is to understand and thereby to deepen awareness and strengthen commitment to act sensitively and virtuously in response to the health needs of others.

Chapter 1 discusses a concept of 'caring' that is frequently cited by writers on nursing and suggests that it is too vague and indiscriminate in what it asks of nurses. The contrasting notion of 'professionalism' is also found wanting in that it makes insufficient allowance for the attitudes proper to nursing practice. In their stead a notion of 'professional commitment' is proposed. Such a commitment is described with reference to its expressions in actions and attitudes rather than to the motivations that enter into making it. The central feature of a nurse's professional commitment is a caring attitude that takes health, rather than the person of the client, as its object.

Chapter 2 questions the Kantian conception of morality that dominates ethical thinking in our society and the rationalist educational strategies that flow from it. In its place it offers an Aristotelian conception of ethics in which sensitivity and feeling are important components of practical reason. It argues that a health care worker's ethical concerns extend further than the bioethical dilemmas discussed in the daily press and that those concerns should be responded to in moral education by a process called 'empowerment'. Empowerment seeks to develop confidence and sensitivity in the making of difficult decisions and does so by training habits, developing attitudes and encouraging reflection on actions performed.

Chapter 3 agrees with the critiques of moral theory offered by such writers as Bernard Williams and Alasdair MacIntyre, and uses ideas from Martin Heidegger and Emmanuel Levinas to argue that caring is a fundamental feature of human existence which takes two forms: caring about oneself (which I call our 'self-project') and caring about others. This dual form of caring is expressed on four levels of human living which are described by Aristotle and which I illustrate with reference to the phenomenon of pain. From this analysis I conclude that those traditional notions of morality that see it as imposing obligations on us should give way to an understanding of ethics as the social forms given to our caring for ourselves and for others. I sketch out a number of implications for ethical theory and draw the conclusion that morality is best understood with reference to the concept of virtue. If I may be permitted to use some technical terms which I will explicate in that chapter, virtue theory suggests that morality is internalist, particularist, pluralist, personalist and objectivist.

A brief description of Helga Kuhse's arguments on the place of caring in moral decision making in her book *Caring: Nurses, Women and Ethics* opens Chapter 4. I challenge Kuhse's position by arguing that she is committed to a position called 'reasons externalism' and to a moderate form of 'motivational externalism'. After explicating these terms I argue that Kuhse compartmentalizes the psychology of moral agency and fails to see caring as the holistic stance towards patients which many nursing theorists have been espousing. I then sketch such a holistic conception and suggest ways of overcoming the difficulties relating to objectivity, to the place of practical reason, and to weakness of will that the new conception raises. This chapter offers a new theory of what caring is in the context of health care.

Chapter 5 challenges Kuhse's view that caring is merely a preparatory stage to moral action and that impartial, principled thinking is required to make action moral. In contrast, I suggest that caring should be thought of as a virtue. If caring is a virtue then acting from that virtue will be acting well. And acting from the virtue of caring involves eight features which include not only that of being sensitive to, and concerned about, the patient, but also that of being aware of, and sensitive to, the relevant ethical principles. In this way caring is seen is an overarching quality which gives action its moral character. The moral character of an action does not derive only from its having been performed in the light of principles.

Chapter 6 is relevant to ethical education. In it I argue that a virtue approach to moral decisions in the clinical setting is more psychologically realistic and theoretically appropriate than a 'principlist' approach. Focusing on virtue allows us to consider a wider range of ethically significant events in the life of a virtuous clinician than an exclusive focus on moral principles. It also allows us to understand that people who act well in everyday life, including virtuous clinicians, have an implicit knowledge expressed through their actions and judgements: a knowledge which I call 'everyday wisdom'. This knowledge and the caring implicit in virtue can hardly be taught, but it can be made explicit, and so deepened and disambiguated. I then describe the method of 'Socratic Dialogue' and illustrate my thesis with a report on a Socratic Dialogue on human dignity in the clinical setting.

If the first part of the book discusses the nature and significance of caring and how it might be inculcated in health care workers, the second part of the book discusses aspects of human life that health care workers should care about.

Chapter 7 begins with the World Health Organization's definition of health and explores the idea that health is a quality of the 'whole person'. This seems to imply that health workers are wrong to focus their attention upon the bodies of their patients. I argue that they are not. I do so first by suggesting that the debate between holists and those who would focus exclusively on the body is misguided because it depends upon an implicit mind–body dualism, and second by arguing that the body is the locus of the full human functioning of the person in social communication and self-definition. This latter argument is mounted in a non-dualist manner. I also briefly draw some implications for the practice of health care.

Chapter 8 is an exploration of health as a state of subjectivity rather than as an observable condition of the body. I analyse subjectivity as involving a pre-intentional, conative dimension distinct from the biological and pragmatic dimensions of living. Using some concepts from Emmanuel Levinas to articulate this conative dimension, I argue that what Levinas describes as 'love of life' – an inchoate feeling that the living of life is enjoyment and nourishment – is the pre-articulated experience of health. Health in this sense is when things go well with us in the conative mode of our subjectivity. Moreover, health in this sense is foundational to our very being as subjectivity. A professional concern for health must be sensitive to all of the modes of subjectivity in which health is experienced.

The philosophical attempt to understand the nature of disease has yielded a great deal of fascinating literature. One theory has it that 'disease' is a value–free concept which describes a particular state of the body in objective terms. The disvalue that is widely attached to disease is merely our subjective reaction to it. In Chapter 9, I argue against this position by adopting a teleological conception of human life and showing that disease is inherently a disvalue because it is a frustration of the inherent purposes of our being. In putting this argument forward I offer a further and fuller elaboration of the Aristotelian model of human existence which informs many of the chapters in this book.

Taking as its starting point a recent statement of the Goals of Medicine published by the Hastings Center, Chapter 10 argues against the dualistic distinction between pain and suffering. In it I suggest that malady, pain and disablement are objective forms of suffering not dependent upon any state of consciousness of the victim. As a result, medicine effectively relieves suffering when it cures malady and relieves pain. This implies that there is no distinct medical mission to confront the spiritual condition of the patient. Central to this chapter is the claim that our conceptions of suffering and pain are often vitiated by dualistic ways of thinking. For example, Eric Cassell's definition of suffering implies that it is a psychological accompaniment to pain. The chapter challenges this approach by applying my Aristotelian conception of the human person and defining suffering as the frustration of the internal tendencies of all aspects of the person. In this way suffering can be seen as an objective condition irrespective of the mental states of the victim. Further, on this conception, suffering can be attributed to animals and other organisms.

It is frequently said that pain is incommunicable and even that it 'destroys language'. It renders us mute and locks us into a non-communicative and isolated stance. Chapter 11 offers a phenomenological account of pain and then explores and critiques this view. It suggests not only that pain is communicable to an adequate degree for clinical purposes, but also that it is itself a form of communication through which the person in pain appeals to the empathy and ethical goodness of the clinician. To explain this latter idea and its ethical implications, I make further reference to the writings of Emmanuel Levinas.

Chapter 12 returns to my exploration of the nature of suffering but approaches it as a spiritual phenomenon. I argue that Western thinkers have usually falsified our experience of suffering in trying to make sense of it. They have tried to see it as part of a greater plan for us, whether that plan be understood in theological, mythical or secular terms. In a postmodern age, however, these accounts seem implausible. We need a way of making sense of suffering while admitting its horror. We need a tragic view of the exigencies of life and yet also one which motivates us to care about the suffering of others.

This book is unified by a common set of concerns and a common theoretical framework. The concern of the book is to understand caring in the context of the health professions and to articulate some of the aspects of human life that such caring is about. Such an understanding will motivate ethical and virtuous action in clinical and other health care settings. The common theoretical framework is Aristotle's four-level conception of human existence which I explicate, using various terminologies, in several of the chapters. While there might be some hint of repetition across these chapters, I have decided not to edit them further, believing that the variety of approaches that I have used to articulate Aristotle's model serve to converge my essays upon a viable, compelling and ethically important theory of caring about health.

Acknowledgements

Most of the essays in this book are edited or expanded versions of articles that have been published in journals and are reproduced here with the permission of the journals and publishers listed below. Chapter 1 appeared as 'Caring and Professional Commitment' in *The Australian Journal of Advanced Nursing* 4/4 (June–August, 1987): 29–38. Chapter 2 was published as 'Moral Education for Nursing Decisions' in the *Journal of Advanced Nursing*, 15 (1990): 210–15. Chapter 3 first saw the light of day as 'Bioethics and Caring' in the *Journal of Medical Ethics*, 22/2 (Spring, 1996): 83–9. An earlier version of this chapter was read at a session entitled 'Foundations of Bioethics' at the second International Congress of the International Association for Bioethics in October 1994, in Buenos Aires, Argentina. I am grateful to the editor of JME and to some anonymous reviewers for helpful comments. Chapter 4 appeared under the title 'Kuhse on Caring' in *Nursing Inquiry* 6/2 (1999): 112–22. Chapter 5 was published as 'Acting from the Virtue of Caring in Nursing' in *Nursing Ethics*, 6/3 (1999): 189–201. I am grateful to Leila Shotton who made valuable comments on this chapter and read it on my behalf at the Australian Bioethics Association Conference in October, 1998.

Chapter 8 is a considerably expanded version of an essay that appeared as 'Health and Subjectivity' in *Health*, 1/1 (July 1997): 23–36. Chapter 9 was a chapter in a book. It was entitled 'Disease and Subjectivity' and appeared in James Humber and Robert Almeder (eds), *What is Disease?* (Totowa, New Jersey, 1997), pp. 287–323. This paper was prepared with the assistance of a research grant from the Faculty of Arts at Deakin University, and with the research assistance of Peter Rzechorzek. Chapter 10 combines two essays that were published separately. One was 'The Suffering Body' which appeared in *Health*, 4/2 (April 2000): 179–95, and the other was 'Suffering and the Goals of Medicine' which appeared in *Medicine, Health Care and Philosophy*, 1/2 (1998): 125–31. An earlier version of this chapter was first read at an international conference in Naples co-organised by Istituto Italiano per gli Studi Filosofici and the Hastings Center in June 1997 on 'The Goals of Medicine: Priorities for the Future'. I am grateful for financial support from Deakin University to enable me to attend the conference. Chapter 11 was published in *Medicine, Health Care and Philosophy*, 6/3 (2003): 255–62. The final chapter, 'The Meanings of Suffering', appeared in the *The Hastings Center Report*, 28/5 (September–October, 1998): 13–19.

PART 1
Health Care, Virtue and Education

Chapter 1

Caring and Professional Commitment

A great deal of writing about the professional life of nurses stresses the concept of caring. It has become almost traditional to distinguish the role of the medical practitioner from that of the nurse by saying that the former seeks to cure the patient while the latter cares for him or her. Even though warnings have been sounded that this distinction between caring and curing may be an ideological cover for the historically contingent nurse–doctor distinction,[1] and that it is improperly based on gender distinctions,[2] it seems clear that there is a role for caring in therapy even if the question as to who exercises that role might receive different answers at different times. Equally clearly it seems that it is the nurse who most centrally occupies that role at this historical juncture. In any case it is imperative that there be some degree of clarity as to what is meant by caring, both in general terms and in terms suitable to the context of a nurse's professional life. It will be my contention in this chapter that not enough discrimination has been displayed by many writers on this topic and that the ideal of caring is consequently in danger of becoming an unattainable goal. I shall then propose an alternative way of thinking of the central objectives of a nurse's professional activities.

The notion of caring

I will begin with some quotations in order to indicate how caring is spoken about in the nursing literature. Firstly, here is Simone Roach:

> Nursing is a personal service, a science and an art practised within a relationship, in itself, therapeutic. This ... presupposes a personal commitment which expresses itself in what may be the most intrinsically human of human acts – the act of caring.[3]

---

[1]   Alasdair MacIntyre, 'To Whom is the Nurse Responsible?', in Howard Murphy and Catherine Hunter (eds), *Ethical Problems in the Nurse Patient Relationship* (Boston, Massachusetts, 1983), pp. 78–83.

[2]   Ann Oakley, 'On the Importance of Being a Nurse', in her *Telling the Truth about Jerusalem* (Oxford, 1986), pp. 180–195.

[3]   Simone M. Roach, 'The Act of Caring as Expressed in a Code of Ethics', *Canadian Nurse*, 78/6 (1982): 30–32, p. 36.

Jean Watson offers the following:

> Caring is viewed as the moral ideal of nursing where there is the utmost concern for human dignity and preservation of humanity. Human care can begin when the nurse enters into the life space or phenomenal field of another person, is able to detect the other person's condition of being (spirit, soul), feels this condition within him or herself, and responds to the condition in such a way that the recipient has a release of subjective feelings and thoughts he or she had been longing to release. As such, there is an intersubjective flow between the nurse and patient.[4]

It seems clear that what is being recommended here is a vocation of service to one's fellow human beings and the establishing of a relationship between nurse and patient of some considerable intimacy: one that is marked for the nurse by deep empathy and rapport, and for the patient by a catharsis of pent-up feeling.

Now it might be suggested that these quotations are not typical and should therefore not be taken as representative. The literature contains a variety of views about what caring is, ranging from the sorts of intimacy just alluded to, to a more level-headed application of caring procedures. However, it is striking that whatever the specific proposal might be for what constitutes caring practice, the notion of caring as such is frequently adumbrated with reference to a quite limited set of authors, a set which almost always features Milton Mayeroff and Martin Buber. So we see Barbara Carper,[5] Doris Riemen[6] and Barbara Blattner[7] alluding to the first, while Madeleine Leininger[8] refers to the second and Watson[9] cites both. Even when these authors are not explicitly cited, they frequently appear in the bibliographies of the literature of caring. But what sort of notion of caring emerges from them?

For Mayeroff, caring is defined as helping the other to grow in a full, personal sense, although he makes it clear right at the outset of his text that 'the other' here might include ideas and ideals as well as persons. However, as this notion is applied to nursing (for example, by Blattner) the proper object for the caring relationship becomes the person. For Mayeroff the special features of caring for a

---

[4]   Jean Watson, *Nursing: Human Science and Human Care: A Theory of Nursing* (Norwalk, Connecticut, 1985), p. 63.

[5]   Barbara A. Carper, 'The Ethics of Caring', *Advances in Nursing Sciences*, 1/3, (1979): 11–20.

[6]   Doris J. Riemen, 'The Essential Structure of a Caring Interaction: A Phenomenological Study', PhD thesis, Texas Women's University, (Ann Arbor, Michigan, 1983).

[7]   Barbara Blattner, *Holistic Nursing*, (Englewood Cliffs, New Jersey, 1981).

[8]   Madeleine M. Leininger (ed.), *Care: The Essence of Nursing and Health* (Thorofare, New Jersey, 1984).

[9]   Watson, *Nursing: Human Science and Human Care: A Theory of Nursing*.

person require that: 'I must be able to understand him and his world as if I were inside it.'[10] In developing this idea, Blattner says:

> Caring is the interactive process by which the nurse and client help each other to grow, actualize and transform towards higher levels of well-being. Caring is achieved by a conscious and intuitive opening of self to another, by purposefully trusting and sharing energy, experience, ideas, techniques and knowledge.[11]

It is striking that along with techniques and knowledge, what is being called for here includes 'trusting', 'sharing' and 'opening' of self to another. Mayeroff's own eloquent text calls as well for patience, honesty, humility, hope and courage. While there is no doubt that these are personal motivational qualities that are inherently valuable and therefore valuable in a nursing context, it may be questioned whether they are sufficiently specific to nursing to constitute features of that particular form of care that nurses should evince. After all, shouldn't any sensitive person display such qualities when they enjoy such an intimate relationship as caring for another? There remains a question of how this applies specifically to nursing.

Indeed, there are striking points made by Mayeroff which call into question the suitability of his model for the profession of nursing. For example, he suggests that any person who cannot grow cannot be cared for in his sense.[12] This would rule out a brain-damaged person who does not have the physical requirements for intellectual or emotional development. Yet such a person needs to be looked after. Can we not call the activities engaged in, in the course of looking after such a person, 'caring'? Even if it were answered that a brain-damaged person has some potential for growth, the point could still be made that making the caring relationship dependent upon an ability of the recipient seems to be inappropriate.

Mayeroff[13] goes on to suggest that the caring relationship breaks down if there is a constant replacement of the person being cared for by another; that there is a degree of permanence and irreplaceability involved in the caring relationship. But surely a nurse owes a duty of care to both short-term and long-term patients. Is the quality of care applicable to the former to be poorer because short-term patients are constantly being replaced by new cases? It becomes clear further into Mayeroff's text that the interpersonal relationship of which he speaks is one of greater singularity and intimacy then is appropriate in a nursing situation. For example, he suggests that 'the other for whom I care is a completion of my own being and as such is partially constitutive of my own personal identity. The other for whom I care is so important to me as to constitute an extension of my very self.'[14] However, it seems less than realistic to expect that a nurse, no matter how

---

10   Milton Mayeroff, *On Caring* (New York, 1971), pp. 41–2.
11   Blattner, p. 70.
12   Mayeroff, p. 33.
13   Ibid., p. 34.
14   Ibid., p. 48.

dedicated, should form relationships with patients that are this intimate and self-defining. This is not to deny that part of the nurse's identity is constituted precisely by the activity of caring and by the various attitudes that are intrinsic to those activities. But it would be strange indeed if every person for whom the nurse cares were to enter into the selfhood of the nurse in this way.

Martin Buber[15] for his part has made the now frequently alluded to (but not so frequently understood) distinction between an 'I–It' relationship and an 'I–Thou' relationship. The first of these is instrumental. As an extreme example one might suggest that the upraised hand of a policeman can be related to in precisely the same way as a red stop sign. There is certainly no necessity to relate to the policeman as to a person when one performs the appropriate response: namely, bringing one's car to a halt. It is tempting to read Buber as suggesting that the contrasting 'I–Thou' relationship is properly an interpersonal one. However a careful reading of his text indicated that this is not so. Most interpersonal relationships are of the I–It kind because they involve some degree of objectification of the other. Even lovers relate in ways marked by routine and patterned behaviour and hence of fixed identities, rather than by the quite extraordinary sense of depth and mystery that marks the I–Thou relationship. This latter relationship is very special indeed. It is marked by an encounter with something deep, mysterious and awe-inspiring. Any conceptualising of what this object of the relationship is limits it and turns it into an It. The Thou to which we relate must remain mysterious and transcendental to ordinary experience. Indeed, as his book progresses it becomes ever clearer that Buber is preparing the way for a description of a relationship to an ineffable God.

That there are privileged moments in human relationships in which elements of transcendence shine though and the relationship is transformed briefly into an I–Thou relationship does not obscure the point that, standardly, our relationships to persons are more mundane and ordinary. It is clear also that the sorts of human encounters that allow for this shining through of the ineffable and awe-inspiring mystery of spiritual being are of a quiet intimate and rare kind. While no human meeting prevents the possibility of such an encounter, it can hardly be expected or called for in such formalized relationships as that between nurse and client. Indeed, the final irony attaching to the appeal of so many writers on nursing to Buber's text is that in an afterward to the third edition, Buber himself argues that the I–Thou relationship is not only unlikely to be present in the healer–patient relationship, but ought not to be so.[16]

It would seem that the rare and intimate mutuality of which Mayeroff and Buber speak is more appropriate to a description of the relationship of people in love than to the caring exercised by a nurse. This point has been noticed by Ann Griffin, who distinguishes caring as 'seeing to the needs of x' from caring as

---

[15]   Martin Buber, *I and Thou*, a new translation with a prologue by Walter Kaufmann (Edinburgh, 1970), p. 177.

[16]   Ibid., pp. 177–8.

'being fond of x', where x is a person.[17] We use the term 'care' in both senses. A dutiful daughter who cares for her ageing mother can be said to care for her in either sense. Moreover, she can be said to care for her in the first sense even though she might not care for her in the second. Perhaps caring for someone whom one is not fond of is neither as satisfying nor as satisfactory as caring for someone whom one does care for in that second sense, but clearly the two senses are distinguishable. It seems that caring for someone in the sense of being fond of them involves some feeling of affection which is not necessary merely to see to their needs. Of course it is not explicitly suggested by the authors mentioned above that what nurses need to feel for patients is affection. But they do seem to require some sort of feeling or motivation as an essential component of the practice of caring. For her part Griffin also shows this tendency by suggesting that a satisfactory nursing relationship generates in the nurse a gratitude for the personal expansion of human experience that the practice of caring brings with it, and through this 'a kind of love' for the patient which is different from affection.

Two spiritual or emotional elements which it does seem appropriate to seek in a nurse–patient relationship are compassion and communication. It may seem odd to refer to this last as a spiritual or emotional element, but I do so because communication is facilitated between people who relate to one another with a degree of empathy. As Gabriel Marcel puts it:

> the person who is at my disposal is the one who is capable of being with me with the whole of himself when I am in need; while the one who is not at my disposal seems merely to offer me a temporary loan raised on his resources. For the one I am *presence*; for the other I am an *object*.[18]

To be *present* to someone in this way is to open channels of communication which are not available in more object-like relationships (of which my relationship to the signalling policeman mentioned above is the most extreme example). It seems clear that this being present to the patient is one of the features of a nursing relationship which the authors cited above are after. Sidney Jourard is one author who spells this out in a very sensible way when he urges nurses to come out from behind a professional manner; which is often adopted as 'character armour' in the face of suffering, and open themselves to the possibility of real communication with the patients in their care.[19] Not only is real communication necessary in order to facilitate the flow of information about the patient's condition to the nurse, and the flow of information about treatment and therapeutic activity from the nurse to

---

[17]   Ann P. Griffin, 'A Philosophical Analysis of Caring in Nursing', *Journal of Advanced Nursing*, 8/4 (1983): 289–95.

[18]   Gabriel Marcel, *The Philosophy of Existence*, edited and translated by R.F. Grabow (Philadelphia, 1971), p. 26.

[19]   Sidney M. Jourard, *The Transparent Self* (Princeton, New Jersey, 1964), p. 180.

the patient, but it is also clear that the patient's recovery is often enhanced by the feeling of warmth and encouragement that a caring nurse can convey.

The question arises, however, whether these therapeutically necessary levels of communication should or can arise out of the deep spiritual rapport which our authors seem to require, or whether they can arise from more mundane and less intimate forms of interpersonal being such as compassion. The reason that this suggestion strikes a new note in my discussion is that compassion is not based upon a feeling of equality with the patient. Quite the contrary, it requires that the nurse recognizes the illness and suffering of the patient along with her own health and abilities. The feeling of compassion is at least partially based upon recognition of one's own power and good fortune in contrast to the patient. This contrasts with the attitudinal stances advocated by our authors, who in their talk of *mutual* growth and rapport seek to place nurse and patient on an equal footing. While this may be admirable from the point of view of an egalitarian humanism, it flies in the face of the obvious fact that the patient is ill and the nurse is well. The patient is in need while the nurse is there to provide what is needed. To say that it must be an objective of nursing to make the patient a participant in his or her own therapy and to encourage the patient to learn to take independent charge of his or her own health is in no way to deny that the nurse as care-giver stands in a superior position in relation to the patient as care-receiver. Compassion is at once the recognition of this superiority and the wish that equality will be re-established.

I should add that compassion differs from pity on just this last point. Whereas pity is content with the inequality what separates the object of pity from the person who feels pity, compassion seeks to overcome that difference by appropriate beneficent activity. Pity involves condescension whereas compassion seeks to promote equality even as it recognizes inequality.[20]

Compassion may then be a feeling which it is appropriate for a nurse to have. On the other hand, it is important to note that not all of a nurse's activity concerns people who are suffering. Work in health maintenance and education is usually work with healthy people. Is therefore not obvious that compassion needs to be a central emotion in the working lives of all nurses. One might care for someone out of compassion or out of some other emotion, or out of no emotion at all.

One last point needs to be made about caring as it is described by our authors. It is interesting to note just how moralistic the authors we have cited can be. Watson, for example, argues that the 'formation of a Humanistic Altruistic Value System ... [is] ... the first and most basic factor for the science of caring'.[21] It is clear also that the virtues that Mayeroff sees as central to caring constitute an ideal of moral human excellence. It would seem not extravagant to say that calling for 'care' as the central commitment of nurses is calling for a particular moral orientation on the part of nurses. Such a call has a long and not always honourable

---

[20]   Lawrence Blum, 'Compassion', in Amélie Oksenberg Rorty (ed.), *Explaining Emotions* (Berkeley, California, 1980), pp. 507–18.

[21]   Watson, p. 12.

history. The call for nurses to care has often licensed a disregard for proper remuneration and working conditions for nurses on the grounds that moral dedication should override the desire for such worldly rewards. I have no wish to enter this debate, but mention of this matter does serve to introduce what the literature presents as the major antithesis to talk of care as it applies to nurses: namely, the notion of 'professionalism'.

Professionalism and caring

Discussion of professionalism ranges from the high-sounding rhetoric of a Norah Mackenzie, who talks of the nobility and responsibility of the nursing profession,[22] to the somewhat cynical views of one Eike-Henner Kluge, who says that 'if nursing is a profession, then whether or not there is a commitment, caring or motivation is irrelevant so long as the professional activities are competently carried out'.[23] The notion of professionalism that underlies the latter view is one that centres exclusively on the exercise of certain activities informed by a relevant expertise rather than on the motivations or attitudes underlying such exercise.

A profession is often defined as a group of people with a definite set of skills and body of knowledge through the exercise of which it defines itself as socially distant from its 'clients' and by virtue of which it claims autonomy for itself in the ordering and regulating of its activities. According to Peter Nokes it is also important to the self-image of a professional that a person who does not belong to the profession is seen as not only not licensed to engage in that profession's activities but as not even able to cope were he or she to try.[24]

Along with these sociological features a profession will have specific ideals and norms. A professional ethic will be that set of norms and standards of behaviour that relate to the specific skills and activities of the profession. Insofar as the knowledge particular to a profession gives its bearer a degree of power in relation to clients and other sectors of society, there is the need to impose ethical constraints in order to ensure the responsible exercise of that power. This notion of ethics relates only to the exercise of professional activities. It is arguably an application of the norms and standards of morality in general to the activities and responsibilities particular to the profession. Unlike morality in general, however, it does not mandate any specific motivation for the practitioner.

The rhetoric of care described above introduces a degree of complication for nurses. On this view, to care for a patient or a client involves more than exercising particular skills in a responsible way. Indeed, not only is caring something more

---

[22]   Norah Mackenzie, *The Professional Ethic and the Hospital Service* (London, 1971).
[23]   Eike-Henner W. Kluge, 'Nursing, Vocation or Profession', *Canadian Nurse*, 78/2 (1982): 34–6.
[24]   Peter Nokes, *The Professional Task in Welfare Practice* (London, 1967).

than the exercise of professional nursing skills and knowledge; it may even be antipathetic to it. It may be that a nurse who has charge of a busy ward is not able to extend to each and every patient within it the degree of care that our earlier authors were calling for. This will be felt as a dilemma and will raise the question as to whether such professional values as efficiency and such set objectives as the administration of medications are enough to constitute a satisfactory exercise of nursing skills. Nokes has argued from a sociological perspective that the helping professions such as social work, education and nursing frequently suffer from such confusions, which arise from the feeling that to be a member of that profession one ought to have a vocation of a moral kind and be dedicated to the general well-being of one's clients.[25] This then expresses itself as distaste for set objectives and efficiency and in the informal imposition of a moral entrance requirement into the profession: namely, that one should be a caring person or be motivated by a caring attitude.

The main criticism that Nokes offers of this tendency is to argue that the broad moral objectives that the notion of a vocation brings with it are usually unattainable. If the goals of a profession are too high then morale is at risk. As Nokes puts it: 'generalized objectives are in fact ideals, and so typically expressed in absolute terms that they provide the practitioner with an almost certain guarantee of failure'.[26] It will immediately be evident that caring understood in the way described above falls victim to this criticism. If the nurse is to be responsible for the growth of the client as a total person in a holistic sense, or if the nurse has to open with every client a depth of communication that allows for the sharing of the most intimate levels of existence, then the practical professional life of that nurse will become impossible. And this is not just because there will not be time enough. It will not be psychologically possible either. A manageable professional life will need to have limited and attainable goals.

Lest it be thought that this implies that a cold detachment is required for a professional approach in nursing, we should again take note of the very sensible advice offered by Jourard.[27] Although he too allows himself such vague formulations as 'nursing is a special case of loving',[28] the practical guidelines he offers propose a level of communication which is attainable in a therapeutic situation and which strikes at a level of depth and intimacy which is no greater and no less than what is required for that therapeutic situation. He concludes with the advice that: 'sincere attempts to know and understand a patient and help him to be comfortable increase his sense of identity and integrity, and this experience seems to be a factor in healing'.[29] It will still be a matter of professional judgement and experience to strike just the right level of rapport with a client consistent with

---

[25]   Nokes, p. 24.
[26]   Ibid., p. 27.
[27]   Jourard, pp. 180ff.
[28]   Ibid., p. 207.
[29]   Ibid., p. 30.

one's professional responsibilities both to this client and to others. Guidelines for this might be meaningfully sought and formulated, but at least the nurse will not be confronted with an unattainably vague requirement to become responsible for a client's whole life. As George Agich[30] and Winnifred Gustafson[31] have suggested, it may be that one of the roles for professional ethics in nursing is the formulation of just such guidelines.

My own view is that such guidelines will be of less use to working nurses than their own experience and sensitivity. My own metaethical views are Aristotelian in that I regard sensitive judgement in particular circumstances as more important than the formulation or following of general rules. The basis upon which one is able to make such judgements is training and reflection. Clinical experience with more mature colleagues and the time and willingness to discuss one's experiences with others and place one's previous judgements under review will develop in the professional nurse the ethical sensitivity required for striking the right balance in relation to individual clients. Being held in thrall by vague ideals or by a generalized set of ethical norms can only harm this process.

However, with all this said we still need to become clear on the proper place of the notion of care in a description of the professional life of a nurse. We can accept that the mere exercise of caring behaviours without regard to the spirit that these activities are engaged in is not adequate. Therapeutically necessary levels of trust and communication with clients are not likely to be set up by nurses who are no more than coldly efficient in the exercise of their professional duties. But can we require of nurses that they be motivated by care for their clients? Professional ethics do not demand specific motivations of anyone. After all, the life experience of every individual differs and he or she will bring to the decision to engage in a particular profession a variety of motivations. Yet the manner in which nurses exercise the activities of their profession does seem to be of ethical importance and the attitudes of the nurse will be partially constitutive of the manner in which nursing is exercised. It seems to follow that we can require as part of the professional ethics of nursing a proper and suitable attitude. We have already seen that this need not mean that nurses must feel affection for their clients or that they should feel compassion for them. What then is the properly professional attitude of the nurse, and is 'caring' an adequate description of it?

Professional commitment

At this point I should like to introduce a new term, namely 'professional commitment'. What is new in this phrase in the notion of 'commitment'. By

[30] George J. Agich, 'Professionalism and Ethics in Health Care', *Journal of Medicine and Philosophy*, 5/3 (1980): 186–99.

[31] Winnifred Gustafson, 'Motivational and Historical Aspects of Care and Nursing', in Leininger, pp. 61–74.

commitment I understand an existential stance towards a specific good that has significant duration, through which the subject defines him or herself, and in the light of which he or she makes particular choices. Commitment is an ethical category developed in contrast to the more traditional ethical category of 'obligation'. To act in the light of obligation is to act in obedience to a perceived duty. It is to do what one 'ought' to do, where the origin of that 'ought' is standardly taken to be something which exists over and against oneself. The commands of God or the categorical imperatives that are to be deduced from pure reason are traditional examples of such origins. Whereas being under an obligation leads one to say that one 'ought' to do something, being committed leads one to say that one feels that one 'must' do it. While linguistic usage needs not to be completely consistent here, the distinction which I am seeking to draw is between a practical necessity which is imposed upon one, and a practical necessity which one adopts because the matter at hand is important to one and requires an urgent response.[32] When Martin Luther said, 'here I stand; I can do no other', he was not reporting on a literal inability or on a moral prohibition, but on his determination not to back off from his own commitment. He was subject to a practical necessity which was self-imposed.[33] He was committed.

A commitment, then, is understood as an existential stance. It is a relatively fixed orientation on the part of an agent towards a specifiable set of projects and concerns. However, my use of the term 'existential' should not be taken to suggest that this stance has no basis other than an entirely free and undetermined choice. A choice made in such a manner would not be a choice that we would feel beholden to maintain through time. My use of this term is meant to suggest, rather, that a particular person defines him- or herself by the commitment made. It is in this way that a commitment may differ from choice. Whereas a choice may concern an insignificant matter in which one's own sense of oneself is not bound up (such as whether to have an apple or a banana for afternoon tea), a commitment implicates one's deepest self. It does this because it arises from one's deepest self and goes on to constitute that self. All one's hopes, loves, fears, character traits, habits, and skills come to expression in the commitments that one makes.

As well, a commitment differs from a choice in that the temporal scope of the significance of a choice is short. The significance of eating an apple as opposed to a banana is typically confined to the time of the eating and a little time immediately after. When I make a commitment, however, the temporal implications are much broader. It may take only a little time to say 'yes', and it may have taken only a short time to decide to do so, but the temporal implication of saying 'yes' is long indeed when that is an answer to such a question as 'Will you marry me?' This one act or choice will be a commitment because it will set the

---

[32]   Bernard Williams, *Ethics and the Limits of Philosophy* (Glasgow, 1985), Chapter 10.

[33]   Harry Frankfurt, 'The importance of what we care about', *Synthese*, 53/2 (1982): 257–72.

pattern of many of my subsequent choices. I will feel myself bound to such a choice in a way that I am not bound to the choice of an apple for afternoon tea. If it transpires that there are no apples available it will not matter much to me to opt for a banana instead. It will be a matter of great importance to me, however, if circumstances intervene to prevent the fulfilment of a commitment. Nor is it necessary that there be a single significant moment at which a commitment is made. It may be that the particular choices that I make over a period of time display a pattern and a systematic set of concerns which I may not have been aware of until I discover and reflect on that pattern. Nevertheless, this pattern will display my commitment.

But it must be stressed that there is no commitment unless there is such a pattern of choices over time. It will be a difficult matter to specify in general terms whether one or more inconsistent choices from time to time prevent one from saying that the agent had a commitment. We are but human and lapses will occur, although there should be moments of regret in a biography marked by lapses. Nevertheless it does seem clear that if there are a great many lapses, even if there is also regret, we would not be inclined to describe the agent as 'committed'.

It will be noticed that I have not said much about the motivation for commitment other than saying that it arises from or expresses one's character. This is an important point in the light of my earlier claim that a professional ethic does not require us to have specific motivations. Now, while we might be morally required to make certain commitments in certain circumstances, the choice of a career is typically not such a case. We make such a commitment freely and whatever it is that leads us to make it is up to us. However, when a commitment has been made (whether we were required to make or not), we can be required to act and feel in ways consistent with it. A commitment sets up not only expectations which we apply to ourselves, but insofar as a commitment may be public, it sets up expectations which others then have the right to impose upon us. While others may not require us to act from certain feelings or motivations on entering into the commitment, they can expect or require us to act on the basis of our commitment when we have made one, and to adopt the proper attitudes that go with it. The committed person can be expected to alter his or her priorities. As a result of the commitment, certain projects, persons or objectives will become more important than they were before. Indeed, their becoming more important in this way is just what the commitment consists in. In the case of a personal commitment such as marriage, the spouse will become more important then any other person, while in the case of a professional commitment, the objectives and ideals of the profession will acquire a pre-eminent importance.

Given this sketch of what commitment is, what do we mean by professional commitment as it applies to nurses? First, it would seem clear that entering the profession of nursing is a commitment in the sense described. It is a choice with long-term implications for one's life. It is normally a choice that expresses one's identity and constitutes a further definition of that identity on the part of the self. Further, the person committed to nursing will undertake to alter personal priorities to the extent of self-imposing a number of practical necessities. The training of a nurse will reinforce, through the formation of habits, the attitudes which will then be experienced as such practical necessities. The feeling that it is important to act in certain ways: that one 'must' do this rather than that, will arise. The nurse will feel not just inclined, but necessitated to act in certain ways in particular circumstances. The nurse will feel that certain sorts of assistance 'must' be rendered; that it would be a failure of commitment not to do so. The terminology of 'duty' and 'obligation' will be out of place here because we are dealing with attitudes which have their basis in commitment.

The reason that I speak of a *professional* commitment is that the commitment which the nurse expresses by entering the profession will be transformed and developed by that nurse's education into a definite set of skills and attitudes which constitute the basis for the professional ethics, or the required and expected set of behaviours and concerns of the nurse. That is, a specifiable range of concerns and actions will become important for that nurse as a result of commitment and socialization into the profession. In situations where these concerns and these sorts of actions are at issue, the nurse will feel called upon to act and to suspend other activities in their favour. A nurse at afternoon tea will feel it to be important to respond to a call for assistance from a patient even through they are not inclined to do so (perhaps because they are tired), or even though they are not obliged to (being at afternoon tea might release the nurse from specific duties for that time). It is important to see that in altering the range of what is important to the professional, a professional commitment involves both actions and attitudes. What then are the activities and attitudes that are given priority in this way by the committed nurse? They are those concerns and activities that relate to health. What the professional nurse is committed to is health. We might express this by saying that what the nurse *professes* is health.

Now here is a crucial point. Unlike a personal commitment, a professional commitment takes 'health' as its object rather than the person of the client. Rather then being committed to the client as such (and his or her 'growth'), the nurse is committed to health and cares for the client insofar as health is to be restored or maintained in the client. The client becomes, as it were, the particular instantiation or embodiment of the nurse's general commitment to health. The ideal of health is the object of the nurse's professional commitment and this leads to caring for the health of the client. Of all the problems that a client might have, it is his health that the nurse is concerned about. A nurse's professional commitment is not to a care or love for the person of this or that client or the persons of clients in general. Neither does it need to be motivated by a love of persons. Motivation, after all, is no longer relevant. The object of one's commitment is health as an ideal to be realized in persons and the attitude that should grow from this is a concern for such health. On whatever biographical or psychological bases, one has adopted the stance that one is going to take the health of people as of central importance in one's life.

But this does not mean the one can be a good nurse and also be misanthropic. One must still adopt a caring attitude. But we now need to discern a further sense of the term 'care'. In this sense to care for something or for someone is to regard it as important. Such care will manifest itself in that one will be vulnerable to disappointment if what one cares about does not flourish. It may be that the dutiful daughter described earlier, the one who is not fond of her mother but cares for her in the sense of looking after her, is after a time no longer able to cope and places her in a public nursing home. The daughter now cares for her mother in neither of Griffin's senses, but she can still be said to care for her mother in my new sense in that she wishes her well and is affected by what happens to her. Morally we can even require the daughter to feel this way. We cannot require her to feel fond of her mother, but we would disapprove of her if she was not affected by some form of grief if her mother's condition deteriorated. Even when one can do nothing it is still appropriate and proper to care. Even a poor person who can contribute nothing to alleviate the suffering of the starving in the third world can and should care for them in this sense. What I am describing is an attitude in which I can care for a person whether or not I feel fond of her or am in a position to do anything for her. In this sense of 'care' it is simply important to me that this person should attain well-being, and it makes a difference whether this person flourishes in the sense that I rejoice in her well-being and grieve at her misfortune.

We can use the concept of commitment to understand how it is that a person can be affected in this way. To care in our new sense is to take something to be important and it is commitment which will have made it important. However, although we have described such an attitude of care in a case where an agent was not in a position to act on her commitment in order to distinguish it from Griffin's 'seeing to the needs of x', it standardly seeks expression in action. To care about something or someone is not just to be vulnerable to disappointment in the way described, but to be inclined to act helpfully when the occasion arises. If we care about something or take it to be important we will feel that we 'must' act in accordance with that attitude when a situation calls for such a response. But this is precisely the action orientation that arises from a commitment. A committed person cares.

To return, then, to our central point. A professionally committed nurse cares about health. What this will mean at the level of the relationship with the patient is certainly that the person of the patient will be important to the nurse. The nurse would be disappointed if things went badly for the patient. But not any disappointment is relevant to the nurse. If the patient's financial investments fail, the nurse might well commiserate but will not feel personally involved in the disappointment. The nurse's commitment-based identity as a health worker will not be implicated here. Should the patient's medical treatment fail, however, the nurse would be properly affected. This is a matter the nurse cares about professionally. What is more important to the nurse is the health of the patient, and this, not the person as such, is what the nurse cares for. The therapeutically required rapport between nurse and client will have to be established on the basis of their mutual perception of the nurse's professional commitment to caring for health. This caring, even though it is not for the whole person, should be sufficient to ground the trust in the nurse that the patient needs to feel.

Finally, it might be objected that in replacing the person with 'health' as the proper object of care in a professional commitment to nursing, I have simply posited a new limitless and unattainable goal. The concept of health is notoriously hard to specify,[34] and its vagueness might lead one to think that the object of the professional commitment of a nurse is to that extent limitless and unrealizable. A brief answer to this would be to suggest that the professional should take the ideal of their particular society as the benchmark and when even this is too vague, should seek to discern what the particular client's ideal is. If that is realistic and adequate, the nurse should work with it. If it is not, the client should be educated to a better ideal. It is the ideal that has priority over the client here. Being the health professional, the nurse should feel entitled to be the final arbiter of what constitutes health for the client. While there may be difficulties relating to patients' rights here, it is a consequence of my view that professional caring has health as its object rather than the client that this order of priorities should be a starting point for reflection about what to do in difficult cases.

Nothing that I have said should be taken to imply that to provide emotional support and comfort for the client is not an important role for the nurse. The nurse should be 'present' to the client in Marcel's sense, and should be perceived as a caring person in that sense. But this will be because the ideal of health includes and requires psychological well-being. It is this ideal of health that the nurse should care about and be professionally committed to.

---

[34]   Leon Kass, 'Regarding the End of Medicine and the Pursuit of Health', in Arthur L. Caplan, H. Tristram Engelhardt Jr, and James J. McCartney (eds), *Concepts of Health and Disease: Interdisciplinary Perspectives* (Reading, Massachusetts, 1981), pp. 9–18.

Chapter 2

Moral Education for Nursing Decisions[1]

My late mother-in-law worked as a military nurse during the Second World War. She served in New Guinea in a field hospital in which the number of medical staff was not sufficient to tend to all the wounded and dying. On an almost daily basis she had to make decisions as to which wounded soldiers would receive life-saving attention. It was inevitable that some deaths occurred because of the priorities that had to be assigned. She had had to work in horrific circumstances. Yet, to her dying day she worried whether she had made the right decision on each occasion. She felt regret at not being able to save every wounded soldier. There is no doubt that she did the best she could. She acted with care, with courage, with determination, and with self-sacrifice. The surviving soldiers loved her and appreciated her devotion. Why did she need to be troubled by the further question whether she acted rightly? What further assurance did she think she needed? And where did she think she could get such assurance from? Perhaps she felt the need to translate this regret into a doubt that she had acted rightly because she was caught up in that web of duty-based moral concepts in which the final verdict must be that she did the right thing. One of the tasks of moral education is to allow moral agents to be free of such worries through understanding the nature of moral norms.

Moral education

Rather than dealing with bioethics or with technical moral theory, this chapter will ask the question of how moral education can lead to the combination of confidence, insight and sensitivity which responsible nursing decisions require, along with the assurance, after the event, that the nurse has acted well. The name that I use for this combination is 'empowerment'. The central idea captured by this term is that acting decisively in a morally difficult or ambiguous situation involves acting in fulfilment of our own moral commitments. This might involve overcoming such internal inhibitions as fear and doubt or such external inhibitions as peer group pressure, social prejudice, or legal, bureaucratic and professional prohibitions. But whether there are such inhibitions or not, ethical action is an

---

[1]   This chapter is dedicated to the memory of Ms Vivienne Fitzpatrick RN.

exercise of internal personal strength. The central purpose of moral education is to enhance such empowerment.

Consequently, there are two approaches to moral education for nurses which I reject. The first of these involves putting ethics into the same context as a study of professional codes of ethics or of law as it relates to nursing. While there is no denying that the law, professional codes of ethics and the policies of hospitals have an influence on nurses' decision making, to impart knowledge of these codes as a way of achieving moral education implicitly suggests that it is by following such external norms that decisions should be made. Professional codes are the specific norms applying to a given profession, while laws might be thought of as the fully worked out or more general norms which operate in society at large. Accordingly, to confine a discussion of ethical decision making to these norms imparts a notion of ethics as a set of rules external to the motivational lives of nurses of which they have to be aware and to which they have to be obedient. Nothing could be more calculated to lead to a lack of confidence and a lack of sensitivity than this.

The idea that we are following rules when we act morally is a tired hangover from the days when the lives of people were controlled by religious and secular absolute rulers who accorded no respect or autonomy to ordinary people. Philosophical doctrines were developed which became the metaphysical counterparts of these social arrangement by positing absolute, objective and universal norms which grounded the inescapable obligations of each and every agent. Two crucial reasons why this will not work are first that, as has been suggested by Alasdair MacIntyre[2] and Bernard Williams,[3] no such metaphysical grounding for morality can be established, and second that it implies a psychology of moral motivation in which anxiety and dependence are primary motivators. This would be the very opposite of empowerment.

My rejection of a second form of moral education will be more contentious. This second form is that of discussing and imparting the moral principles on the basis of which it is said we should act. Proponents of this view argue that ethical theories (such as deontology, utilitarianism, teleology, or natural law theory), even if they are not the initial focus of teaching, should be introduced at some point in order to give nurses a basis for ethical decision making. Ethical discourse is thus seen as having as its function the provision of knowledge of principles and of meta-ethical theories which provide their justification. These principles and theories will then constitute a basis for making decisions by way of a rational process of deriving particular imperatives from the general principles.

2   Alasdair MacIntyre, *After Virtue: A Study of Moral Theory* (London, 1981).
3   Bernard Williams, *Ethics and the Limits of Philosophy* (London, 1985)

Kant

The major historical figure in this rationalist way of conceiving of morality is Immanuel Kant (1724–1804). He taught that persons act morally well only when they act out a sense of duty without regard to their inclinations, and that their duty consisted in treating all persons with the respect that arose from seeing them as autonomous rational agents rather than as mere means to be used for their own ends. The test for whether you were acting in this way would be to see if you could turn your own policy in acting into a rule by which everyone should act: a sort of sophisticated version of the Golden Rule. Now, there is nothing morally questionable about any of this. Kant was able to justify the basic norms of Western ethics by these criteria. However, there is the problem that this is a morality which is aimed at generating ethical principles on the basis of pure reason which the agent is then obliged to obey. Despite all its talk of autonomy, Kant's moral theory makes the agent obedient rather than empowered. Yet this is the moral theory that underlies most moral education today. It is a theory that says that what moral agents need in order to act morally is to know the principles by which they should act and to use their reason in order to apply such principles to the possible actions that their situations call for.

Many currently available books and articles exemplify this approach. So we have Raanan Gillon[4] arguing against the view that mere appeals to conscience, integrity or good character are enough to secure morally good behaviour for medical practitioners. What is needed, he argues, is clear thought and knowledge of principles. Gillon offers two main arguments for this conclusion. First, he says that we must still engage in rational philosophical discourse to decide exactly what terms like 'conscience', 'integrity' or 'good character' mean and how they enter into moral decision making. Second, he argues that two practitioners who act from conscience, integrity and virtue might nevertheless adopt different courses of action. How shall we decide which one is right? Moral discourse will still be needed. I counter these arguments with two comments. First, it might indeed be worth knowing what virtue and good conscience are. However, our question concerns how we should impart these and it is not obvious that a rational discussion aimed at discovering what they are would lead to their acquisition. Second, the idea that two virtuous agents doing different things in similar circumstances constitutes a problem implies a view of morality which asserts that in any situation there is only one morally right course of action available. This is precisely the view that ensnared my mother-in-law.

This assertion arises from the very heart of what Kantians take morality to be. On this view, morality is conceived of as an objective guide to action. Knowing what morality as such dictates allows us to infer what we should do in any specific situation. This is a juridical notion of morality. A clear judgement is always possible. There is no room for ambiguity in the moral life. For Kantians, morality

---

[4]   Raanan Gillon, *Philosophical Medical Ethics* (Chichester, 1986)

tells us objectively what we are obliged to do or not to do. With this notion of morality, two moral agents should indeed do the same thing in similar circumstances. However, I would argue that in the complexity of human life no two circumstances are exactly the same. The biographies of the persons involved in the situation will be different and hence their attitudes to it will also differ at least in some minimal way. The material circumstances, too, will never be exactly duplicated. I think this is enough to make this view of morality at least inoperative. There are no principles both broad and specific enough to apply to any two situations in the same way. However, I want to do more than assert that this view of morality is inoperative. I want to suggest that it is wrong. It is undeniable that we must not act without thought and that such thought must be both clear and well reasoned. However, I would question whether it follows that moral action must always be preceded by clear thought about, and knowledge of, moral principles. I would suggest that what we need to think about is what values are at issue in the situation.

Nor is my argument merely centred on the question of whether reason has a role as part of what leads to a decision, or whether its role is that of justification for any such decision at a time other than when it is put into effect. There are many authors[5] who argue that the function of ethical discourse is to set up a structure of justification for action such that an action can be defended to others and be accepted as normative by the agent's community. People should not perform actions that they cannot justify in this way. Once again, this is essentially a juridical notion of ethical thought and one that does not address the question of what leads agent to perform their actions, unless it be to suggest that fear of the sanctions of that community is the most central consideration. Reason occupies the central place in this moral theory as a curb to inclination rather than as the originator of action. Even when we move from the justification of particular actions to discourse about norms and principles, the motivation of actions is left mysterious while reason is given the task of justifying what these motivations lead us to. In this way reason becomes merely the means for justifying and codifying our pre-existing moral intuitions.[6]

Weakness of will

That pure reason is not the sole basis for our moral decisions is also shown by the phenomenon which classical authors referred to as 'weakness of will'. Merely rationally knowing that something is the right thing to do is not enough to give an agent the courage or the determination to do it. This courage must come from within that agent. No amount of exhortation or reasoning can get a person to act

---

5   For example, see Peter Singer, *Practical Ethics* (Cambridge, 1979)

6   For a fuller elaboration of these arguments, see Stan van Hooft, *Understanding Virtue Ethics* (Chesham, 2005).

well if that person has no internal resources or reasons to act in that way. To argue that ethical theory can lead to good actions by itself is to accept the motivational efficacy of what Bernard Williams calls 'external reasons'.[7] These are the reasons that rational and impartial observers of the agent rightly judge should apply to the agent. But for agents themselves these are not necessarily reasons in a practical or motivational sense. An 'internal' reason is needed: a motivational and cognitive stance which needs to include the conviction born of reflection and commitment that the action is incumbent upon the agent.[8] The basis for moral decision making remains a mysterious mix of emotion, knowledge, determination, commitment, ideals, thought, and the agent's character.

To fully explain this I need to mention another classical author from our tradition of ethical discourse: namely, Aristotle (384–322 BCE). For Aristotle, to act well was not to act in obedience to rules or justifications, but to act in a way that fulfilled us as persons. The whole object of ethical discourse for Aristotle was to help us to live well and to be aware of doing so. His was not a juridical notion of morality, but a humanistic notion of ethics as a means to living a flourishing life. We use reason, not to find out what we are obliged to do, but to become more aware of ourselves and of our practical environment. Aristotle used a technical term here: 'practical reason', (the ancient Greek word was *phronēsis*). One important point about this notion is that it is not confined just to the intellect. For Aristotle, human agents were many-faceted and their actions involved their emotions and desires as well as their pure reason. Morally sensitive practical reason leads us not only to think rightly about our actions, but also to feel rightly.

On an Aristotelian view, the task of moral education for nurses would not be just to impart knowledge of moral norms or to train the intellect to think in certain ways about moral problems, but also to develop the sensitivity and caring which would motivate nurses to act well. Such education would proceed by three steps: first, the training of habits, second, the development of attitudes, and third, reflection upon the nurse's actions. Let us start our discussion with the second of these.

I start here because attitudes provide the motivational basis for making all of our decisions, including morally difficult ones. It is a consequence of my arguments against juridical notions of morality and against Kantian moral rationalism that the making of sensitive decisions will be facilitated to the extent that nurses have been given the power to believe that their attitudes are appropriate for the making of such decisions. Despite the existence of codes of ethics, law, and other apparently 'objective' norms, no public, rationally grounded norm and no bureaucratic pressure needs to be blindly followed. Of course, it may be that a particular decision leads to our being disapproved of, or even punished, by others.

---

7   Bernard Williams, 'Internal and external reasons', in Bernard Williams (ed.), *Moral Luck* (Cambridge, 1981), pp. 101–13.

8   Stan van Hooft, 'Obligation, Character, and Commitment, *Philosophy*, 63 (1988): 345–62.

Our ethical freedom may not be socially or institutionally acknowledged and so may lead us into conflict with others. However, even when it is made with full knowledge of those consequences, our decisions are still our own. Any decision is motivated from within and therefore based on our attitudes. The implication of Aristotle's dictum that we must not only think rightly in order to act well is that our attitudes as well as our thinking are appropriate objects for ethical education.

I am not talking about what some educators refer to as 'values clarification' here. This process certainly involves reflecting on our attitudes, but it accepts as given the attitudes which we reflect upon. This process assumes a pluralist position which asserts that people are entitled to the attitudes that they in fact have and need only to reflect on them in order to make them more conscious and thus more strongly motivational. It may be an absurd consequence of this view that the antisocial attitudes of the criminal should be accorded the same right to exist as the altruistic attitude of the law abiding citizen, but it is not an illogical one. Against such pluralism, I assert that educators do have the right to instil certain attitudes rather then merely to seek the clarify already existing ones, even though this right must be exercised with sensitivity and supported by practical reason.

It is widely accepted that the central professional attitude for nurses is that of caring. As I argued in Chapter 1, the role of such an attitude for nurses is that of being the foundation for a commitment to caring for the health of patients with all the efforts and skills that that entails. It follows that nurse education may and should concern itself with the formation of specifically caring attitudes.

Caring attitudes

How do educators develop caring attitudes in student nurses? Seeing as educational processes centre on the imparting of knowledge, it would seem to be important to impart the sort of knowledge that leads us to care. What sort of knowledge is this? Clearly it would not just be knowledge of facts. Certainly nurses need to have a large amount of factual knowledge about bioscience, clinical techniques, counselling and listening skills, and so forth. But all of these bodies of knowledge have a meaning. They are not just 'brute facts'. All of the facts of the relevant sciences and all of the techniques for dealing with clients have the significance that they do within the context of a culture in which nurses and clients are participants. This means that neither nurse nor patient understands these things in a purely neutral way. They are matters which already have values built into them. The relevant bioscientific facts are valuable insofar as they are part of those sciences through which a patient's health is restored and they also share in the more general cultural significant that science has for us all. The interpersonal techniques have a value insofar as they are functional within the caring process and also share in the more generally held cultural understandings of what it is to be a person, to live, to enjoy good health, to suffer illness, and to die. Nurses cannot just acquire the necessary facts and skills without also acquiring an attitude to them and to such notions as that of science and of the human person. These attitudes, in turn, are a combination of the individual's attitudinal stances, of the particular culture of nursing practice, and of the more general cultures of the surrounding society. In these contexts, everything that student nurses learn has significance.

This significance can be recognized by nurses because it forms part of their motivational stance. To see the significance of something is to have a motivational stance or attitude towards it. When nurses recognize the significant place of scientific knowledge in caring processes, they will be motivated to acquire that knowledge and to apply it with care. When they acknowledge the significance of persons, their hopes and their fears, they will be motivated to develop interpersonal skills and deal sensitively with clients. It is important for nurses to embrace the culture of science with the notion of practical, objective and rationally grounded knowledge which it encapsulates. Nurses must be taught to recognize and respect this knowledge even as they acknowledge its limitations.

These limitations become apparent when we consider the deep human significance that living and dying have for people. Bioscience has little to say on this. Yet nurses must, above all else, have both clear and sensitive attitudes to these matters. For many cultures and cultural groups within our own society these matters fall within the purview of religion. Nurses, therefore, whatever their own religious convictions, should develop a sensitive understanding of religion and of the way it provides a meaning-giving matrix for the living of the most crucial episodes in a human life. They should also be helped to develop for themselves attitudes to these ultimate matters which will allow them not only to cope with the constant confrontations with crises of life and death which they will experience, but also to be of aid and comfort to those of their clients who face such crises, irrespective of the relevant beliefs and understandings of these clients.

Forming habits

This leads us to the first and third stages of ethical education: that of the forming of habits and that of reflection on actions performed. These two processes interact with one another and with the inculcation of attitudes. Nevertheless, I will extricate them from one another for the sake of analysis. The role of reflection in the education of attitudes and feelings is primarily to make the latter more conscious and so more strongly motivational. However, the object of the reflection that nurses should engage in includes not only their attitudes, but also the actions that they have themselves performed on previous occasions and the example of actions that others have performed. In this way their motivational attitudes and feelings will include not just the compassion and concern which should motivate nurses to act caringly towards their clients and the respect for science and for the life meanings held by nurses and clients, but also the confidence which comes from having acted in these ways before and having found it good on reflection. When nurses reflect on actions previously performed and are able to generate a level of self-approval, they develop a level of practical confidence which can be invoked consciously or which can operate unconsciously on future occasions. New situations do not have to be similar to old ones in order for the confidence that arises from such reflective self-approval to be empowering since, as I have noted, no two situations are ever completely alike. Moreover, we do not always need to completely approve of our own previous actions. We can acquire a lesser form of practical confidence even when we disapprove of what we have done, provided we understand what went wrong. In these ways, moral empowerment enters into the nurse's motivational stance as a preparation for future action.

As well, student nurses can gain courage to act from the example of their peers and seniors. If the object of nursing education is to empower nurses to act well, it requires nurses to reflect on examples arising from the practice of others, as well as on their own actions. That an impressive nurse has done something difficult can help others to do it. Those daily adjustments to the demands of institutional routines and of difficult patients which nevertheless preserve sensitivity and caring can be taught and imparted more by display and example than by the articulation of guidelines or the discussion of principles. Teaching ethics to nurses is not just about teaching conformity to codes or how to avoid litigation. It is about empowering nurses to act in difficult or stressful situations in which objective guidelines are not, and possibly cannot be, available. This is achieved by giving student nurses examples of ethical behaviour of which they can approve because they accord with the attitudes that are being inculcated into them. This is one of the ways in which the three stages of moral education interact. Attitudes are reinforced by approving of their realization in the actions that they perform themselves and which they see others performing

I turn now to Aristotle's first phase of moral education: namely, the forming of habits. How can we explain what could lead us to act well the first time that we do so? If the motivational force to act well requires reflection on previous actions along with well-formed attitudes, then how do we get started on the path to ethical living? What motivates our first good action? Aristotle answers this question by saying that our first good action requires not an internal motivation, but an external stimulus. He argues that moral education must begin with the formation of habits which are externally induced by teachers or exemplars. This is the first step of moral education because our attitudes arise from what we have been trained to do habitually. For nurses this training involves the process of socialization into practices and attitudes which arises within the clinical experience of the trainee. Nurses must be inducted by habituation into ethical and caring nursing practice and into the attitudes which such a practice encapsulates. Having established this unreflective mode of ethical behaviour, the nurse educator is then in a position to invite reflection on that behaviour and thereby continue the process of empowerment. Acting habitually in the way that nurses have been trained to leads to the development of suitable attitudes to the extent that trainee nurses internalize the meanings that those actions have within nursing practice and to the extent that they are encouraged to reflect on them.

Of course, these processes of reflection may still make use of the sorts of rational discourse found in most ethics text books. But the function of ethical discourse in this reflexive context is not to underpin with rational considerations that attitudinal and motivational stance which leads to the action so as to legitimate that stance, but to accept the actions which were performed more fully. If empowerment requires self-approval, then reflection must seek to align our attitudes with our past actions. I do not mean that agents must use moral theory in any cynical way in order to make their actions look good no matter what. Some actions may be found to be unacceptable in any way. What I mean is that, insofar as any action in a moral dilemma is accompanied by doubt and questioning even after it is performed, if nurses are to approve of the actions that they have performed, they will want to be able to lay them to rest and give them a sense that they can live with. To this end they could use the methods and categories of ethical theory. Acceptance involves giving meaning to actions which allows nurses to say that they have acted well so as to empower those nurses to perform difficult and caring actions again on future occasions.

It is also possible that the ethical intuitions of student nurses come into conflict with the values implicit in the modes of nursing practice into which they are being inducted. If the practices in the training institution are less than ideal, the trainee nurses may come to feel a dissonance between those values and their own caring attitudes. This situation, too, will generate the need for critical thought structured and informed by ethical theory as much as by the attitude of caring. To be able to articulate a critical position on the inadequate practices will require a good grasp of ethical concepts and principles.

Conclusion

Strength of will comes from feeling good about ourselves insofar as we have had the courage to act well in the past, as well as from the feeling that we are acting in accordance with our deepest commitments, motivations and attitudes. These latter will have been formed in us by our socialization and by the example of others. Nurses who are empowered to act by way of an ethical education such as I have described will act decisively and responsibly in both routine and morally complex situations. They might not act in the same way every time, but they will on each occasion be able to feel that they have done what was best on that occasion, fulfilled their deepest commitments, and answered the most pressing expectations placed upon them.

Chapter 3

Bioethics and Caring

Bioethics is often seen as an instance of 'quandary ethics'[1] of which the purpose is to provide guidelines for making difficult decisions: decisions for which there are no precedents arising from a pre-technological age. It is thought to require deductive thinking in which guidelines for a particular action are drawn from general principles or rules which tell us what it is obligatory or good for us to do. These principles or rules are said to be imperative, real, and universal and it is the task of moral philosophy, as it was of theology in the past, to tell us what they are. For their part, bioethicists combine knowledge of these obligations with knowledge of particular fields of endeavour such as medicine and health care in order to solve the practical quandaries which these fields throw up.

It follows that the quest for the 'Foundations of Bioethics' would be conceived as a quest for knowledge of the universal principles of morality. However, there has been much discussion in the philosophical community in recent years about whether such a quest could ever succeed.[2] A key point that has emerged is that theorists should be more concerned with what moves people to act well in the way of 'internal' motivations rather than with what they are obliged to do because of 'external' impositions of duty.[3] The quest for foundations in bioethics should no longer be the quest for any such 'external' set of norms.

I would argue that what we do in situations of moral difficulty or practical quandary is an expression of what we care about most deeply. It follows that a quest for the foundations of bioethics will be an exploration of the ontological

---

[1]   Edmund L. Pincoffs, *Quandaries and Virtues* (Lawrence, Kansas, 1986).

[2]   The most notable examples of this trend are Bernard Williams, *Ethics and the Limits of Philosophy* (London, 1985) and Alasdair MacIntyre, *After Virtue: A Study in Moral Theory* (London, 1981). For a more recent discussion of more limited scope in which impartial reason is criticized as a basis for ethical judgement, see Anne MacLean, *The Elimination of Morality: Reflections on Utilitarianism and Bioethics* (London and New York, 1993).

[3]   Even recent discussions of 'virtue ethics' can fail to note this distinction. The demand to be virtuous is often seen as just another external demand rather than one that arises from the motivational structure of the agent. For example, see Robert B. Louden, 'On Some Vices of Virtue Ethics', and Tom L. Beauchamp, 'What's So Special About the Virtues?', both in Joram Graf Haber (ed.), *Doing and Being: Selected Readings in Moral Philosophy* (New York, 1993).

being of the agent and, through this ontology, of the deepest levels of motivation within the agent.

Caring

What do I mean by 'caring' in my title? Caring can be thought of as behaviour or as motivation. As behaviour the word often refers to looking after people and seeing to their needs, whether in the context of the health care professions, social work, teaching, parenting and other familial relationships, and so forth. As motivation the word can refer to being fond of someone, feeling sympathy or empathy for them, being concerned for their well-being, or having a professional commitment to seeing to their needs. It can be said that the best caring professionals exemplify both of these senses of the word. As I argued in Chapter 1, they are good at seeing to the needs of others and they are motivated to do so by their caring attitude. Such a person is described as a caring person.

In contrast to these familiar usages, I propose a technical notion of 'caring' in which that word designates a fundamental structure of human living which would be the basis for these caring attitudes and behaviours and also for any sense of obligation that we might experience as arising from traditional moral norms. I will be arguing that this concept provides a basis for ethics, and hence for bioethics, that is more fundamental than either rules or virtues. After all, the value of rules and of virtues must be assessable. A rule is a good one if it meets standards of rationality or leads to approved consequences, and virtues are admirable if they lead to a good life for the individual and for society. These further goods are a yardstick against which both rules and virtues must be measured. My argument, developed fully in an earlier book,[4] is that it is a mistake to appeal to some objective good to be this yardstick, whether such a good be the will of God, the Moral Law, the preferences of rational individuals, or the self-fulfilment or happiness of rational agents (described by Aristotle as *eudaimonia*). In order for any good or principle to be a yardstick against which both rules and virtues can be measured, we must care about it.

Deep caring

Caring in my sense is developed from the ideas of Aristotle, Karl Jaspers, Emmanuel Levinas and Martin Heidegger. It does not designate a motivation or a desire of which an agent could normally be aware, but a deep and innate quest which does not have definable objects. It is the kind of quest that existential phenomenologists like Jean-Paul Sartre captured with terms like *being-for-itself*

---

[4]   Stan van Hooft, *Caring: An Essay in the Philosophy of Ethics* (Niwot, Colorado, 1995).

and *being-for-others*.[5] But I prefer to use Heidegger's ontological notion of *sorge* (care) which describes the way a human being exists at the deepest level.[6] The phrase I use to distinguish this from the familiar concept of caring described above is 'deep caring'. To use technical philosophical language, deep caring is not intentional. It is not a quest for anything specific. But it provides the impetus for all of our concerns, our objectives, and our desires. Its fundamental purpose (but not conscious goal) is the formation and maintenance of both the integrity of our selves and also of our relationships with others and the world around us. I represent deep caring in this sense on the following diagram:

PAST ⬅➡ PRESENT ⬅➡ FUTURE

THE SPIRITUAL LEVEL
>   Thinking which integrates and gives meaning to all the levels of our functioning (for example, creative art, pure science, philosophy, morality, religion, transcendent or ultimate values).
>   This level is uniquely human.

THE EVALUATIVE–PROACTIVE LEVEL
>   Voluntary, purposive behaviour informed by plans and values and the rational pursuit of needs arising from lower levels (includes most of what we do in our everyday, practical, self-conscious lives).
>   This level is distinctively human.

THE PERCEPTUAL–REACTIVE LEVEL
>   Involuntary ways of seeing and reacting to things around us – consciousness and affect (including learnt responses, emotions, desires, bonds of affection and group membership.)
>   We share this level with animals.

THE BIOLOGICAL LEVEL
>   involuntary physical functions and growth (such as metabolism, instinctual drives, reflexes)
>   We share this level with plants.

Most of the content of this diagram requires explication which goes beyond the scope of this chapter. Moreover, it would be interesting to explore how it describes levels of human living which can be distinguished in a number of ways: for

---

5   Jean-Paul Sartre, *Being and Nothingness: A Phenomenological Essay on Ontology*, translated by Hazel E. Barnes (New York, 1956).

6   Martin Heidegger, *Being and Time*, translated by John Macquarie and Edward Robinson (Oxford, 1973), sections 64 and 65.

example, as to their intellectual sophistication, as to the degree and kind of their presence to consciousness, as to their being individualistic or communitarian, and so forth. But the most crucial point to note is that these levels are levels of activity; or even better, levels of engagement with a person's environment in the richest sense of that word. The model does not represent 'parts of the soul' in Aristotle's sense, as if it were describing parts of a living entity. What it is describing are levels of functioning and engagement.

This is the meaning of the top line of the model in which the 'temporality' (to use Heidegger's term) of human existence is highlighted. What this means is that a human being is constantly oriented towards the future and acting from out of his or her past. This notion of the temporality of human living highlights the dynamic nature of our being. We are constantly engaged, constantly striving, constantly doing (except when we are asleep and not dreaming). The phrase 'human being' should be read as a verb rather than as a noun. It does not so much designate a biological entity as a mode of engagement with the world around us. And this mode of engagement can be called deep caring. The world, the future, and other people all matter to us in some way. On my model, temporality is the horizontal axis of our deep caring. Insofar as this caring is, by its very nature, an active engagement with the world, so our being is outwardly oriented: a being-for-others.[7]

And this deep caring can be described on the four levels of the model. Many things in the world matter to us biologically. Our mothers when we are infants, the air we breathe, the food we eat, the sexual partners with whom we mate are all entities that engage us because of the biological dynamic that constitutes our deep caring at this level. Notice that it is difficult to describe these examples, especially the last, in purely biological terms. The further levels of our being and of our caring are engaged with these matters also. This is the significance of the arrow on the left of the model. A fully functioning human being does not operate on any one of these four levels by itself. To be a 'whole person' (if I may use that overworked phrase) is to be engaged with the world at all four levels and to have those four levels interact with each other so as to constitute the meaning and significance of our living. I call this vertical cohesion of human being 'integration', and I suggest that integration in this sense is an inherent goal or *telos* of deep caring. Insofar as our deep caring is oriented towards this integration of our lives, I call it a 'self-project'.

Integration in my sense is not the achievement of control on the part of the higher levels of the model (especially the spiritual level) over the lower levels. Aristotle's model of the soul was hierarchical and allowed him to say that the higher parts should control the lower. Reason should control the emotions. In contrast, my model is 'holistic'. Our breathing is not controlled by the higher levels of my model and yet is a matter of deep caring for us, as is evidenced by the

---

[7]   I am not using this phrase in the somewhat defensive and solipsistic way that Sartre uses it in his analysis of 'The Look' in his *Being and Nothingness*, pp. 340ff.

shift in our priorities when we experience breathing difficulties. More ethically interesting biological functions such as sex only become a matter about which we might ask ethical questions, such as whether control should be exercised over them, after they have been shaped by all the levels of our being so as to take on ethical significance. The question of whether a sexual desire should be controlled is not a question that arises from the higher levels so as to be directed to the lower. It is a question about how one's integration as a being which functions at all four levels should be preserved.

To illustrate the model further, consider pain. Pain is a biological phenomenon arising from dysfunctions or lesions in the body. At level one of our being (the biological level) there will be the cries and grimaces that are the involuntary expressions of pain. But pain is experienced and so is lived out on the second level of our being as well. At this level there are not only feelings of pain and distress, but also emotions and reactions which are constituted socially and interpersonally but which are experienced as arising pre-consciously. At this level there is suffering. The involuntary expressions of my pain will be partially structured by the cultural formation that allows me to express my pain in that way. In our society, for example, men are less likely to express their pain directly than women. Pain behaviour is a learnt response and this learnt response is the expression of our deep caring about pain at the second level of our being. And, given that we are related to others at all levels of our being, another expression of our deep caring at this level will be our spontaneous compassion with the pain of others.

At the third level of my model will be those many behaviours of avoidance and palliation which constitute our rational and practical response to pain, whether that pain is actually being experienced or merely being envisaged as a possibility in our lives. In the case of a particular pain episode, our visit to a doctor or our reaching for the aspirin will be our living out our deep caring about pain, our expression of the fact that pain matters to us. Further, as we move to the third level of our being, there will be individual and collective deliberations and plans ranging from buying more aspirin to setting up hospitals. The rational basis for this collective action will be the recognition that others too can suffer pain and that cooperation is needed to deal adequately with it. The social provision of health care is a collective expression of deep caring focused at the third level of our being.

But most importantly, and most frequently neglected, there is the fourth level of our deep caring in which people will seek to integrate biological pain episodes and the sets of reactions and activities that respond to them into their conception of themselves and of their deepest values and relationships. People suffering pain will seek to understand their suffering in the context of their lives and beliefs. A religious person will see it as the will of God, whether as a test or as punishment. A secular person will see it as bad luck or as an opportunity for personal growth, and so on. The numbers of ways in which pain can be given meaning and made into an integral part of the narrative of a life are many and varied. These ways include how people feel called upon to respond to the pain of others. The fourth level of our being will be the level at which the whole set of reactions, feelings and activities relating to pain will be given their meaning in ultimate terms.

Deep caring is an engagement along both the horizontal and vertical axes of my model. It is an engagement with the world, with the future and with others, but, given the vertical axis, it is also an engagement the innate purpose or function of which is the constitution of our integration as whole persons. Caring is both being-for-others and self-project. I said earlier that caring has no object; it is not intentional. I am not now suggesting that it is the true object of our caring to live out our lives over time and to establish and maintain our integration in doing so or to relate to others in determinable ways. Our goals and purposes are what they are given to us as being in our own self-consciousness (even if it may sometimes require difficult and honest reflection to discover them). But that they matter to us arises from a deeper and pre-conscious mode of our being. The caring which I am seeking to describe is not a caring about this thing or that, or about this person or that. And it is not a caring about ourselves and our integration. If we care about anything or if we care for anyone, it is because deep caring is the very nature of our being. These familiar and intentional forms of caring are expressions of our ontological being as deep caring. The function of deep caring is to integrate our living and to give it world-relational and intersubjective meaning.

This function is exercised when our deep caring is given form. Things in the world, our projects, and the persons that we relate to, as well as the social solidarities and the faiths that we have, give structure and direction to our deep caring. They are important to us because they are the occasion for our innate caring to become focused. Our intentional concern for these things will then be the expression of our deep caring.

Implications for ethics

And so it is for ethics. Ethics is an expression of our deep caring in the sense that it is a socially constructed form through which we constitute the integration of our being and the quality of our engagement with the world and with others. This does not imply egoism. I am not saying that while being seemingly concerned for ethical values, we are actually only concerned for our own integration or relationships. What we are actually, consciously, and authentically concerned with is the ethical object of our current projects. But the force of our concern, its engine so to speak, is our own nature as deep and implicit caring: our fundamental and inescapable engagement with self and world.

How does this help us understand ethics and, by implication, bioethics? In a chapter that is already too schematic, I can only give a sketch of an answer by alluding to a number of current debates in ethical theory and indicating how my model might be relevant to them.

1. My model can be used to suggest that most ethical theories are reductionist in that they highlight just one of the levels of human existence rather than all four.

If ethical theory, along with ethical agency, is an expression of our deep caring, and if my model gives a holistic picture of four levels of that deep caring, then we would expect that ethical theory would be an expression of all those four levels in my model. However, this is seldom the case.

An extreme example would be socio-biology, which explains ethics in terms of genetically grounded traits. Such a theory is clearly reductionist in that it focuses only on the biological level of our being. But various forms of intuitionism and emotivism would be reductionist in a similar way. The second level of our deep caring is where our socially formed reactions and pre-conscious intuitions come to expression. On my model, moral convictions and intuitions which seem self-evident and inescapable to an agent would be seen as only a part of the ethical life. I would place most rationalistic ethical theories on the third level of our being. Consequentialism requires us to deliberate about actions in relation to their outcomes and this activity is an expression of the third level of our deep caring. And in most versions of utilitarianism, happiness seems to me to be a third-level value. It is at the fourth level of our being that we adhere to values in an ultimate commitment. For example, a deontologist might adhere to the value of duty in an ultimate way and various ethical theories of a Platonic stamp (including Christianity) involve a faith in ultimate values, sources of value or 'moral facts'.

My model would suggest that no ethical theory could be an adequate expression of our deep caring if it did not relate to all four levels of our being. Moreover, no description of ethical agency or moral psychology would be complete if it did not show how such agency was an expression of all four levels of our deep caring. This, in turn, points to the concepts of character and of virtue.

2. My model gives us the subjective and motivational basis for ethics, and hence for bioethics, which I have argued we need. In doing so, it supports 'internalists' in their debate with 'externalists'.[8] Externalists believe that there is a distinction between knowing what is the right thing to do and wanting to do it. Along with a belief, there must be a relevant desire if an action is to occur. A belief cannot motivate by itself. Hence a belief about the world (that a patient is suffering, for example) is not, by itself, a motivation for acting. One must also have a desire (whether it be based in compassion, or in a moral commitment to beneficence, or in other comportments) to cause us to act.

My model departs from this explanatory paradigm of human action.[9] On my model, the human subject is not an ontological isolate comprising a combination of cognitive input and conative output. By virtue of our ontological being as deep caring, we realize ourselves by reaching out to the world and to others. We are primordially intersubjective and related to our world. The world is always already

---

[8]   For a thorough exposition of this debate, see Jonathan Dancy, *Moral Reasons* (Oxford, 1993).

[9]   The paradigm that both beliefs and desires are needed to explain actions was articulated by Donald Davidson in recent times in his *Essays on Actions and Events* (Oxford, 1980), but is at least as old as Hume.

meaningful rather than a neutral field available to our scrutiny and evaluation. In this sense I am an internalist. If the situation is such that I am in a position to help, my belief that another is suffering is a moral reason for me to act and will be immediately motivational. The suffering of another typically calls out to us immediately for a response. (We are, of course, free to reject this call, but at a cost to our integration as self-project and being-for-others.)

3. There is debate as to the nature of moral obligation or 'practical necessity'. Moral realists give a metaphysical grounding to moral obligation by suggesting that it is a matter of obedience to objective moral norms. In contrast, Bernard Williams has said that the feeling that we 'must' do something 'goes all the way down' into our characters.[10] My model suggests what this might mean. Our ontological being as deep caring can express itself imperiously when objects with which we are engaged and our integration are at stake. Moral 'oughts' are an expression of deep caring.

4. My model is consistent with ethical theories such as those of David Hume and John Stuart Mill that appeal to 'natural sympathy' or a 'natural motivation to be ethical' as basic to morality.[11] But there is the important difference that deep caring is an implicit and non-intentional comportment which is concerned both with self and with others. It can be expressed as sympathy in the context of situations that call for it, but it might on other occasions be expressed as anxiety for oneself.

5. My model can throw light on the current debate between those who argue for a 'different voice' in ethics as theorized by Carol Gilligan[12] and those who argue that Lawrence Kohlberg has fully described moral development along Kantian lines. Gilligan has suggested that, when making ethical judgements, girls are more concerned with maintaining caring relationships and bonds than with following general rules. It would be too easy to say that Gilligan's concepts are appropriate for describing the second level of our being where our bonds and relationships come to expression, while Kohlberg's describe the third (or perhaps, fourth) level of rational thought. Both theorists purport to describe the same thing; namely, the growth and development of our moral thinking. It might also be tempting to see my model as a developmental one and to suggest that the women studied by Gilligan arrested their development at the second level, while Kohlberg's subjects went on to develop levels three and four. But my model is not developmental or hierarchical. Rather it hypothesizes a deep level of caring in all human beings which comes to expression at various levels. It is possible that social formation will favour one form of expression over another, and it is likely that such social formation will differ between people in gender-specific ways.

---

[10]   Williams, p. 188.

[11]   John Stuart Mill, 'Utilitarianism', in Alan Ryan (ed.), *John Stuart Mill and Jeremy Bentham: Utilitarianism and Other Essays* (London, 1987), p. 303.

[12]   Carol Gilligan, *In a Different Voice: Psychological Theory and Women's Development* (Cambridge, Massachusetts, 1982).

(However, there is no suggestion in my model that deep caring is a feminine quality.) Gilligan is right to have reminded us that expressions of deep caring at the second level of our being are as valid as expressions at other levels. However, it would be reductionist to stress this level to the exclusion of others.

6. My model suggests an account of the purpose of ethics as an expression of our deep caring. Deep caring is concerned with solidarity with others (especially those with whom we have some bond) and with integration. Ethical discourse is a way of seeking to secure this solidarity and integration in the face of actions, ways of life, or personal characteristics which might threaten them. While there are many theorists (especially in the field of bioethics) who see the purpose of ethical discourse as the formation of social policy and law, and while I would not deny that this purpose has importance, I would place stress on the personal task of making ethical decisions. Of course, our actions in morally complex situations are not only expressions of our deep caring. They are also, by virtue of their occurring in a realm of intersubjectivity, public declaration of where we stand ethically. In this way they enter into the sphere of public discourse and are subject to criticism and the need for justification. But this is distinct from the engagement with public policy issues which is chosen as a vocation by some as an expression of their deep caring. The latter generates the more abstract and theoretical ethical discourse of which the bioethics literature is an example.

7. To those who debate whether the basic motivational structure of human lives is altruistic or egoistic, I suggest that deep caring looks both outwards and inwards at the same time. Not being intentional, deep caring cannot be described as either altruistic or egoistic. It is an ontological mode of being which is both self-project and being-for-others. This is not to deny that social formation might favour one orientation over the other. But in the hidden depths of our being, we are neither exclusively altruistic, nor exclusively egoistic. In an ideally formed human being, integration and solidarity will be equally strong motivations.

8. There is a debate as to whether ethical obligations are 'real' from an impersonal point of view. Realists would argue that impartial thinking or 'the view from nowhere' gives us a surer grasp of what is morally required of us than a point of view which takes account of our particular and personal relationships and properties. I favour the personal point of view.[13] Insofar as it is our integration and intersubjective solidarity which lie at the heart of our concerns, the scope of our moral obligations will emanate from our being so as to embrace those whom we love with greater urgency than those we do not. Moreover, insofar as we might be committed to ideals of justice at the fourth level of our being, the call upon us of those who suffer injustice will be more urgent than of those who suffer simple need and hardship.

---

[13] For an interesting discussion of these issues, see Lawrence A. Blum, 'Vocation, friendship, and community: limitations of the personal-impersonal framework', in his *Moral Perception and Particularity* (Cambridge, 1994), pp. 98–123.

This does not mean that the call upon us of morally salient features in a situation is not 'objective'. It is there to be apprehended by anyone with the educated sensitivity required to sense it.[14] The ethical formation which we receive in our communities and the ethical discourse of these communities will create a set of standards of moral excellence which will be objectively present for us in our lives.

9. My model is descriptive of our ontological being and gives an account of how it is that we feel we have obligations. As such it is not prescriptive. Rather than telling us what we should do, my model explains why we have the moral notions that we do. By showing how all four levels of our being come to expression in such notions, my model explains why ethics matters and why morally relevant situations call out to us so as to demand our response.

10. It follows from my model that moral education would not consist in explanation of moral principles or instruction in moral theory, but in showing how the deep caring of moral neophytes can be fulfilled in a variety of ways in a variety of situations. As opposed to a teaching that would address only the third level of our being, moral education will consist in showing what is morally salient in a situation. Rather than teaching medical or nursing students about the principle of beneficence so that they will know that they ought to respond when a patient is in pain, educators would teach those students what pain is and what it may mean so that they will respond to it in accordance with all four levels of their natures as deep caring. This teaching will be phenomenological, reflective and anthropological, rather than instruction in moral theory. It is a consequence of my 'internalist' position that any agent who understands a situation as involving pain that she can alleviate, will be moved to do so. If she were not so moved she will not have understood the situation correctly, with regard to its moral salience. Accordingly, as I argued in Chapter 2, moral instruction must aim to enable such an understanding of the situation.

11. There is currently a debate about whether we always apply a single set of moral principles and a single form of moral judgement in various situations. Those who deny this are 'pluralists'. Pluralists argue that we may think deontologically in some situations, consequentially in others, while in others again we might be more concerned to preserve or develop virtue. Again, some pluralists point to a number of incommensurable overarching values or principles which might guide our lives (and which, on my model, would be operative at the fourth level of our being). My model is pluralist in this sense. Rationalism is no more the final arbiter of moral norms than emotivism or intuitionism would be. My four-level model embraces all of these approaches at the various levels, but sees them all as expressions of deep caring as self-project and as being-for-others. As such it provides a theoretical

---

[14]   The nature of this objectivity is explored by Julius Kovesi in his *Moral Notions* (London, 1967). Following Wittgenstein, Kovesi develops the idea that moral notions are objective although tied to the practices of particular language communities.

basis for pluralism in that it gives various ethical theories their (limited) place as expressions of deep caring.

Insofar as moral theory and moral thinking are culturally formed and contingent expressions of deep caring, the importance and value of our lives centre on integration and solidarity rather than on the ways we might have developed for achieving these, or the values we might have articulated in order to express them. Accordingly, there might indeed be a number of generalizable decision procedures, moral principles, rules of thumb or ideals of character for solving ethical dilemmas. But what matters is that each situation calls out to us in its own terms and calls out to all four levels of our being. What being ethical calls for is that we act so as to constitute and preserve our being as self-project and as being-for-others.

12. In relation to the debate between 'generalists' and 'particularists', I would agree with the latter.[15] A generalist holds that a moral judgement or decision takes the form of a deduction from general principles or rules, while a particularist stresses the sensitive attention that a moral agent should give to the morally salient features of the specific situation. These approaches need not be mutually exclusive, but there is an issue in descriptive moral psychology as to which takes priority. Given my conception of human being as involving a primordial orientation towards others and towards oneself, caring attention to the situation will be a framework in which any judgement or decision takes place.

A moral agent may use moral principles to articulate her motivational stance in any given situation and she may even express her thinking during or after the decision by way of a practical syllogism, but these will be forms given to her pre-conscious deep caring. Such forms are learnt in a given culture. In our post-Enlightenment culture, most of us learn to express our deep caring in response to morally relevant features of a situation by thinking of principles, rules or virtues. In another culture agents might respond in terms of what they take to be the will of the gods. And even understanding what is morally relevant in a situation will be a culturally learnt response operating at the second level of our being. What is regarded as a routine matter in one culture might be a matter that calls for moral deliberation in another. The more individualistic a culture is, the more freedom it gives its members, the greater the scope for asking what ought to be done.

Generalist ways of thinking are appropriate at the third level of our deep caring, while particularist ways of reacting are expressive of the second level. A full ethical theory will embrace both approaches. However, ethics is important in particular situations rather than as a matter of theoretical discourse. What we care about deeply is our integration and our belonging. These are particular concerns. Our concern with general ethical norms is derivative from this particularity.

---

[15]   For an introduction to particularism, see Lawrence A. Blum, 'Iris Murdoch and the domain of the moral', in his *Moral Perception and Particularity*, pp. 12–29.

13. In the debates between 'virtue ethics' and 'rule-based ethics', I would side with the proponents of virtue.[16] If the issue here is between considering what a moral agent should *be* rather than what he should *do*, then my model focuses on the first. The fundamental moral motivation is the twin motivation of preserving relationships and integration. This is an orientation to what we should be. What we should do becomes a derivative question that gains its urgency from this deep caring. Indeed, I would suggest that virtue-based ethical theory might be the only adequate way of holistically embracing all four levels of our deep caring. The key idea of virtue theory is that something deep within an agent comes to expression in moral action. What this something deep is will be described on my model as involving all four levels of our being. With this model, virtue theory can be internalist, particularist, pluralist, personalist and objectivist.

The rule-based ethicist says that we must make our ethical decisions on the basis of reasons. And if these reasons are to sway us, or to explain and justify our actions to others, then they must be general in form. That is, they must be understandable by other people in terms of how they apply to such situations in general, and agents must understand them and be prepared to apply them in other similar situations. On the other hand, virtue ethics is 'particularist'. What a virtuous person is able to do is to attend to all the morally relevant features of a particular situation and respond to them appropriately. She may not be able to say why she acted as she did and she may not be able to say ahead of time how she would act in a situation like the one at issue. Nor would she be able to say that she would act that way again in a similar situation (given that there can be morally salient differences in similar situations).

This point can be brought out with an analogy. Tom loves Mary. Jim asks Tom, 'Why do you love Mary?' Tom is unable to answer clearly, but when pressed he says that Mary has a sweet disposition, lovely hair and a cute smile. Jim now says that Jill has a sweet disposition, lovely hair and a cute smile too. Why doesn't Tom love her as well, or instead? If love were based on reasons, this point would confound Tom because reasons are general and what applies to one case should apply to others which are similar. But love is not like that. It is particularist. Something deep in Tom is attracted to Mary and reasons are only a superficial gloss on this. My point is that moral decisions are particularist in just this way. Something deep in the agent responds to what is morally relevant in the situation (the pain of the patient, or their loss of hope, say). The agent might be able to give no clear reason for her decision and offer no clear principle that she is following or would follow in similar circumstances. All that can be said is that this 'something deep' motivates the agent to do what she sees is best. This is her virtue.

But is such a non-generalizable account of ethical decision making of any use to us? This depends on what we think ethical theory is for. If it is to give us guidance as to what we should generally do, then such a notion of virtue is useless.

---

[16]   I have developed my position more fully in Stan van Hooft, *Understanding Virtue Ethics* (Chesham, 2005).

Because it does not trade in general reasons, it cannot offer guidelines or even rules of thumb. If these are what we want, then an ethics of duty is what we need. But if ethical theory is for giving us a description of moral psychology (and this is of practical importance for understanding moral education), then it should accept the particularist nature of moral decisions. The discourse of bioethics may contribute a general form to the innate desire to create and preserve relationships and integration, but there is no ultimate guidance and no safety offered by the pronouncements of professional ethicists.

Chapter 4

Towards a Theory of Caring

The notion of caring as used by nurses and as informing the self-understanding of nursing practice has been thematized and critiqued recently by Helga Kuhse in her book *Caring: Nurses, Women and Ethics*.[1] In this wide-ranging work, Kuhse acknowledges the importance of caring in the profession of nursing, but also criticizes its shortcomings. Situating her discussion in the history of the nursing profession and the ideologies which have circumscribed it, both inside and outside the profession, Kuhse espouses a strong patient advocacy role for nurses. However, she argues that caring by itself is inadequate for performing such a role and for the ethical life of nurses.

Analysis of Kuhse's argument

Practical reason is at the very heart of Kuhse's conception of ethics. Like many other philosophers in the Anglo-American tradition, she sees ethics as essentially a branch of practical reason. As she puts it, 'Living according to ethical standards is thus tied up with giving reasons for what we do, with justifying and defending the way in which we live.'[2] Moreover, Kuhse's conception of ethics is that of a social practice designed to achieve and maintain social harmony. Therefore, it requires an impartial consideration of the interests of all and an ability to engage in public discourse about one's actions. What she calls her 'minimalist conception of ethics' involves objectivity, consistency, clarity of thought, impartiality and universality.

Kuhse is committed to such a strong focus on practical reason because she is a utilitarian. Put simply, utilitarians maintain that an agent must calculate the consequences or anticipated consequences of the action options that a situation presents, and perform that action that will have the most beneficial consequences. (I leave open the question of just how the notion of 'beneficial' is to be specified.) The focus here is on the calculation. This decision procedure is an exercise of practical reason.

I should add here that it is important to discuss utilitarianism because it is, as it were, the default position in nursing ethics and in bioethics more generally. While

---

[1]   Helga Kuhse, *Caring: Nurses, Women and Ethics* (Oxford, 1997).
[2]   Ibid., p. 77

there is no room to critique utilitarianism in this chapter, my argument is informed by a general concern about its dominance of contemporary ethical discourse.

But a stress on practical reason will inevitably raise problems as to how to assimilate a concept such as caring into ethics. Caring is seen by many theorists as fundamentally a matter of emotion, where the emotions in question are those that give motivational impetus to actions required by interpersonal relationships of various kinds. Drawing on the literature generated by the work of Carol Gilligan, Kuhse acknowledges that this emotional conception is important. Gilligan is said to have made 'an attempt to articulate a theoretical approach to ethics that would capture the moral experiences of women'.[3] These experiences highlight the personal and private sphere of ethical motivation, especially in the realm of particular interpersonal relationships. While Kuhse argues that this is neither feminine nor masculine and should not be appropriated by feminism, she does acknowledge that mainstream ethics focuses too much on reason and on universality at the expense of the emotional or motivational aspects of our ethical lives. In this way, her argument establishes the *prima facie* relevance of caring to the professional and ethical lives of nurses.

But how does Kuhse understand 'caring' in the context of nursing? Kuhse suggests that nurses use the notion of care in two senses:

> The first involves an emotional response – concern for the other, emphasis on relationship, on attachment, openness, and on attentiveness and responsiveness to the needs of the cared-for. The second sense suggests looking after or providing for the needs of the other.[4]

While the second of these notions is behavioural, the first is a mode of being or a virtue. It answers the question 'How should I, the carer, meet the cared-for?' rather than the more standard ethical question, 'What should I do?' But, referring to the work of Nel Noddings, Kuhse argues that this conception seems to call just for emotion and that this does not do justice to the ethical demands of the patient–nurse relationship. In its place, Kuhse proposes a dispositional notion of caring which she explains thus: 'If we understand "care" broadly in the sense of willingness and openness to apprehend the health-related reality of the other, then it seems to me, we have captured what I want to call a "dispositional notion of care".'[5] This notion of caring focuses the attention of nurses on patients as particular others with needs, desires, and health-related problems. It sees caring as a form of perception which is open to the other as a vulnerable and unique person.

Utilitarianism is usually silent on how the action options of a situation present themselves to an agent. How an agent even notices that an action is called for, or how she notices that the options have a moral significance, is seldom explained by

---

3   Ibid., p. 99
4   Ibid., pp. 146–7
5   Ibid., p. 150

ethical theorists who stress practical reason. Where such explanations are offered, they refer to the principles that such theories already propound.[6] For example, most utilitarians would see as morally salient only those circumstances that are relevant to the possible beneficial outcomes of a situation. It is to Kuhse's credit, therefore, that she does recognize this problem and acknowledges that the caring perspective provides a means for solving it. This concept of caring is an important contribution to the utilitarian outlook since it addresses how an agent comes to confront a morally complex situation and to recognize what is ethically salient in it, even when this does not relate directly to preference satisfaction. On this view, caring is an attentiveness that leads agents to put their ethical principles into effect. Conceived as perceptual in this way, caring is necessary for ethical action.

But Kuhse also maintains that caring is only a part of the structure of a complete moral action. She insists that impartial practical reason should still be predominant in the ethical lives of nurses. She suggests that 'Dispositional care is ... a necessary but not sufficient condition for an ethics that will serve patients and nurses well. An adequate ethics needs impartiality or justice as well as care.'[7] The reason for this is that beyond dispositional caring, 'We need to be able to identify the nature of the good we are pursuing, and we need universalizable principles and rules to counter arbitrariness and caprice.'[8] The reasons for our caring (which make it ethical) must be found in the object of caring rather than in the feeling or emotion of the nurse. For example, should a distressed dying patient be kept alive by heroic medical means or be allowed to die? What would caring suggest here? One sense of caring for the patient (seeing to physical needs) suggests keeping alive. The other sense (compassion) suggests letting die. Kuhse's point is that caring by itself leaves the nurse not knowing what to do. It is the patient's wishes or the principles that are agreed to apply to such cases which should indicate the right course of action rather than the feeling of compassion or the general imperative to see to the patient's needs. So it is not only a cognitive attentiveness that is needed, but also action that can be discursively justified in the light of impartial principles.

Kuhse asks how a nurse who cares but does not think rationally could balance the demands arising from several patients. And how would a caring perspective deal with preventive care policies in cases where no particular patient was at issue? But Kuhse's most important argument is that a relational ethics of care silences nurses: 'To eschew all moral principles is to withdraw from moral discourse and to retreat into an essentially dumb world of one's own.'[9] And she adds:

---

[6]   Owen Flanagan, *Varieties of Moral Personality* (Cambridge, Massachusetts, 1991), Chapter 4.

[7]   Kuhse, p. 145.

[8]   Ibid., p. 157

[9]   Ibid., p. 162

If nurses eschew all universal principles and norms, they will not be able to participate in ethical discourse. They will not be able to speak on behalf of the patients for whom they care, nor will they be able to defend their own legitimate claims.[10]

In this chapter I want to explore the dispositional notion of caring that Kuhse has developed and the relationship between caring and practical reason which is implicit in her position.

Motivations and reasons

Moral psychology is important for anyone seeking to understand the place of caring in our decision making. For example, Kuhse's concept of dispositional caring raises the problem of adjudicating the various and sometimes conflicting claims upon us of our motivations and inclinations on the one hand and of practical reason on the other. This problem has a long history. Hume thought of reason as the slave of the passions. This implied that reason was a purely instrumental faculty which we used in order to obtain more effectively what our 'passions' or desires indicated as leading to our satisfaction. On this view, we feel wants and desires and then calculate how we will achieve what we desire. The role of reason is thus limited to that of a means for attaining satisfaction. It is necessary for the possibility of our being moral, therefore, that sympathy is to be found among our desires. Without this essentially altruistic 'passion', egoism would hold sway in our lives since practical reason cannot ground an altruistic ethics by itself. For his part, Kant held that reason was the pre-eminent faculty for ethics and that we were ethical only to the extent that we followed the dictates of reason. In order to have a 'good will' we should disregard our 'inclinations' entirely, think rationally and consistently, and be moved by the sheer respect that we felt for that logical rigour to act in accordance with what practical reason indicated.

Kuhse's discussion of Gilligan's work restores such 'inclinations' as caring and concern for others to importance in our ethical lives. But Kuhse does not accept the Humean alternative that reason should be nothing more than the instrument of our achieving what we care about and that caring should be the sole guide of our ethical lives. Even though she accords more importance to caring than do many rationalistic ethicists, Kuhse still gives the principle of utility fundamental importance in ethical thought. Dispositional caring discloses what a situation demands, but the rightness or wrongness of an action derives from its status as disclosed by reason.

Accordingly, Kuhse explicates the relationship between a disposition to see and act upon what is ethically needed in a situation on the one hand, and an ethical decision guided by practical reason on the other, by referring to the two-level

---

[10]   Ibid., p. 166

utilitarian approach of Richard M. Hare.[11] For Hare, our moral actions can be motivated by immediate moral intuitions and then justified later in a rational reflection that appeals to principles or to a consideration of the preferences of individuals impartially conceived.[12] On this view, caring might lead in an immediate way to action but this action will be legitimate only if it can be subsequently justified by offering reasons. In this conception, practical reason operates as a sort of house of review.

Yet it is clear that Kuhse also wants practical reason to play a constructive role in the making of ethical decisions. Reason will need to enter into the formation of decisions and thus play a role in the moral psychology of agents alongside caring perception and motivation. To see how this might work we need to understand Kuhse's notion of dispositional caring more fully. We have seen that she sees caring as a structure of perception whereby the morally salient features of a situation are noticed. By describing caring as dispositional, Kuhse skirts around the problem of whether it should be primarily understood as a mode of perception or of motivation (or whether these are inherently connected). The notion of a disposition is an operational notion used within behaviourist discourses which points to whatever it is in the agent that leads to action in typical or characteristic circumstances. The key point is that it does not matter to a dispositional analysis what the internal elements in the agent are. It matters only that there are such elements and that they should lead to appropriate action in circumstances that demand it. So Kuhse can afford to be neutral on the question of whether caring is a mode of perception or a motivation or both. Yet we do need to ask how whatever it is that operates within the agent characteristically leads to action in order to understand the role of reason in that process.

Perhaps Kuhse assumes that, along with seeing what a situation demands, a sensitive agent will be motivated to act accordingly. But this assumption does need justification. If we think of caring just as a sensitive mode of perception, then we have the problem of showing how such perception leads to action. As aesthetic perception in the context of the dramatic and narrative arts shows, it is possible to attend to the particularity of a person, with their needs and their suffering, and simply to enjoy this as an aesthetic experience. We may empathize with a character who is badly treated in a novel, play or film, but such experience does not, and should not, lead to action to alleviate the suffering. Sensitive awareness of another's needs does not necessarily motivate action or give us a reason to act. And, of course, we can also imagine an immoral, psychopathic or sadistic person who sees the genuine suffering of another in a real life situation and does nothing to alleviate it.

Even if we think of caring as a motivation, we still need to ask how it leads to action. That there is a gap that needs to be bridged here is shown by the

---

[11]   Ibid., pp. 139 and 151

[12]   Richard Mervyn Hare, *Moral Thinking: Its Levels, Method and Point* (Oxford, 1981).

phenomenon of weakness of will. One can be motivated to do something and yet fail to do it. Indeed, this gap is presupposed by Kuhse's argument. She envisages that caring nurses might be motivated to act towards particular patients in particular ways but that they should still ask themselves whether that is what they ought to do. And if they decide that it is not, then they should not proceed. So it is not only weakness of will but also what we might call 'ethical hesitation' which shows that there must be a gap between being motivated to act and actually going to act: a gap to be filled by practical reason and decision.

And yet, on the Humean conception which Kuhse partly shares, reason by itself does not motivate either. Kuhse has the problem of explaining how impartial reasons can be motivational for particular agents. Practical reason should be more than a review of actions after they are performed or an impartial calculation whose purpose is to decide what is to be done. It must itself be motivational. Practical reason too should have a role which is internal to the processes that lead to action. In order to see how this might be possible, we will have to explore the psychological structure of moral action.

Internalism and externalism

There would seem to be three stages involved in the moral psychology of behaviour that expresses caring. First, there is the sensitive awareness of the clinical situation and the needs of the persons in it. This perceptual stage will give us a reason to act in a certain way. It is cognitive and subject to the criteria of 'true' or 'false'. Our beliefs about the situation have to be true. But we need to have more than an accurate description of the situation. We also need to see what should be done in that situation. In this way seeing the situation accurately will disclose to us what ought to be done in it. Sensitive perception leads us to internalize what Robert Audi calls a 'normative reason' to act.[13] Second, having this reason to act will have to become a motive for the agent. I might know on the basis of sensitive perception what the situation is and what I ought to do and still not be motivated to do it. So where does the relevant motivation come from? Perhaps we need a general desire to do what is right or a commitment to a general principle such as that of utility. Either way, this stage is not cognitive and is separated from the first by a fact/value distinction. Seeing the situation for what it is does not logically entail that the agent will want to do what should be done. (Though the situation may entail that it *should* be done. The is/ought distinction works differently from the fact/value distinction. It may be that if a nurse sees that a patient needs help, this directly entails – in the context of a nurse–patient relationship – that the nurse ought to give that help. However, this entailment says nothing about whether the nurse will in fact be motivated to help.) Third, this motivation will have to lead to

---

13   Robert Audi, *Moral Knowledge and Ethical Character* (New York, 1997), pp. 217–47.

the performance of the action. Is the fact that the agent is motivated to perform the action sufficient to lead the agent to act if nothing prevents the action? It would seem not, since I have already noted that agents can fail to act in the way they are motivated to act or that they can change their minds.

The first stage of this sketch of agent psychology: that of obtaining a normative reason for action through sensitive perception, raises the problem of understanding how reasons can become normative. In discussing this problem, many philosophers use the term 'externalism'. More specifically, Robert Audi speaks of 'reasons externalism'. This suggests that no motivational states are necessary to make a reason normative. Reason can establish what ought to be done independently of the motivations, wishes or commitments of the agent. Although Kuhse does not explicitly espouse it, reasons externalism is implicit in her analysis. The utilitarian calculus appeals only to consequences and can thus establish what it is right to do irrespective of what anyone wants to do (though not irrespective of what anyone wants to have happen). It also suggests that, whether I make the judgement or not, it makes sense to say that there is a moral reason for me to do something and that that reason can be identified on grounds that refer to actual outcomes rather than on grounds that depend upon or involve the agent's expectations, dispositions, moral stances or virtues. Accordingly, reasons externalism would suggest that dispositional caring is irrelevant to practical reason when it discerns what ought to be done.

The opposite position is 'reasons internalism'. Of this, Audi says:

> In a generic form, it is roughly the view that normative reasons for action must be grounded in some internal conative or at least non-cognitive motivational state, such as a want, desire, passion, or emotion.[14]

This is an alternative view about what makes a reason normative. While a reasons externalist would say that only something external to the agent could make a reason normative, an internalist would say that an action is right if it accords with a morally good motivation of the agent. On this view, moral judgements provide reasons for action because they tap into basic desires. If these desires include altruism or caring, then these motivational judgements can also be, fortuitously and contingently, normative. Here the implication flows from their being motivational to their being normative. However, this would mean that the normativity of reasons is based on the contingent fact of our having desires (broadly conceived) which are moral in their object. As a result, reasons internalism is contentious. Most moral theorists, whether consequentialist or Kantian, require that the moral reasons one has for acting should be normative whether or not they are supported by desire. Kuhse would certainly require that nurses' perception of what ought to be done in a clinical situation, or the reasons to act which sensitive perceptions would give

---

[14]   Ibid., p. 221

them, should gain their moral normativity from the external consequences of such actions rather than from the dispositional caring of those nurses.

I now want to focus on the transition from stage one to stage two of the model of action given above: the transition from having a normative reason to act to being motivated to act accordingly. How can we be moved to act by the perception of what ought to be done in the situation? The technical term used by Audi to highlight this problem is 'motivational externalism'. Motivational externalism is the view that an agent can have accepted a reason to act but fail to act on it because the reason does not provide the necessary motivation. It is the view that there is a gap between having a reason for doing something and being motivated to do it. It implies that reasons as such can fail to motivate. In contrast, Robert Audi takes:

> *motivational internalism proper* to be the view that some degree of motivation is intrinsic (and in that sense internal) to the holding of a (self-addressed) moral judgement – especially the kind that is for or against some particular action or type of action clearly representing one's future possible conduct.[15]

Notice that Audi speaks of a moral judgement here. A moral judgement is a peculiar form of judgement in that its appeal to moral concepts would tend to make it inevitable for non-psychopathic agents that it will motivate. Motivational internalism seems the most plausible view in relation to such judgements.

But, for Kuhse, caring is preliminary to moral judgement. For her, caring as sensitive perception is not yet a moral judgement. If such caring also motivates it will not be because of its already having a moral quality. Therefore, it is not clear whether she is a motivational internalist. If the moral judgement is put to one side, then the problem for Kuhse becomes that of showing how the sensitive perception which is said to be central to dispositional caring would motivate the caring agent to act. In other words, how does a normative reason (provided by the sensitive perception) become motivational for the agent? Kuhse assumes that it does, but does not show how. I will suggest that, were she to address this problem, she would tend to the motivational externalist position.

In its most extreme form, motivational internalism is the view that having a normative reason for action provides a degree of motivation that is not only necessary for the performance of an action but also sufficient. Of course, outside circumstances ranging from the unavailability of tools to sudden paralysis in the agent's body may prevent the action from taking place, but the extreme motivational internalist will argue that the motivation inherent in the having of reasons for an action will be sufficient to produce that action if such inhibitive external circumstances are absent. In contrast, motivational externalism is taken to be necessary to explain how an agent can have reasons to act in a certain way and yet not do it because of a lack of motivation. (Such an explanation would differ from an explanation for not doing it which appeals to a weakness of will or to the

---

15   Ibid., p. 224

presence of countervailing reasons. Such explanations are consistent with agents' being motivated to some degree to act in accordance with the reasons they have.)

In arguing that practical reason should intervene so that dispositional caring does not lead directly to action, it would seem that Kuhse is a motivational externalist and that she is committed to understanding caring in externalist terms. For practical reason to be able to intervene in this way, caring must not lead directly to the action. Whatever motivation is present must not be sufficient to produce the action. Kuhse must reject extreme motivational internalism. It is not so clear whether she must also reject the more moderate form of motivational internalism which would suggest that there could be 'some degree of motivation' arising from sensitive perception. Admittedly the best way for theory to ensure that motivation must not be sufficient to produce the action is to argue that there is no motivational impetus at all to be derived just from having the reason that dispositional caring gives us. Such an argument would lead to extreme motivational externalism. But I have assumed that Kuhse's account of dispositional caring suggests that caring is needed not only to allow the agent to see what action is called for by the situation so as to give the agent reasons to act, but also as a motivational additive to those reasons. If this is what Kuhse means, nurses will not only have a reason to help a patient when they notice that the patient is in need, but also, if they care about the patient or about some relevant feature of the situation, they will be motivated to act on that reason. In this way it would be dispositional caring which turns normative reasons into motivations and which leads the agent to action. This is a form of motivational internalism. It is because caring can motivate in this way that dispassionate moral reasoning is required as a process of review to monitor what caring would lead one to do.

But Kuhse also has reason to espouse a moderate form of motivational externalism in which dispositional caring does not completely motivate an agent to act. Not only could Kuhse not accept extreme motivational internalism because it would leave no room for weakness of will and for ethical hesitation but also because it would threaten a return to a Humean outlook in which caring could not be subject to rational appraisal. For Hume, reason was the instrumental slave of the passions. On such a view, caring would have to be accepted ethically at face value. If the passions are independent of reason, their moral standing would have to derive just from their own nature. Moreover, such a view would threaten the ability of reason to review an action before it is performed. On this reading, Kuhse would have inherited Hume's problem of desires being intrinsically motivating and valuable and thus *prima facie* beyond the range of a critique by reason. In fact, Kuhse wants reason to be both independent and dominant. And in order to ensure the latter, Kuhse is committed to reasons externalism, as we have seen, and also to motivational externalism. For her, reasons do not need to be motivational in order to be normative and neither are they compelled to become sufficiently motivational by their being normative.

Enlightenment conceptions of the agent

This complex and compartmentalized account of reasons and motivations for action needed to understand the role of Kuhse's notion of dispositional caring in our moral psychology would seem to leave practical reason quarantined from perceptual and motivational elements in decision making. Kuhse seems to have inherited a conception of the human person that became dominant during the Enlightenment. This conception was dualistic in a number of ways. As is well known, it was dualistic in that it distinguished body from mind as two metaphysically distinct kinds of entity. But it was also dualistic in that it distinguished reason from emotion (and from a cluster of other non-rational functions including perception, imagination, and motivation). Indeed, various theorists of that tradition have spoken of a number of 'faculties of the mind', including belief, sensation, desire, the will, reason, cognition, fantasy, feeling, emotion, imagination, consciousness, and so forth. In identifying such 'faculties', philosophers reified a number of mental functions, thought of them as somehow distinct from each other, and thereby gave themselves the task of showing how they interact.

It is such a compartmentalized and reified conception of the human person which leads to problems of reasons externalism and motivational externalism and which a more holistic way of thinking inspired by a more recent phenomenological tradition of thought is striving to overcome. The concept of caring, I will now begin to argue, should be understood from within this latter tradition so that it does not take its place as yet one more faculty or function in an interactive mental system within which the connections await theoretical exposition.

A new conception of caring

I would suggest that when a typical proponent of the caring perspective in nursing such as Simone Roach says 'Caring is the human mode of being' and 'Nursing is the professionalization of the human capacity to care',[16] what she is wanting to stress is the holism of caring. Rather than the dualistic or faculty-based conception of moral decision making common to both the Humean and Kantian traditions, contemporary caring theorists have wanted to stress that caring should infuse all aspects of our moral lives. More specifically, if we are going to use practical reason as either the key to a decision procedure or as a reflective device for assessing the moral worth of what has been done, then caring theorists would want such reasoning also to express caring. It is not enough, from this perspective, that caring will have entered into the moral decision as a necessary first step – whether

---

[16]   Simone S. Roach, 'The Aim of Philosophical Inquiry in Nursing: Unity or Diversity of Thought?', in June F. Kikuchi and Helen Simmons (eds), *Philosophical Inquiry in Nursing* (Newbury Park, California, 1992), pp. 38–44, 41.

as perception or as motivation – or as the executive impetus needed to put a rational decision into effect. Caring must also infuse practical reason itself. For example, to adapt a frequently discussed example, imagine a situation in which two children are in mortal danger and an adult is close at hand who can save just one of them. Suppose further that that adult is the parent of one of the endangered children. Many of those who adhere to an impartialist ethics would argue that in such a case, agents have a *prima facie* duty to be impartial and to seek to save the child whose prospects of survival are the best or who most clearly deserves to be saved. Both a commonsense and a caring approach, on the other hand, would say that it was at least permissible for parents to prefer their own children regardless of such impartialist considerations. While there are some impartialists who decide in favour of the common sense intuition that it is legitimate to prefer one's own child by appealing to such a utilitarian ground as that such a policy would lead to the greatest preference satisfaction for the greatest number over time, it is striking that they still prefer impartial practical reason where an immediate caring response seems to be what is called for. There is something odd about parents who need externalist reasons to justify actions that stem from their parental love. What we would admire more is a person whose caring suffused their reason in such a way that both their actions and their reasoning are expressions of their caring.

So how will we develop a notion of caring which is holistic and which infuses the whole of our moral being? While it will not be possible to complete such a grand project within the compass of this chapter, in order to indicate how it might unfold, it is helpful to note one feature of the Descartes/Hume/Kant tradition of which so many modern moral theories are a part. The dominant concerns of this Enlightenment tradition were epistemological. Given the great challenges to religious and social orthodoxies which the development of science and an emerging belief in individual autonomy were creating, the most important philosophical problem facing that age was the basis of knowledge. Was knowledge to be gained by obedience to authority – whether in the form of religious tradition or kingly power – or was it to be gained by unshackled inquiry? And if the latter, what should be the rules of such inquiry so as to guarantee truth? Important as these issues were, they resulted in a focus on the human being in which the dominant question was how human beings received knowledge from the world around them. In order to secure the veracity of knowledge, it was crucial that our perception should register the way that the world actually is and that our beliefs should accord with reality. In other words, so far as their reason was concerned, human beings had to fit in with the objective reality of the world. Human beings should be receptive of information from the world in a way that was minimally distortive of that world. Empiricism, with its positing of sense data as the building blocks of knowledge, was the most direct expression of this approach, but even rationalism sought to reject any suggestion that human subjects could cognitively create a world by using the concepts with which the mind was furnished. So far as knowledge was concerned, human beings were relatively passive. The direction of fit between human subjects and the world was such that the world was what it was and human subjects had to fit themselves to it.

In the field of ethics this style of thought has expressed itself variously as moral realism, objectivism, or cognitivism. Broadly, these views suggest that moral norms or principles have an objective existence of some kind and that being moral consists in apprehending or discovering these rules and then living in accordance with them. While the philosophical issues here are too complex and our sketch of them too brief for us to critique this position here, it will be clear that reasons externalism is an expression of this tradition in moral psychology and that utilitarianism also belongs in this tradition. For utilitarians, it is an objective fact that certain action options have certain consequences. Even if it is too difficult for a specific agent to know what those consequences will be, they have an objective existence in that they will be realized in the fullness of time if the envisaged action is performed. It is these factual consequences which dictate whether the action is right or wrong. The agent's task is to discern them as accurately as possible and to act accordingly. The rightness of the action is an objective matter received, as it were, by the agent from the world. In relation to this objective rightness, the agent must be subservient. Although the agent is active in relation to the action options that the situation presents, and in relation to the perception, understanding, and reasoning which must be engaged in, it is the world and what happens in it that dictates what should be done.

We could perhaps illustrate the notion of the human person which is implicit in this tradition of thought by thinking of persons as a cinema screen upon which the world projects itself. What happens on the screen (in the person) is, or should be, a reflection of how the world is.

But there is another tradition of thought in modern philosophy as well: a tradition that includes Spinoza, Hegel, Nietzsche and the existentialist thinkers. So far as epistemology is concerned, this tradition stresses the active construction of knowledge on the part of human beings, and in relation to ethics it places a greater stress on the creativity and dynamism of human agents.[17] If I can use the analogy of a screen again, we might think, this time, of a television screen onto which images are projected which come from within the television set and which seem to be created by it. This screen does not reflect the world around it. It creates a new reality within it. Another way of putting this point is to note that there is another direction of fit with the world, other than the one stressed by the mainstream tradition: namely, the direction of fit in which the world is made to fit with the way the subject is.

While it is true that this way of thinking can lead, in the sphere of knowledge, to an acceptance of ideology and superstition (seeing the world in accordance with our desires, fears and hopes, rather than as it really is), it is also true that this orientation makes for creativity and change. The most central human 'faculty'

---

[17]   For an excellent overview of these issues, see David E. Cooper, *The Measure of Things: Humanism, Humility, and Mystery* (Oxford, 2002).

which is involved in this orientation towards the world is that of desire. When I desire something, I want the world to become as I desire it to be. When I desire a piece of cheesecake, I want the world to be such that cheesecake is in my possession or even in my mouth. It will be clear that, if we are developing a philosophical understanding of action, we will need to be very conscious of this orientation towards the world. Action is not just a set of reactions to the way the world is, it is also, and most importantly, an engagement with the world which seeks to change it in accordance with our creative and desired conceptions. In action we do more than understand the world, we change it.

Now ethics involves thinking about what we should do, and how we should be. Accordingly, it is about changing the world rather than merely reflecting about it. It is creative of value rather than merely subservient to value conceived as existing objectively within it. There are very large philosophical issues at play in these claims, and for the sake of keeping this chapter within manageable proportions I want to shrink back from exploring all of them. Suffice to say that from this perspective the most important issue in ethics is not that of discovering what it is right to do by the use of an externalist practical reason and then obeying, but that of developing a form or style of creative orientation towards the world which will lead us to create value in it. The dynamic and creative aspect of our own human existence must be shaped in such a way as to result in ethical behaviour.

In order to explain this it may help to use some existentialist ideas. The notion of the human person of the existentialist tradition is that of human being, where 'being' is a verb. The self is seen as a 'project' in which the goal is that of creating and maintaining one's own identity and integrity. Although Jean-Paul Sartre may have fetishized freedom to an untenable degree, the basic idea which he expressed was that of the creative self-making of the human individual in the context of a material and social world the meaning of which could be structured by the individual to fit with his or her projects. This way of thinking goes back to Spinoza's concept of *conatus*. This term points to the dynamic, desiring, creative aspect of human being. It designates the way a human being reaches out to the world and shapes it. Human beings do not just react to the world and seek a state of equilibrium or contentment. Human beings are active and pursue their projects in such a way that fulfilment only comes if effort has been expended and difficulties overcome. Without challenge there is no satisfaction. The mode of being which is characteristic of human beings contains a conative (proactive) aspect as well as a cognitive (receptive) one. The conative aspect of our being is our projecting ourselves into the world in order to fulfil our projects within it. It is the aspect of our existence that seeks to change the world in order to bring it into alignment with our needs and aspirations.

In using the notion of desire to illustrate the idea of the conative aspect of our existence, I am in danger, not only of limiting the concept to that of seeking contentment, but also of reintroducing the compartmentalized and reified 'faculty' model of the human person, as if 'desire' or 'conation' was one of the faculties that go to make up the complex system of mental functions that constitutes our selfhood. However, I do not want to return to this model. The notion of a conative aspect of our being is the notion of a creative and motivational impetus which infuses our whole being. All of the mental functions or faculties that have been described by philosophers in the past as making up our mental lives are suffused through and through with this dynamic self-projection into the world.

We can illustrate the conative aspect of our being by returning to our example of the television set. In projecting its image onto the screen and into the world, the television set might use a number of different functions and components. One part of the set assembles the colours while another shapes the picture and another again throws it onto the screen. But the analogy only helps to illuminate what conation is if we consider the electric current which enlivens and makes possible all those processes. It is as if the conative aspect of our being enlivens or electrifies our whole being, including all of our faculties. It provides the impetus and the enthusiasm with which we live our lives. We may want, for reasons of analysis, to distinguish the mental functions or faculties of reasoning, perception, motivation, and so on, but without the infusion of the enlivening element of conation all this would be just so much biological processing and triggering of reactions. Conation is not another mental function or faculty to be assembled into a complete picture of our subjective existence along with such other functions as reason and will. It is the very enthusing of those functions with our lust for life, our existential self-project, our relationships with others, and our love of the world. Our existential being as project-for-living is the fundamental drive and creativity which makes us who we are.

But who we are is also the result of the shaping which this conative form of our being receives from our society, our families, our habits and our decisions. The narrative of our lives is the story of the shaping of our conative being into a social form comprising character, relationships, social roles, and ethical responsibilities.

The conative aspect of human existence can take ethically admirable forms or ethically deplorable forms.[18] If all I ever want is my own satisfaction and if I am prepared to use others and even to exploit them in order to achieve this, and if I see others just as means for my own satisfaction, then the form of my conative orientation towards the world will be egoistic and deplorable. It will not be virtuous. It may even result in my performing actions which my society regards as immoral. Whereas if my wants and desires and my outlook on others embrace helping others and giving attention to my friends and family, then the form of my orientation towards the world will be altruistic and admirable. It will be virtuous and it will result in my characteristically performing actions which society considers moral.

It can be argued, though there is no room to do so in this chapter, that the egoistic orientation is contrary to our most fundamental nature as human beings. It can be argued that concern for particular others is more consistent with our natural orientation towards the world and our concern for ourselves than an exclusive self-

---

[18]   Michael Slote, *From Morality to Virtue* (New York, 1992), p. 93.

regard.[19] Be that as it may, it is important to see that the conative aspect of our being is not only an expression of egoistic desire. Such egoistic desire seeks to change the world by appropriating it. It is dynamic and creative, but its goal is to make use of things and people in the world for the purpose of the fulfilment of our own projects. But there is also a dynamic and creative aspect of our being which consists in giving. There is a fundamental stance towards the world which is that of expressing our own fullness in a way that enhances the world. If desire is *eros*, then this further dimension of our creative dynamism is *agapé*. Artistic creation and parenting are but two examples of how this fundamental conative drive towards giving comes to expression. Whenever we take pride in an achievement of ours in the world, we are acknowledging a satisfaction that comes from having added to the value that the world contains. Whatever our egoistic rewards and desire satisfactions might be in such an achievement, part of what we relish is the feeling that we have made a contribution out of our own being. We all want to enhance the world in some way even as we change it.

If we direct this *agapé*, this drive towards giving and enhancing, upon other people with whom we have some kind of relationship, whether remote, professional or intimate, then we have captured the notion of caring which I want to develop. My central thesis is that other-directed caring is an orientation of the self-giving conative aspect of our being towards other people. More specifically, the caring of which the nursing literature speaks is the conative and giving orientation of nurses towards those people with whom their professional responsibilities bring them into direct or indirect contact.

Making ethical decisions

It would follow from this analysis of caring that we should revise the two-dimensional model of ethical decision making which Kuhse espouses in her book. Rather than seeing caring just as a perceptual, emotional and motivational stage of ethical decision making which needs to be supplemented or reviewed by impartial practical reason, caring should be seen as a holistic, giving orientation of nurses, which directs and focuses all of their professional attention and motivation towards the needs of their clients, whether conceived as individual patients or as groups and sectors of the community.

This conception of caring would overcome the problems arising from motivational externalism and reasons externalism and which are troublesome for Kuhse's account. The gap between sensitive perception and the having of a normative reason to act – the problem of reasons externalism – and the problem of being motivated to act on one's normative reasons (and also the problem of

---

[19]   This has been argued, for example, by Jonathan Lear, *Love and its Place in Nature: A Philosophical Interpretation of Freudian Psychoanalysis* (New York, 1990), and by Stan van Hooft, *Caring: An Essay in the Philosophy of Ethics* (Niwot, Colorado, 1995).

bridging the gap between being motivated to act and actually going to act) – the problem of motivational externalism – are bridged by caring. But they are not solved by a notion of dispositional caring which sees it as another faculty or element such as Humean desire or Kantian inclination which stands in problematic relations to reason. What reasons externalism separates – having a sensitive and accurate perception of the situation and having a normative reason to act (or making a judgement about what ought to be done) – is linked by caring. And what motivational externalism separates – having a normative reason to act and being motivated to act in accordance with that reason – is also linked by caring. If caring is an orientation of the subjective reality of the agent which suffuses his or her whole existential being, then the having of an other-regarding reason will be inherently motivational. And its being motivational will make it normative. The having of a reason will not only be a neutral belief about what action a situation calls for, it will be a call to action. Seeing a patient in need will not only give the agent a further belief about the world or a normative reason to act. Such an experience will be felt as a call to action. It will involve a judgement about what should be done and it will directly motivate the agent because the caring will enliven the cognition in such a way as to turn it into a motivation. Again, whereas motivational externalism separates having a motivation from actually putting that motivation into effect, my notion of caring will bridge this gap. For a person who cares about the matter at issue, a motivation to act in a certain way, being an expression of a sensitive perception of what the situation calls for, will, all other things being equal, lead directly to action.

Whereas motivational externalism is about what makes a normative reason into a motivational reason or a motivation, reasons externalism is about what makes an objective circumstance into a normative reason for an agent. Both explanations can be given if caring is assumed as a holistic context and as a motivational background for the moral psychology of the agent. But such a context will then yield an internalist analysis of moral psychology. Unlike Kuhse, I am committed to both reasons internalism and motivational internalism.

However, reasons internalism and motivational internalism leave problems about weakness of will, ethical hesitation, changing one's mind, and the role of objective reason. The last problem is easily solved. There is no completely objective reason. Nor is there an *a priori*, universal set of norms in ethics. External reasons (of which objective reasons and universal moral values are subsets) should not be called reasons at all. There may be circumstances in the world which, were we to be sensitively aware of them, would call upon us to act. But unless we are aware of them, it begs the question to call them normative reasons to act. Externalism in all its forms involves a kind of 'overobjectification' of normative reasons which is not available to real human agents.[20] Of course, I do not want to suggest that we cannot take the views and claims of others into account when we engage in practical reason. We may even be able to place their needs or demands

---

[20]   Thomas Nagel, *The View from Nowhere* (New York, 1986), p. 162.

ahead of our own. But when we do so, we do it because we care about those others or about such values as justice which might be relevant to the situation. We can only act on the best lights and best motivations that we have. It is these lights and motivations, arising from our caring orientation towards the world, that constitute worldly situations as ones that have both a normative and motivational call upon us.

Some difficulties

Of course, there are serious difficulties with this view. It seems to suggest that for a correctly motivated person impulsive action will be acceptable. And this leads directly to the problems that Kuhse has identified. There will be no room for reflection and for the consideration of other relevant matters. Action becomes dumb and immune to rational revision or decision. But I answer this objection by saying that caring also infuses such revision or decision. What this means is that caring infuses the exercises of practical reason that might, on occasion, need to give the agent pause. The model of responsible and ethical action is neither that of impulsive action (where the impulse arises from the ethically positive stance of caring) nor is it Kuhse's two-stage model where the impulse should be checked and reviewed by an impartial form of practical reason.

The account of our moral psychology that I need to give in order to leave room for ethical hesitation is similar to the account that I would give for weakness of will. The problem of weakness of will goes back as least as far as Plato and Aristotle. Plato was a motivational internalist in that he thought that once we apprehended the Form of the Good we would be directly motivated to follow it so that it would change our lives. In this sense knowledge was virtue. Knowing the good would immediately make us good. For Plato weakness of will was not possible. When persons fail to do what they judge to be good to do it is because they did not in fact correctly apprehend the Good. Aristotle, for his part, would have no truck with such an idea of the Good. Yet he, too, was a motivational internalist. He argued that when a virtuous person apprehended what was to be done in a situation and judged that that was what the situation called for, she would be directly moved to act in accordance with that judgement. In the event that she did not do so – in the event, that is, that there was an instance of weakness of will – it would be because another motivational judgement to the effect that something else was good to do interfered with and, as it were, short circuited the initial judgement. I would endorse this motivational internalist analysis of weakness of will or of changing one's mind. It acknowledges that agents can undergo internal conflict without requiring a postulation of 'faculties' between which there would be that conflict.

Applying this analysis to Kuhse's example, nurses can be motivated towards helping a dying patient achieve relief from suffering, and they can be motivated towards honouring the value of life. In both instances there is caring involved. It is not a conflict between caring and principle. It is a conflict between one expression of caring and another expression of caring. There is caring for the individual patient, and there is caring about the perceived values. Given my Aristotelian account of weakness of will, ethical hesitation, or changing one's mind, there is one cognition (of the particular suffering patient) which is normative, motivational, and action-producing and another cognition which is also normative, motivational, and action-producing but which is caring in relation to other more general considerations. The conflict between these cognitions may produce weakness of will or ethical hesitation.

One can be a motivational internalist and still accept weakness of will, hesitation, and the rational review of ethical action. And such a rational review will be caring rather than impartial. Caring might be a holistic concept but it is not a unifying one. It describes the motivational psychology of agents in an all-embracing way, but it cannot guarantee that there will not be conflict within that psychology.

But then, does the integration of our moral lives require a second-order level in our moral psychology at which such conflicts can be resolved? Rationalistic systems of ethics have thought that such a second-order level would be provided by a single overarching principle such as the categorical imperative or the principle of utility. But on my view there is no universal practical reason to provide or justify such principles. Perhaps there are caring theorists who suppose that such an overarching resolution can come from caring. Such theorists might suppose that, provided we care enough, the single right course of action will present itself. Like Kuhse, I believe that this is an empty promise. Far from providing a second-order solution, caring about the issues and the persons who are involved in a morally complex situation is what makes such problems so difficult and seemingly intractable. In such situations, a decision just has to be made and it has to be made with sensitivity and responsibility. It is part of caring to acknowledge that, sometimes, there is no objective guarantee that one is doing what others would judge to be right.

Chapter 5

Acting from the Virtue of Caring

Helga Kuhse has recently argued that, taken by itself, caring is inadequate as a guide to ethical decision making in nursing.[1] While caring is necessary to ensure that nurses are sensitive to the morally salient features of a clinical situation, it is not sufficient to ensure morally justifiable action. A more objective principle-based form of ethical thinking is also required in order to ensure that nurses act well and are able to justify what they do in public ethical discourse. Kuhse argues that practical reason must be rational, principled, impartial, universal and publicly justifiable. She suggests that, by itself, caring does not meet these criteria. Kuhse sees caring as a necessary but not sufficient preliminary to moral action: namely, a stage of sensitively seeing the patient's needs. For her, the moral quality of an action arises from the moral reasoning that leads to it or justifies it, rather than the caring that might have been a preliminary to it.

Against this I will suggest that caring is a virtue and I will argue that the virtue of caring embraces all aspects of action, including the emotions, motivations, knowledge, and ethical thinking that enter into it. In my view, caring is central to all aspects of nursing practice and is the basis of its moral quality. This need not imply that acting from principle or on the basis of impartial reasoning is irrelevant to acting well. There will be occasions when caring nurses will make use of such principles. But the moral quality of their actions will not depend solely upon such reasoning as Kuhse suggests. I do not argue that caring ethics can replace principle-based ethics or render it irrelevant. Rather, I argue that principle-based ethics is embraced by caring conceived as a virtue, and therefore that caring is central in the lives of nurses.

Caring as a virtue

Virtue ethics claims that, if an agent acts from virtue, this will be sufficient to make the action good. Acting from virtue is not only necessary but also sufficient for the goodness of the action. No impartial or detached appeal to principles is needed as a supplement to the action in order to give it its moral quality.

A virtue is an ethical orientation of the self towards the world in characteristic ways. It is not manifest only in the behaviour of virtuous persons but is an aspect

---

[1] Helga Kuhse, *Caring: Nurses, Women and Ethics* (Oxford, 1997).

of their inner lives. And yet a virtue is not just emotional or motivational and nor is it only a form of thinking. It is a comportment or orientation of the whole of our internal life, whether emotional or rational, and of our intentional actions. I understand virtue as an ethical form of dynamic orientation towards the world and to people: an orientation that leads to actions that society will describe as good or right.[2]

I define the virtue of caring as the comportment of the self towards others which has the inherent goal of enhancing the existence of those others – whether they are others in intimate relation to me, others for whom I have professional responsibility, or others with whom I identify simply because they are compatriots, co-religionists or fellow members of the human race. Accordingly, nurse caring, or caring in the context of professional health care, will be the comportment of the nurse towards others which has the inherent goal of enhancing the health-related existence of those others for whom the nurse has professional responsibility. Of the three alternative but not mutually exclusive bases for caring mentioned above – intimacy, professional responsibility and group identification – nurse caring should be primarily based on professional responsibility.

I do not propose to spend a lot of time in this chapter arguing that nurse caring, understood in this way, is a virtue. Others have done this adequately.[3] I will be content with one brief argument to make this idea plausible. The most obvious argument for saying that caring is a virtue is to suggest that when we describe a nurse as 'caring' we are praising that nurse in a way that refers to what the nurse characteristically does and to the way that it is done, and also in a way that attributes admirable traits of character or typical motivations to that nurse. According to Michael Slote, such praise is definitive of the discourse of virtue.[4] It is worth adding that even someone like Peter Allmark, who argues against the notion of an ethic based on care, unwittingly agrees that caring is a virtue when he says that for caring to be moral a 'person must care about the right things ... [and] in the right way'.[5] This is precisely what Aristotle takes to be definitive of virtue.

The focus of my argument will be that seeing caring as a virtue allows us to see all the aspects of professional nursing practice as participating in the moral quality which caring brings to it. This will include the impartial and principle-based thinking which nurses will need to engage in from time to time as well as the sensitivity and emotional rapport which nurses will have with patients from time to time. There is no reason, on my view, to give moral priority to principle-

---

[2]   For a fuller account of my views on virtue, see Stan van Hooft, *Understanding Virtue Ethics* (Chesham, 2005).

[3]   Chris Gastmans, Bernadette Dierckx de Casterle and Paul Schotsmans, 'Nursing Considered as Moral Practice: A Philosophical-Ethical Interpretation of Nursing'. *Kennedy Institute of Ethics Journal*, 8/1 (1998): 43–69.

[4]   Michael Slote, *From Morality to Virtue* (New York, 1992).

[5]   Peter Allmark, 'Can there be an ethics of care?', *Journal of Medical Ethics*, 21/1 (1995): 19–24, 23.

based thinking in the way that Kuhse argues. Nor is there need to give moral priority to emotional rapport with patients as others argue.[6] When we analyse what it is to act from caring, we discover that a great many aspects of the practice of a professional nurse can be the basis of the ascription of the virtue of caring.

Acting *from* virtue

Kant had said that for an action to be morally worthy, it should not just conform to duty, it should also be done from a sense of duty. The moral quality of an action derives from its motivation rather than from its description. Similarly, a virtue ethicist says that for a person to be virtuous, it is not enough that his or her characteristic behaviour should accord with the standards of virtue. There must also be virtuous states of the agent from which this behaviour arises. Again, for an action to be virtuous it is not enough that it accords with standards of virtue. It must also be done from the virtue of the agent. So what is it to act *from* virtue?

Aristotle says:

> If the acts that are in accordance with the virtues have themselves a certain character it does not follow that they are done justly or temperately. The agent also must be in a certain condition when he does them; in the first place he must know what he is doing, secondly he must choose the acts, and choose them for their own sakes, and thirdly his action must proceed from a firm and unchangeable character.[7]

This quotation specifies the internal states of the agent which are necessary for us to be able to say that an agent acted from virtue. This description of what it is to act from virtue has recently been elaborated by Robert Audi.[8] For Audi, to act from virtue it is not enough to act in accordance with virtue and nor is it enough to act for the sake of virtue: that is, for the sake of honouring it or acquiring it. Acting *from* virtue involves acting intentionally in relation to a field of concerns relevant to the virtue. This is what Aristotle meant when he said that the agent must choose the action for its own sake. We can do this directly, as when we recognize that a virtue is involved; for example, when we act justly because we recognize what would be just in the given situation. Or we can do this indirectly, as when we do things for reasons which relate to the virtue but without being aware that this is so: for example, when we act justly because we feel an inchoate sense of fairness in acting in this way. Audi also agrees with Aristotle that the action must be

---

6   For example, see Jean Watson, *Nursing: Human Science and Human Care: A Theory of Nursing* (New York, 1988), and Anne Boykin and Savina O. Schoenhofer, *Nursing as Caring: A Model for Transforming Practice* (New York, 1993).

7   Aristotle, *Nicomachean Ethics*, 1105A28–34.

8   Robert Audi, *Moral Knowledge and Ethical Character* (New York, 1997), pp. 174–92.

expressive of our characters. It is not enough if our action is virtuous by accident. But the motivational field that constitutes our character is a complex structure. Aristotle identifies it as including knowledge, choice and disposition. What is the nature of the knowledge that Aristotle requires a virtuous agent to have? What sorts of beliefs and desires must an agent have in order to act from virtue?

Let us explore this in more detail. Audi offers a more elaborate account of acting from virtue which is in the spirit of Aristotle but which suggests that there are six features present in virtuous action:[9]

1. the field of virtue, or what range of matters and sorts of things the virtue concerns itself with, or what sorts of situation call for the virtue in question
2. the targets of the virtue, or what virtuous actions of this kind seek to achieve in that field
3. the agent's understanding of that field
4. the agent's motivation
5. the agent's acting on the basis of that motivation
6. the beneficiaries of the virtue.

It is when agents instantiate these factors in the way a virtuous person does that they act virtuously. In this way, these features, specified in an appropriate way for the case at hand, become criteria for the ascription of a virtue term to an agent or to an action. We could define actions as being expressions of a virtue, or agents as being virtuous, if these features are present in the appropriate form. It follows from this that we need not specify a particular class of actions as being expressions of the virtue. An indeterminate range of actions can be virtuous in the relevant sense. I will illustrate what this means presently.

Bearing in mind Aristotle's point that a virtuous person should feel rightly,[10] I would add to Audi's list, the feature of (7) the agent's feeling the appropriate emotions or inclinations in relation to the field of the virtue and feeling them in the appropriate degree. Lastly, in consideration of such all-embracing virtues as integrity, I would add a further feature which is necessary for its being true that an agent acts from virtue: namely (8) a preparedness on the part of the agent to reflect on what they are doing or have done. It is this preparedness which leaves room for the agent's sense of integrity.

Let us take an act of distributive justice as an example to illustrate these features. In this case the field of the virtue will be the distribution or allocation of material goods or opportunities. It is a situation in which goods are to be distributed that calls for the virtue of distributive justice. To be acting from distributive justice, we must be acting within such a field. In contrast, if the field in question was a situation containing physical dangers, then we would suppose that the relevant virtue being called for was that of courage. Again, if the situation was one in which we owned more goods than we needed and there were people in dire

---

9   Ibid., p. 180
10   Aristotle, 1106b17–23

need, then the virtue called for would be that of generosity or charity. In these ways, we see a conceptual link between a particular type of virtue and the kind of situation in which it is to be exercised. We designate a virtue in the way that we do with reference to the field of the virtue or the situation.

The target of the virtue of distributive justice will be a fair or equitable distribution. In contrast, the target of the virtue of courage will be the doing of the deed which fear inhibits. The target of a virtue delineates the right things that the agent should be concerned with. As Allmark points out, it is not moral for a 'good' torturer to be good at causing intense pain in his victims. This is because torturing people is not a goal that would constitute an ethical practice. Calling an action virtuous suggests that the aim of the action is good and that its field is an ethical practice.

Third, the agent's understanding of that field will have to comprise some kind of grasp of the social realities and of the consequences of what might variously be done (though not necessarily of the concept of justice as such). The virtuous agent will have to understand what the goods are that are to be distributed and why they are important. Fourth, the agent will have to be motivated towards the achievement of justice in some form. As Rawls has argued, the agent will have to be motivated by a sense of fairness if the actions are to be expressions of the virtue of distributive justice rather than of, charity, for example.[11] And the fifth feature of acting from virtue requires that this motivation will have to be the reason for the agent's action. Moreover, according to Audi's sixth point, the agent who acts from distributive justice will have to have given consideration to the people who will benefit by the distribution just as the person who acts from courage will have to have given consideration to the values, persons, or goods which the action in the face of danger is intended to save or preserve. That there are such beneficiaries in these situations is what makes the actions actions from distributive justice and from courage respectively.

As for the appropriate feeling, we would expect just persons to have a sense of fairness so that they are pleased when justice is done and angry when it is not, whether or not they themselves are the recipients of the goods being distributed. Speaking of these emotions, Robert Solomon speaks of a 'passion for justice'.[12] Last, the eighth feature suggests that a just person would be prepared to reflect on how effective their actions towards the goals of justice have been. If all eight of these conditions are met then the agent acts from the virtue of justice whether what he is doing is actually distributing goods, working in the public service sector, writing letters to the press, organising political activity or engaging in any of the myriad activities that might conduce to justice.

---

[11]   John Rawls, 'The Sense of Justice', *Philosophical Review*, 72 (1963): 281–305.

[12]   Robert C. Solomon, *A Passion for Justice: Emotions and the Origins of the Social Contract* (Reading, Massachusetts, 1990).

It is worth quoting Audi's comment about his own account of acting from virtue to the effect that:

> moral action, in the full-blooded sense of action from moral virtue, need not be rule following conduct or performed under the conception of the virtue in question or indeed under any explicitly moral concept, such as that of (moral) duty. Moral autonomy is roughly the capacity for self-government under moral standards.[13]

Acting from the virtue of caring in nursing

How would this account of acting from virtue apply to caring as a virtue for health professionals? Above, I suggested that, applied to the professions of health care, the virtue of caring should be seen as a practical comportment towards others which has the goal of enhancing the health-related existence of those others. I can now offer a brief and schematic expansion of this account using the eight features of acting from a virtue which I have identified.

The field of the virtue

The field of the virtue of caring in the context of health care is obviously health care itself. The range of matters and sorts of things the virtue concerns itself with will be connected to health care. The sorts of situation that call for the virtue of nurse caring will include clinical situations, community health programmes, health education, and even public policy advocacy on behalf of health needs. I do not propose to spell out the very large range of health-related activities which the health care professions are involved in. There will be debates as to what should or should not be included under this heading (for example, is drug addiction a health problem considered apart from the physical effects of the addiction?). Many personal and social issues are health issues or can become health issues in one way or another. It is enough to say that the key unifying concept which specifies the object or central issue of all these activities in one way or another is health. We will be able to say that nurses are acting from the virtue of nurse caring when they are acting in the field of health care. It will be important to define the boundaries of the field of the virtue of caring in order to ensure that the arguments of some nursing theorists for the wholeness of the person of the patient are not taken to imply that nurses should become involved in all aspects of the lives of their patients.

The target of the virtue

The target of the virtue of caring in health care, or what virtuous actions of this kind seek to achieve in the field of health, is the enhancement or preservation of

---

13   Audi, p. 292

the health of individuals, families or communities. Once again, we will be able to say that nurses are acting from the virtue of nurse caring when they are acting with this target in mind. The clinical situation will be the most obvious example of this, but the range of activities that have this target will be quite large. It might include, for example, political action aimed at preserving a clean air environment, or legal action taken against tobacco companies, or counselling or education of individuals in relation to their health needs along with the more obvious clinical practices. Administrative tasks can also be regarded as having this target and could therefore also be expressive of the virtue of caring. Notice that tasks such as these are usually not done with an accompaniment of caring emotions and are not usually described in a direct way as behaviours that see to the needs of others (though they may have that effect indirectly). Yet, on my account, they can be seen to be caring actions in the sense that they are performed from the virtue of caring.

Of course, there may be difficulties if the target of the action is conceived differently by different people in the situation. A nurse may have a different conception of the target of health in relation to a specific patient than does that patient, or the doctor, or the patient's family. It will be important that such differences do not lead to stalemate in the clinical context or to the imposition of treatment regimes that threaten the autonomy or well-being of the patient. It is for this reason that the feature I am about to describe – the knowledge base of the nurse – is important. Indeed, it should be noted that the eight features of acting from virtue that I am describing should be taken to be a package deal. A nurse can only be said to be acting from the virtue of caring if all of these features are present in some way. Only with all these features present will there be the possibility – if not the guarantee – that these quandaries will be resolved.

The agent's understanding of the field

As we turn our attention to the nurse's understanding of the field of the virtue of health care, we begin to analyse the knowledge base of the health care professions. This will be an extensive body of knowledge. The most obvious bodies of knowledge will be physiology, anatomy, and other medical sciences, but 'nursing knowledge' and the bodies of knowledge used by alternative medicine will also be relevant to specific health professions. As well, virtuous nurses in this field should have knowledge of human psychology, sociology, and relevant parts of economics. I will make no attempt here to specify what this range of relevant knowledge will be. What it is important to note, however, is that possessing this knowledge is constitutive of the virtue of caring in the health care context. True to my Aristotelian inspiration, I am stressing that caring is not just a matter of feeling rightly, it is also a matter of thinking rightly. And this involves having the required knowledge. Only a person with the relevant knowledge can act effectively and virtuously in the world. If an ignorant person does the virtuous thing, it will be by accident and they will not be acting *from* virtue. For example, if a nurse, in his anxiety to help, were to administer a medicine in an emergency which was merely the first medicine that came to hand, and if, perchance, this procedure turned out well, we would not be inclined to say, despite the happy outcome or the solicitous motivation, that the nurse had acted virtuously.

The general background knowledge without which doing the virtuous thing would be purely accidental includes knowledge of how to do those things that are central to the activity. The skill or practical knowledge that health care workers bring to their professions results from their training and experience in applying their knowledge to their practices. Although there are some virtues, like justice, which do not seem to involve characteristic skills in their application, holistic virtues like integrity and caring do. Caring applied to a health care context would seem to imply a definite set of competencies. I would suggest that if a nurse were to be described as acting from the virtue of caring, we would expect to see a skilful performance of tasks as well as a careful and caring performance.

Among the competencies that a caring nurse will display are those of critical thinking. For nurses to be described as acting from the virtue of caring, they would have to think clearly, be able and willing to distinguish genuine science from pseudoscience, and be able and willing to discuss professional matters with others clearly and persuasively. This will mean that such nurses will have an effective grasp of informal logic and scientific thinking as well as the ability to discuss matters of policy.[14]

The knowledge that is relevant to acting well as a health care worker will also include ethical knowledge. By this I mean knowledge of the ethical codes and policies that apply to the profession and of the law as it applies to health care practice. The ethical self-understanding of the profession may also be expressed in particular principles such as those of respect for autonomy, beneficence, non-malevolence, and justice.[15] Less formalized will be knowledge of what exemplary health care workers have done or would do. I would argue that knowledge of moral theory and of those overarching theoretical principles such as the principle of utility or the categorical imperative are less useful and can be dispensed with, but knowledge of the moral standards that apply in the clinicians' society or in the society that they are working in will be important. Knowledge of their own ethical standards and self-knowledge more generally will also be relevant, though such knowledge is more likely to be implicit and operational than explicitly articulated.

Another form of knowledge that it will be necessary for clinicians to have if they are to be described as acting from the virtue of caring is an empathetic awareness of what is important in clinical and health-related situations. What I mean by this is that a health care worker should have a grasp of what is valuable about health and life. Such workers should have an understanding of what pain and

---

[14]   For a fuller elaboration of this critical thinking, see Stan van Hooft, Lynn Gillam and Margot Byrnes, *Facts and Values: An Introduction to Critical Thinking for Nurses* (Sydney, 1995).

[15]   Tom L. Beauchamp and James F. Childress, *Principles of Biomedical Ethics* (4th ed, New York, 1994).

suffering are and how people deal with them. They should have an understanding of the concept of disease as more than just a physiological or mental dysfunction but also as a human condition with a negative meaning for its victims. They should have thought about death and the conditions under which it is either tragic or a peaceful resolution of the condition of the patient. They should understand what it is to be a person with autonomy and the role that health plays in grounding the dignity of persons. Such knowledge will ground the feeling of caring and of responsibility that health workers feel towards their patients and will motivate their helping actions. In short, a philosophical grasp of the health-related aspects of the human condition will also be a necessary condition for acting from the virtue of caring.[16]

The knowledge and understanding that a virtuous nurse brings to health care practice is not just general background knowledge, however. It also includes specific and particular knowledge of the case at hand. Not only does this include the diagnostic knowledge that would appear on the patient's chart, but also relevant personal knowledge about the patient. Being aware of the patient's life circumstances and needs is important in the clinical setting. Understanding how these circumstances impinge on their health status and enhance or inhibit the patient's progress will also be important, as will an understanding of the patient's state of mind. It is this particular, personal knowledge which recent nursing writing has stressed.[17] It is under this heading of knowledge that I would want to put Kuhse's stress on sensitive perception. Noticing the health-related needs of clients is clearly part of the knowledge that a nurse needs in order to be acting from the virtue of caring. It is this particular and contextual knowledge that is essential to my Aristotelian conception of what it is to act from virtue. It is necessary to act with the range of knowledge gestured at in these paragraphs in order to be acting from the virtue of caring in health care.

Given this stress on knowledge and given the range of knowledge that is relevant to acting virtuously as a caring nurse, it follows that the activities that express the virtue of caring will extend beyond directly clinical and caring actions. Caring can also be expressed by study, for example. A health care professional who takes the time to study the scientific basis of the profession and to acquire the competencies required for it can be expressing caring. Similarly, the professional who endeavours to become familiar with the ethical rules that apply to the profession, or who reflects about and discusses with others the meaning of health, disease, suffering and death, or who takes the time to come to know the patients at a personal level can, just in those efforts, be acting in a caring manner.

---

[16] For a fuller account of these matters, see Stan van Hooft, *Life, Death, and Subjectivity: Moral Sources in Bioethics* (Amsterdam and New York, 2004).

[17] Barbara A. Carper, 'Fundamental patterns of knowing in nursing' *Advances in Nursing Science*, 1/1 (1978): 13–24.

The agent's motivation

The nurse's motivation has been the focus of much of the discussion of caring in the nursing literature. There have been debates in that literature about whether nurses should be motivated by a kind of love for the patient, or whether their motivations should arise from a relationship of intimacy with the patient. For myself, in Chapter 1, I have espoused the notion of 'professional commitment' as the basis for the motivation of caring in the health care professions. The first and second conditions for acting from the virtue of caring described above cover this point to some extent. Without arguing the case at length here, I would suggest that the motivation of caring is importantly other-directed as opposed to selfish. A person whose primary goal in health care is making money would fail to be virtuous in this sense. Caring involves a sense of concern for the needs of others. Caring is giving. This is not to suggest that care-givers have to be totally self-sacrificing, but it does imply that, considered just as health professionals, the primary motivation should be to help others in relation to their health needs. There will be other motivations and purposes present in the inner life of the health worker including the quite valid one of making a living, but enhancing the lives of others in relation to their health should be the pre-eminent motivation while acting professionally.

There is a distinction to be drawn between the target of the practice (point 2 above) and the motivation of the professional. The target of the practice is the enhancement of the health status of clients or the alleviation of their suffering when health enhancement is not possible. The primary motivation of the professional should be to advance the goals and targets of the practice. In this way it is not necessary for nurses to have specific motivations in relation to each and every patient or client. It is enough that their motivation is to perform their professionally defined tasks well. This will be a suitably other-directed motivation but it leaves room for those many nursing tasks, such as administration and record keeping, which do not centrally involve a caring relationship with another. We can express and fulfil our other-directed motivations in the professionally defined tasks of a practice the target of which is to help others without having to feel motivations which are specifically directed upon particular others. There will be times when caring is expressed in the context of empathetic relationships with specific patients. But there will be many other times when this personal dimension is absent or would even be counter to the effectiveness of the tasks at hand. And, of course, there will be those patients who for one reason or another fail to inspire any caring motivation in their professional carers. Nevertheless, health care workers can still be said to be acting from the virtue of caring if their motivations are in line with the other-directed health-enhancement goals of their profession.

The agent's acting on the basis of the appropriate motivation

It is perhaps obvious that the nurse's acting on the basis of the motivations just described is central to their acting from the virtue of caring. However, it is important to make this point in order to distinguish that use of the word 'caring' which merely describes the behaviour of a health professional from that use of the word that ascribes a virtue to them. A person may act in a caring way out of habit, or because the routines of the hospital guarantee that they will be effective in their caring regimens. But this will not be acting *from* virtue. To act from virtue requires that caring actually be the motivation.

What does this mean? Whether this means that the health worker must always be in a self-consciously caring frame of mind or must always be fully conscious of the health needs of particular patients is debatable. I have already suggested that it need not mean that the nurse be motivated by a specific empathetic feeling for a particular patient, though there is no denying the value that such feeling can have on particular occasions (and there is no denying either, as Kuhse has argued,[18] that they can be harmful on other occasions). A general commitment to the professional goals of health care will be sufficient. Also, it does not mean that the worker must have a self-image which includes their understanding of themselves as caring persons, although such a self-image may be motivationally helpful. That an agent conceives of their action as falling under a virtue is not necessary for that agent to be described as acting from that virtue. A courageous person does not need to think that they are being courageous in order to be acting courageously. In the same way nurses do not have to think of themselves as caring in order for them to be acting from the virtue of caring.

Acting from caring does mean that, having noticed the health-related needs of patients or clients, nurses are motivated by seeing those needs to respond to them. That motivational link between sensitive perception and caring response is what caring consists in. And this link arises in more contexts than the bedside. A motivation of caring also means that, having noticed the organizational needs of the institution in which they work, health professionals will be motivated to do something about them; or, having noticed the political need for changes to health care policies, health professionals will be motivated to do something about them; or, having noticed the need for more knowledge and understanding in their own professional lives, health professionals will be motivated to do something about that, and so forth. The range of actions that can be expressive of nurse caring is large and underdetermined.

The beneficiaries of the virtue

Consideration of the beneficiaries of the virtue of caring may seem redundant. It would seem obvious that the beneficiary is the patient in the clinic or the client of

---

[18]   Kuhse, pp. 152–6.

health services. However, there are two questions that can be asked here: how wide is the scope of this category? and under what concept is the beneficiary best understood? The first question includes such quandaries as whether the immediate family of the patient is also to be cared for and to what extent. For community nurses, the question might be whether the whole community or the wider society is the beneficiary of the caring. While engaged in political advocacy it might be the wider community, while in the event that the nurse is acting in a surgical setting, the beneficiary of the caring might be thought of as the particular patient. The second question raises the more abstract issue of whether the beneficiary of health caring is best thought of as a 'patient', a 'client' or even as a 'customer'.[19] Clearly, different connotations attach to these terms and they will shape caring practice in different ways. If the beneficiary is thought of as a 'customer' or consumer of health care services, for example, the health professional may well think of themselves as traders in a market of health care services. Such an outlook will clearly effect whether the worker is acting from the virtue of caring.

The agent feeling appropriate emotions

The nurse's feeling the appropriate emotions or inclinations in relation to the field of the virtue has also been a focus of discussion in the nursing literature. I tend to agree with Kuhse that too much importance can be given to emotion in our understanding of caring as a virtue. It does not seem to me to be obvious that a health worker needs to be in an emotional state of concern in order to be acting from the virtue of caring. Insofar as the work is difficult, stressful, and requires concentration, it might be best to engage in it with as little distracting emotion as possible. However, I would argue that health workers need to have a strong and affective commitment to the goal of health. This would mean that they consider health to be important and are prepared to give it priority in their lives. Such a commitment will be primarily motivational. Moreover, at an emotional level it will mean that they will be pleased when their patients experience positive health outcomes and they will be angry when policy makers make decisions that compromise such outcomes. Health will matter to them. As well, they will feel a degree of sympathy with the suffering of individual patients. Even patients who are difficult and whom they find it hard to like will attract a sufficient degree of sympathy and sensitive awareness in order to enhance the motivation to caring behaviour that arises from professional commitment. While health care workers do not need to be too gushing in their emotional responses to clinical situations and health issues, they do need to be sufficiently involved emotionally in order to be fully present to the patient. The patient must not be made to feel that their nurses are merely doing their job. Only in this way will nurses be acting from the virtue of

---

[19]   Phyllis R. Schultz, 'Clarifying the Concept of "Client" for Health care Policy Formulation: Ethical Implications', in Janet W. Kenney (ed.) *Philosophical and Theoretical Perspectives for Advanced Nursing Practice* (Sudbury, Massachusetts, 1996), pp. 133–40.

caring in the health care setting. To be cold and dispassionate would make being virtuous in this way more difficult.

Let me reiterate the point that it is important to distinguish between the emotions that it is appropriate for a nurse to feel and the motivations that lead a nurse to act. It would be a mistake to suppose that emotions, no matter how worthy, altruistic or sympathetic, can be valid motivations for action by themselves. It would be a mistake to go to help a patient simply because we felt sympathy for them. Such sympathy might be an appropriate and useful additional motivation, but it can never, by itself, be a sufficient reason. If we acted to assist others simply because we felt sympathy for them, we might well end up imposing our attentions where they are not wanted. We also need to decide what it is best to do in the situation. This patient may not want the attention that we are moved to give. Or this patient may be being looked after by someone else. Caring does not consist in emotion alone. Therefore, to act on emotion alone is not to act in a caring manner. We act from the virtue of caring when our actions are marked by all the features I have elaborated, including that of judgement and understanding. It is a mistake to think of caring just as an emotion and then to suppose that the feeling of that emotion justifies any action that that emotion motivates. Sometimes the caring thing to do for a patient is to leave them alone in their suffering.

Preparedness to reflect

The preparedness to reflect that marks all virtues is especially important in the context of caring. Given the complexity of health care practices in their various settings and given the depth of the ethical considerations to which they give rise, it will be important for health care workers to reflect on their practice and to establish formal mechanisms that make this possible.[20] Not only does the constant growth of relevant scientific knowledge make it necessary for professionals to update their knowledge, but the ambivalences that inevitably attend clinical practice make it imperative to review the moral quality of motivations that lead to actions in professional settings. A nurse could not be described as caring who was not prepared to reflect on matters in this way.

Caring as sufficient for moral action

What is clear from this analysis of acting from the virtue of caring in the health care setting is that caring embraces both thinking rightly and feeling rightly, and having the right goal in the context of an ethical practice. It suffuses all aspects of the person of the health care worker and becomes a full and total orientation of their professional being. In this way both their feeling and their thinking will have

---

[20]   Christopher Johns and Dawn Freshwater (eds), *Transforming Nursing Through Reflective Practice* (Oxford, 1998).

the quality of caring. It is not the case that caring is only a preparatory part of being virtuous or acting well, as Kuhse argues. Acting from caring, or acting well in the health care context, involves sensitive awareness, proper motivation and rational, evaluative judgement. Accordingly, being a caring health care worker is enough to ensure that you will act well.

Those who argue that caring is an interpersonal emotion that nurses must feel fail to notice the cognitive and behavioural aspects of the virtue. Those who hold that caring is merely helping behaviour fail to notice the motivational, cognitive and emotional aspects without which such behaviour would not be caring. And Kuhse, who would argue that caring is merely a disposition to perceive the health needs of patients that is preparatory but not sufficient for acting well, also misses the way in which ethical considerations are present in caring as part of the knowledge base from which the caring nurse acts. For Kuhse, 'acting from virtue' (if she were to use that phrase) or 'acting morally' is secured only when action is seen by the agent to be in accord with universal principles. Against this I would argue that, provided that principles – even if held in an implicit and inchoate form – are present in the knowledge base of the action, and provided the other eight features that I have identified are present, nurses can be truly described as acting from the virtue of caring. My analysis provides both a more inclusive and more demanding standard of what caring is than the limited views of the emotionalists, behaviourists, and of Kuhse. And insofar as it is a virtue we are talking about, it also provides the only available guarantee that when nurses act from the virtue of caring they will be doing what anyone could judge to be right.

Chapter 6

Socratic Dialogue and the Virtuous Clinician

Despite an increasing literature about virtue in the professions[1] and, more particularly, in the clinical professions such as medicine[2] and nursing,[3] the branches of applied ethics that are relevant to clinical practice are still dominated by what has been called a 'principlist' approach.[4] Let me explain what this means.

The philosophical literature on ethics makes a distinction between a concern for what we should *do* on the one hand and the way we should *be* on the other.[5] The first of these focuses attention on action and the principles or rules in the light of which an action can be said to be right or wrong. It can also focus attention on the goods which an action might achieve or promote and on whether these goods make the action right or wrong. Or it can direct attention onto the type of action that it is and on the moral status of such an action in the light of universalizable reasons or of natural or divine law. A focus on the way we should *be*, on the other hand, leads us ask about whether an agent is a good person, has admirable character traits, feels appropriate emotions, has appropriate motivations, acts with integrity, or acts in a way that expresses a positive disposition. In short, a focus on how persons should *be* generates a discussion that has come to be known in the philosophical

---

[1]   Dean Cocking and Justin Oakley, *Virtue Ethics and Professional Roles* (Cambridge, 2001).

[2]   Diana Fritz Cates and Paul Lauritzen (eds) (2001), *Medicine and the Ethics of Care* (Washington, DC, 2001) and Edmund D. Pellegrino, 'Towards a Virtue-Based Normative Ethics for the Health Professions', *Kennedy Institute of Ethics Journal*, 5/3 (1995): 253–78.

[3]   Chris Gastmans, Bernadette Dierckx de Casterle and Paul Schotsmans, 'Nursing Considered as Moral Practice: A Philosophical-Ethical Interpretation of Nursing', *Kennedy Institute of Ethics Journal*, 8/1 (1998): 43–69.

[4]   Stephen E. Toulmin, 'The Tyranny of Principles', *Hastings Center Report* 11/6 (1981): 31–9, Tom L. Beauchamp and James F. Childress, *Principles of Biomedical Ethics* (4th ed, New York, 1994), and J.H. Evans, 'A Sociological Account of the Growth of Principlism', *Hastings Center Report*, 30/5 (2000): 31–8.

[5]   Joram Graf Haber (ed.) *Doing and Being: Selected Readings in Moral Philosophy* (New York, 1993).

literature as 'virtue ethics'.[6] If the major progenitors of the principlist approach to morals are Thomas Aquinas, Immanuel Kant and John Stuart Mill, the founder of virtue ethics would be Aristotle.

The recently renewed interest in virtue ethics in moral philosophy was inspired by the suggestion that, in some circumstances, a person who acts from principle would actually not be acting well. Take the case of a person who visits his friend in a hospital.[7] If he made this visit on the basis of duty, we would think that there was something lacking. In such a context, we consider that acting well would consist in visiting the friend out of friendly feelings. Similarly, we might suppose that a clinician who looked after patients efficiently and effectively but did so purely because she felt it to be her duty to do so, would be lacking in some way. We would like caring to add to the moral quality of the activity through being part of its motivation. Indeed, when we turn our attention to clinicians, it has been suggested that there is a range of virtues that is of central importance to that practice. Edmund Pellegrino lists the following: fidelity to trust and promise, benevolence, effacement of self-interest, compassion and caring, intellectual honesty, justice and prudence.[8]

What are the implications of a shift from a focus on principles, rules and obligations to a consideration of virtue? First, by focusing on virtue ethics we are actually considering a wider range of matters than are covered by the principlist perspective of ethics. When we speak of actions being right or wrong we refer to a set of moral standards with a finite range of applicability. They include actions that honour or violate rights, or actions that honour or violate requirements of duty. Clearly this is a limited range of actions. One of the authors who revived contemporary interest in virtue ethics[9] did so by suggesting that the standard moral terminology centred on such words as 'right' and 'wrong' was too abstract and 'thin' to be of much day-to-day applicability. It would be better to use 'thick' concepts which gave more substance to the moral judgement that we were making: words like, 'courageous', 'considerate', 'generous', 'insensitive', 'callous' or 'just'. This use of specific virtue or vice terms enriches our moral discourse. Moreover, when we speak about virtue and the evaluation of persons or actions as virtuous, we embrace a much larger range of matters. A doctor may be cheerful at her work and will be liked and admired on that account. This involves a positive evaluation, though not a moral one. Clinicians might be efficient, courteous, punctual, neat, sensitive to the needs of patients, or any one of a range of positive

[6]   Justin Oakley, 'Varieties of Virtue Ethics', *Ratio (New Series)*, IX/2 (1996): 128–53, and Daniel Statman, 'Introduction to Virtue Ethics', in Daniel Statman, *Virtue Ethics: A Critical Reader* (Edinburgh, 1997), pp. 1–41.

[7]   Michael Stocker, 'The Schizophrenia of Modern Ethical Theories', *Journal of Philosophy*, LXXIII/14 (1976): 453–66.

[8]   Pellegrino, p. 268.

[9]   Elizabeth Anscombe, 'Modern Moral Philosophy', *Philosophy: The Journal of the Royal Institute of Philosophy*, 33 (January 1958): 1–19.

features which we do not normally think of as explicitly moral matters. Yet we consider them admirable. We think of cheerfulness, efficiency, courtesy and neatness as virtues. It has also been argued that virtue is needed in other areas in which right or wrong are not at issue.[10] Examples would be matters about which the principlist approach in ethics is largely silent: like courtesy, respect, trust and caring for others. Without these interpersonal sensitivities the ethical life is arid. As well there are intrapersonal qualities like integrity and authenticity. Without these virtues the moral life is cold, harsh and meaningless. Insofar as it does not encourage consideration of these matters, the principlist approach seems too shallow.

We can see this by reflecting on the term 'a good clinician'. If we were to spell out what it was to be a good clinician, would we use only moral terms? Would we spell this out only with reference to a clinician's universalizable and publicly justifiable duties, or with reference just to their adherence to the law and to ethical guidelines enunciated by the institutions that they work in? I suggest that such a description would contain terms which allude to admirable traits most of which will go well beyond what morality or public norms require. And if we disapprove of what a clinician has done, are we always saying that that clinician has done the morally wrong thing or broken the rules? Could it not be that the clinician has made a mistake or been careless? We might be saying that they seem a bit surly today or that they are being a bit sloppy or off-hand with a patient. In short, our disapproval does not always imply that we are referring to a moral issue. We will, however, be referring to standards of behaviour that we regard as virtues. Michael Slote has argued that the discourse of virtue is marked by praise of people that is based on attributing admirable traits of character or characteristic motivations to them as well as on admiring their characteristic behaviour and the way in which they do what they do.[11] And what we mean when we criticize people in the discourse of virtue is that we find their behaviour and the character which it expresses deplorable. In this way, when we speak of a 'good clinician', we are engaging in the discourse of virtue. In a similar way, when we describe a clinician as caring, we are making use of the concepts of virtue ethics.

A second implication of a focus on virtue is that it highlights the inner life of the agent. Principlism directs our attention onto the action or its consequences. It asks whether the action is in accord with law, duty or reason, or it asks whether its consequences are beneficent. In contrast, a virtue is an ethical orientation of the self towards the world in characteristic ways. It is not manifest only in the behaviour of virtuous persons, but is also an aspect of their inner lives. It includes our emotions and motivations, as well as our deliberation and other forms of thinking. It is a comportment or orientation of the whole of our internal life, whether emotional or rational, and of our intentional actions. I understand virtue to

---

[10] J. Griffin, 'Virtue Ethics and Environs', *Social Philosophy and Policy*, 15/1 (Winter, 1998): 56–70.

[11] Michael Slote, *From Morality to Virtue* (New York, 1992).

be an ethical form of dynamic orientation towards the world and to people, an orientation that leads to action that society will describe as good or right.

This is well illustrated by the virtue of caring. In Chapter 5 I defined the virtue of caring as the comportment of the self towards others, which has the inherent goal of enhancing the existence of those others, whether they are others in intimate relation to me, others for whom I have professional responsibility, or others with whom I identify simply because they are compatriots, coreligionists, fellow members of the human race, or simply sentient beings.

Everyday virtue and everyday wisdom

There is a further implication of turning away from a principlist approach to clinical ethics in favour of a virtue approach that has not been frequently noted: namely, that virtue is expressed in everyday situations even when there are no dramatic moral issues at stake. To highlight this, I have coined the phrase, 'everyday virtue'. Everyday virtue is the disposition to act well in everyday situations, in accordance with the goods of everyday life. Because mainstream ethics has often focused on relatively dramatic and problematic situations or on questions that relate to public policy, the recent revival of virtue ethics has been a timely reminder that living well involves many decisions and judgements that were thought to be too humble to attract the attention of professional ethicists. Even though Aristotle spoke about courage as a virtue required in the situation of threats to life that even in his bellicose times must have been relatively unusual, he also focused on everyday situations and the moral demands implicit in them, such as giving to each person their due. While heroic virtue may be admirable and may serve as exemplars for the teaching of virtue, most people most of the time are not called upon to emulate the dramatic actions which situations of mortal danger or high moral stakes call for.

Everyday virtue is largely hidden. Because it is exercised in the everyday context of the private sphere and the sphere of work, rather than in the public sphere of policy formation or the making of grand moral gestures, it remains largely unnoticed by others and even by virtuous agents themselves. Everyday virtue is part of the fabric of life, both in its personal dimension and in the public dimension. The small courtesies with which we lubricate the daily exchanges with family, shopkeepers, bus conductors, teachers, students and colleagues, are all part of this pattern, as are the small decisions that have to be made from minute to minute in our interactions with others and our work. Paul Komesaroff, speaking of the relationships between clinical health workers and patients, speaks of a 'microethics'.[12] This refers to the bearing of doctors towards their patients: the tone

---

[12]   Paul A. Komesaroff, 'From bioethics to microethics: ethical debate and clinical medicine', in Paul A. Komesaroff (ed.), *Troubled Bodies: Critical Perspectives on Mostmodernism, Medical Ethics, and the Body* (Melbourne, 1995), pp. 62–86.

of voice in asking questions, the sensitivity of touch during a physical examination, and so forth. In other contexts, bidding a shopkeeper the time of day, stepping out of the way of a pedestrian in a busy street, returning the excess change wrongly given at a supermarket check-out, ensuring that the next person has their turn in the queue when you could jump in yourself, being fair in the filing of your tax return, being prepared to listen without interrupting at a meeting, and the many other occasions when virtuous persons put a slight brake on their own inclinations in order to respect the presence of another or of a value, are all examples of everyday virtue. They involve micro-judgements of which the agent is barely aware. Insofar as the agent is virtuous there is no need to make those judgements explicit and no need to problematize them. Virtuous persons simply find themselves doing things sensitively, considerately, and honestly and they seldom give this a second thought. One would be concerned about the ethical character of a person who needed to ask themselves whether they should step out of the way of a person sharing the footpath or who engaged in an internal debate with themselves before they could find reason to return the overpaid change.

Virtue and knowledge

The implicit micro-judgements that characterize everyday virtue are expressions of a form of knowledge that is itself virtuous: a knowledge of what matters in an everyday situation and of what is morally salient in it. It is a knowledge that expresses what the agent cares about and which, in a virtuous agent, will guide everyday judgements in a way that will usually ensure that the agent acts well. I will call this knowledge 'everyday wisdom'. It is important to see the link between this knowledge and a motivational state such as caring about what is salient in the situation. Everyday wisdom is not abstract or value-neutral knowledge. It relates directly to what the agent cares about and, as such, it is directly motivational.

As I detailed in Chapter 4, there would seem to be three stages involved in the moral psychology of behaviour that expresses caring. Such behaviour begins with sensitive awareness of the situation and the needs of the persons in it. But for this awareness to lead to action there needs to be a predisposition within the agent. Such a predisposition is precisely what I meant when I defined a virtue as 'an ethical form of dynamic orientation towards the world and to people, an orientation that leads to action that society will describe as good or right'. What is needed to turn a recognition of what should be done into a motivation to do it is a pre-existing state of virtue. Moreover, virtue is needed to ensure that weakness of will or a change of mind does not waylay the motivation. Only this time, it is the so-called 'executive virtues' that are at issue. These are the strengths of character that allow an agent to overcome internal or external inhibitions to acting well: forces such as fear, laziness, or distracting desire. The executive virtues, accordingly, include such predispositions as courage, commitment and constancy.

The virtue of caring suffuses all three stages of ethical decision making, as described in Chapter 4. It is because of what we care about or whom we care about that we notice what needs to be done. The sensitive awareness that alerts us to the need for action is, in part, a product of our concern for what is salient in the situation. Second, it is caring which provides the motivational impetus which turns the sensitive awareness into an intention to act. And third, we exercise the necessary executive virtues on behalf of values that we are committed to or care about. We do not display courage for its own sake, as an exercise of bravado. We exercise it because we are committed to a value and to a course of action in pursuit of that value from which we do not want to be deflected by fear. This commitment is itself an expression of our caring.

Everyday wisdom

In contrast to the principlist approach, a virtue ethicist focuses upon the internal motivational power that reasons have for a virtuous and caring agent. Everyday wisdom provides internal reasons for action. That is to say, having a reason which arises from everyday wisdom and everyday virtue is motivational. Indeed, insofar as the stage of explicit reflection and deliberation is frequently absent from everyday virtuous actions, everyday wisdom needs to be directly motivational. Having such wisdom includes being motivated to act well in the situation in which we finds ourselves. There is seldom a self-conscious stage of holding or entertaining a reason. We simply see what a situation calls for in the way of moral response and we are motivated to do it. The way of seeing that allows this direct path from sensitive perception to ethical action is precisely the knowledge or practical wisdom that is a mark of virtue. Scholars of Aristotle familiar with the notion of *phronēsis* will find this analysis quite familiar.

Although it is knowledge, everyday wisdom is not expressed in general propositions, principles or objective reasons. It is pre-reflexive in that most agents would have difficulty articulating it clearly even as they express it in their actions and decisions. Insofar as it is expressed in action, it is particular rather than general. It comes to expression in specific and concrete everyday situations. This is not to say that agents could not, with suitable effort or assistance, come to articulate the maxims of their actions as principles or rules. My claim is simply that they need not have an explicit awareness of such rules or principles in order to act well or to know that they are acting well. Contrary to the common reading of Socrates which suggests that agents need an explicit knowledge of what virtue is in order to be virtuous, I would suggest that such abstract and theoretical knowledge is secondary in the practical life of agents. The knowledge that underwrites virtue takes the form of the particular judgement that an agent makes in a concrete situation and which is expressed in the virtuous action that is taken. A thorough-going virtue ethics – one that rejects all forms of principlism – needs to be able to show that the micro-judgements of everyday life are sufficient for being virtuous and that, however helpful or interesting general ethical principles or propositions might be, they are not necessary.

All this is not to deny, however, that becoming articulate about the ethical norms or standards of behaviour that we are implicitly following is without value. While it may be true that most virtuous people, most of the time, act well pre-reflexively and express their virtue or their caring without having to give themselves explicit reasons for doing so, it can also happen that situations will be of such complexity or ambiguity, that a more or less intuitive response to them will be either impossible or inadequate. There may be a clinical situation in which our caring for the patient and one's caring other values inherent in that situation will come into conflict and will produce a kind of motivational short-circuit which prevents a clear motivational flow into action from arising. The kinds of cases which are the bread and butter of bioethical discussion – such as effecting an abortion to save the life of the mother, or hastening a terminally and painfully suffering person's death – will exemplify this dilemma. But so will more everyday situations where the caring attention of a clinician towards a patient might be compromised because of the needs of efficiency or the lack of a just distribution of resources. In cases such as these the clinician's implicit everyday wisdom may not be adequate to the situation. In such cases, there is need for thought, for reflection and for explicit consideration of ethical values and options.

In response to this need, the ethical principlist will reach for the compendium of objective, universal, moral norms which will have been developed within our theological and philosophical traditions. The assumption will be that there are objective truths within morality which have to be acknowledged and followed. Whether these truths are based on God's law, on the findings of pure rationality, or a utilitarian calculus, or on what will be claimed to be the collective wisdom of the ages, they will be seen as standing over and against the agents who are called upon to follow them. Moreover, it will be assumed that disinterested rational thought will be able to resolve any moral quandary in principle. The resources for solving moral dilemmas will be seen to exist externally to the motivational life of the agent.

It is my contention, in contrast to this position, that the resources virtuous agents need in order to overcome the dilemmas which their more or less intuitive adherence to the ethical standards relevant to their lives as persons and as clinicians give rise to are present within them all the time. While a pre-reflexive expression of caring and of other virtues may not be adequate to the complexity of the situations in which they find themselves, reflection will disclose levels of understanding and of motivation which can resolve those dilemmas in particular and specific situations. There is no need to appeal to general principles or norms or to the theoretical pronouncements of ethicists and to follow them more or less blindly. Rather, what is needed is a sustained and deep reflection on the motivations and understandings that the agent already has and which can, with further clarification and articulation, be a guide through the moral complexities that contemporary clinical situations often give rise to.

If there is a role for professional ethicists, it is not that of handing down normative pronouncements or permissions from the realm of theoretical speculation, but to assist virtuous clinicians to come to a more articulate understanding of the values that they already hold and of the commitments that they already adhere to. In the cases where an articulation of such values and commitments discloses a conflict or a contradiction between them, it will be the role of the ethicist to assist the clinician to understand which of their commitments is the more profound or overarching so that a clearer and less ambiguous course of action can be suggested by that commitment. As John Rawls has argued, the purpose of ethical discourse should be to produce 'reflective equilibrium': that is, a coherence and relative gradation amongst the values that one holds so that the motivational short circuit which moral dilemmas produce can be overcome.[13] This is not to suggest that the life of virtue can be made simple. Difficult ethical decisions will often come with a moral cost as we see the need to override values that we hold dear even as we pursue other values which we deem to be more important. But such a cost can be offset by clarity as to what is at issue and confidence that we have acted as well as we could in that situation.

In this way the role of ethical thought is not that of deriving actions from principles in some logical or algorithmic manner, but rather that of balancing the motivations and inclinations towards virtuous action that we feel through becoming more articulate about the significance of those virtuous feelings. This means that we exercise reason as a form of reflection on our understandings and motivations. We does not ask what reason (or an objective moral norm) tells us to do. We ask how we understand this situation and what we really care about most in it. Having an answer to this second question will guide us as to what we have to do.

I believe it was this thought that led Socrates to say that the unexamined life is not worth living. Even though Plato presented a Socrates who sought eternal and indubitable definitions of concepts so as to uncover an objective and absolute form of knowledge by which we could orient our lives, I believe the actual Socrates urged us simply to reflect on our own convictions and world views so as to deepen our understandings of them, become more articulate about them, and be able to communicate them to others and so test them against the shared understandings of our communities. Moral truth is not the product of theoretical speculation. It is the product of an examination of our authentic commitments.

But this does not mean that such ethical insight is solely the product of individual inspiration or intuition. It is the product of debate, discussion and dialogue. The articulation of what we already hold in a context of discussion which tests and refines those beliefs gives them a warrantability which no degree of individual conviction or individual cognitive processing can give them. The life of virtue requires caring, commitment and understanding produced by reflection and dialogue. When Socrates said that knowledge is virtue, I take him to have meant

---

13   John Rawls, *A Theory of Justice* (Oxford, 1971), p. 20.

that in a morally complex world, we cannot be virtuous without also being articulate about our convictions. We need not only to be motivated to act well; we must also understand our motivations and the values by which we are moved. And such understanding is achieved by more than just individual reflection. It is achieved by the rational testing which arises from dialogue and debate. We know from what happened to Socrates that such testing could have unsettling and even dangerous consequences. But living virtuously was never meant to be safe.

Socratic Dialogue

Rather than argue further for this thesis in a theoretical way, I want now to illustrate it. I do so by reporting on a day-long conversation held with twelve people who were nurses, doctors, or social workers and moderated by me following the format called 'Socratic Dialogue'. The topic of this conversation was 'What, in the clinical setting, is Human Dignity?' and I will show in my report on it that the twelve participants had an implicit knowledge of what human dignity was which contained not only conceptual content, but also ethical and imperative content. Without being overly sophisticated and, more importantly, without being theoretical or abstract, the understanding implicitly held by this group and expressed in the everyday actions and judgements of the individuals in it, was the basis of their everyday virtue and of the many micro-judgements they made in their professional lives. Further, these judgements were often ethical in nature. Their understanding of human dignity included a sense of the moral demands and responsibilities that a virtuous understanding of this concept brings with it.

Let me first explain what Socratic Dialogue is. Based on the ideas of German philosopher Leonard Nelson (1882–1927)[14] and his pupil Gustav Heckmann (1898–1996), and developed by the Philosophical-Political Academy in Germany, the Society for the Furtherance of Critical Philosophy in the UK, and by Jos Kessels with the Dutch Association for Philosophical Practice, Socratic Dialogue is a powerful method for doing philosophy in a group.

While the Socratic Dialogue derives its name from Socrates, it is not a simple imitation of a Platonic dialogue, though there are some similarities. A Socratic

---

[14]   Leonard Nelson, *Socratic Method and Critical Philosophy* (New Haven, Connecticutt, 1940). See also Rene Saran and Barbara Neisser (eds), *Inquiring Minds: Socratic Dialogue in Education* (Stoke on Trent, 2004); Dries Boele, 'The 'Benefits' of a Socratic Dialogue. Or: Which Results Can We Promise?', *Inquiry: Critical Thinking Across the Disciplines*, XVII/3 (Spring, 1997): 48–69; Stan van Hooft, 'What is Self-Fulfilment? A Report on a Socratic Dialogue', *Practical Philosophy*, 4/1 (March 2001): 47–54; Paolo Dordoni and Stan van Hooft, 'Socratic Dialogue and Medical Ethics', in Patricia Shipley and Heidi Mason (eds), *Ethics and Socratic Dialogue in Civil Society* (Münster, 2004), pp. 205–12, and Les Fitzgerald and Stan van Hooft, 'A Socratic Dialogue on the Question: What is Love in Nursing', *Nursing Ethics*, 7/6 (2000): 481–91.

Dialogue begins with a general question, like the one Socrates asks in the *Euthyphro*, 'What is piety?' Note that both Socrates and Euthyphro are at the law court for urgent personal reasons. This ensures that their purpose in discussing this question is not purely theoretical. Euthyphro's assertion that it is piety that motivates him to bring an action against his father contextualizes the question of what piety is and relates it to an actual judgement that Euthyphro has already made: namely, that piety consists in bringing the legal action against his father. However, Socrates' response to this judgement is not of the kind that a modern Socratic Dialogue would make. Whereas Socrates denies the importance and validity of Euthyphro's particular and concrete judgement and seeks a general and theoretical definition of piety instead, a modern Socratic Dialogue would explore the reasons behind Euthyphro's judgement and the ethical knowledge that is implicit in it. I will explain this in a moment. Further, perhaps the most significant difference between a modern Socratic Dialogue and a Platonic one is that the facilitator does not contribute any content and does not seek to lead the participants to a pre-conceived conclusion in the way that the real Socrates clearly did.

While 'What is piety?' is an archaic question for us, it is a good illustration of the kind of question about which a Socratic dialogue can be conducted. General questions such as 'What is X?' where X stands for a concept such as happiness, health or a virtue, along with questions of the form 'What is the significance of X?' where X might stand for something like death or suffering, are suitable questions for a dialogue. I have also conducted dialogues on questions of the form 'When is X a success?' where X stands for a caring process such as pain management. Other forms of dialogue questions can also be devised. The common characteristic will be that they seek a general answer. Notice that it is not appropriate for a Socratic Dialogue that it seeks a practical solution to a practical problem either in real or hypothetical terms. It is not appropriate to ask 'What should we do in this case?' or 'What should we do in a case like this?' While many courses in applied ethics discuss cases in terms such as these and while there is much pedagogical value in doing so, such questions do little to challenge the existing ethical convictions of the participants and do not force participants to be articulate about these convictions or to reflect on them further. While participants in such case studies will be asked reasons for their decisions and while this brings many implicit moral commitments to light, there is little opportunity for participants to seek to understand or question those commitments in deeper terms. It is only when we ask the classical philosophical question 'What do you mean by that concept?' that true Socratic inquiry can begin. And, as I argued earlier, it is when a deeper and more articulate understanding of the key concepts and realities that are present in a clinical situation is gained that a more virtuous response to similar clinical situations can be elicited on future occasions. Sensitive awareness, which is the first step in ethical decision making, requires such a deeper understanding of what is ethically salient in morally complex situations. This is why the Socratic Dialogue approach is fruitful in the context of teaching ethics even though it differs from the case study approach and the hypothetical approach that is so widely practised in clinical education.

Another reason that Socratic dialogue does not ask what one would do in a hypothetical situation is that such questions often elicit answers infected by bad faith. It is all too easy to give lip service to the official values of one's profession or community when answering such questions. The fact is that in a truly difficult or extreme situation which we merely envisage we often have no idea what we would do. We only know what we would do when the situation actually arises and we are actually called upon to act. And we may then surprise ourselves. It follows that the most epistemologically secure way of discussing our actual commitments and convictions is to discuss cases in which we have really participated and in which we have made actual decisions and judgements. It is also the case that even with real cases such as these, we can be vague on what our own action and judgement have meant and what conceptual understanding of the salient features of the situation were implicit in that action and judgement. So in offering an example to the dialogue group we are allowing ourselves to discover ethically important facts about ourselves which no answers to questions of the form 'What would you do if X happened?' could elicit.

Accordingly, the key to the modern dialogue method is that members of the group begin by proposing examples from their own lives in order to illustrate the theme of the question. Such examples must be specific incidents, rather than attitudes or habits, in which the dialogue question or its theme has come to mind in some way. The group then decides which one of the examples offered looks most promising for the purpose of answering the discussion question. From that point on, that example becomes the focus and the touchstone for the entire discussion. By grounding the discussion in a concrete and real example in this way, Socratic Dialogue avoids discussing the question in general and hence vague and theoretical terms. If the group were to ask the general question 'head-on' as it were, it could only respond with participants offering conflicting definitions. They would have no means available to them as a group to adjudicate which of these conflicting suggestions were correct. Consensus would then be all but impossible to achieve.

Moreover, a concrete example avoids the kind of artificiality which philosophers' examples such as 'Jim and the Indians'[15] or 'the fat man stuck in the mouth of the cave'[16] bring with them, and it also avoids the dependence on theory that many ethical debates seem unable to avoid. After all, examples such as 'Jim and the Indians' or 'the fat man stuck in the mouth of the cave' are devised expressly to make or challenge a theoretical point in moral philosophy. If you try to understand what Jim or the fat man's desperate companions might actually be thinking or might actually be like as individual persons, you have stopped playing

---

[15]   J.J.C. Smart and Bernard Williams, *Utilitarianism For and Against* (Cambridge, 1973), p. 98.

[16]   Hugo A. Bedau, *Making Mortal Choices: Three Exercises in Moral Casuistry* (New York and Oxford, 1997), Chapter 2.

the philosophical game and you are likely to disrupt the theoretical elegance which such discussions are designed to preserve. In contrast, taking an actual real-life example threatens the theoretical tidiness of the discussion, but promises contact with the way actual people think and feel about morally interesting issues.

The next step in a Socratic Dialogue, after an example has been decided upon, is for the group to explore that example by asking for more details from the person who offered it. The purpose of this stage of the discussion is to ensure that everyone understands the example with enough detail and empathy in order to be able to place themselves into the situation of the example giver. Most often the example will involve the person having made some decision or performed some action or come to some realization which can be summed up in a judgement. It is crucial that the whole group can understand what this judgement is and can imagine themselves also making it. (This does not imply that everyone has to agree with it. Others in the group may well imagine themselves making a different judgement. Nevertheless, they must be able to understand the situation well enough to be able to come to this view and also to understand sufficiently the judgement that was in fact made by the person who offered the example and actually experienced the incident.)

When this phase of the dialogue is over, the facilitator asks the group to consider how the judgement that was made, and which they can all now understand, throws light on the topic. How does the judgement express an implicit understanding of the issue or concept which is the focus of the Dialogue? What does Euthyphro's judgement that piety demands his laying a charge against his father say about Euthyphro's understanding of what piety is? What must he take piety to be if he makes that judgement? And what must other members of the discussion take piety to be if they can understand his making that judgement?

An important technique which the facilitator will use in a Socratic Dialogue is to write the answers that participants give to this and further questions on a flip chart. By doing this the facilitator ensures not only that the discussion proceeds at a slow enough pace to allow everyone to consider what is being said and to listen as well as contribute, but also that everyone agrees on the way that ideas and answers are formulated. It is the seeking of this agreement that makes the Dialogue such a painstaking and thorough instrument for philosophical exploration. Most of the one-day Dialogues that I have conducted have been felt by participants to be too short to reach a final conclusion and many dialogues are generally conducted over several days. By this and other techniques the facilitator ensures that all participants can contribute fully, that they listen carefully to each other, and that they proceed to further discussion only when they are satisfied that they understand each other and agree with each other at every stage of the exploration.

Further, no participant is permitted to say anything that does not relate to their own experience or beliefs. Purely theoretical or book-based considerations are banned. Moreover, every proposal must be tested against the example and only this example. To what extent does the example illustrate the proposal or to what extent does the proposal clarify the example or contribute to answering the question with reference to the example? A proposal fails if it does not illuminate the example. Moreover, it is not permitted to challenge a proposal by showing that it would not apply to a different example. In this way the specificity of the discussion is preserved throughout.

It is only when the question has been thoroughly answered in the specific context of the example that the group is invited to proceed to the final stage of the Dialogue: that of asking the general question in its general form. The strategy here will be to learn from the example what, in general, can be said in answer to the question. If health in the example consists in P (where P is the understanding that the group has reached in relation to the specific example), then a more general understanding of health can also be reached. Indeed, one technique that is available to the facilitator, if there is time at the end of this phase of the discussion, is to go back to the examples that were offered at the beginning of the Dialogue but which were not selected, to see whether the definition that the group has agreed upon will help in the understanding of those examples. In this way, a group consensus can be reached on an answer to the Dialogue question, a consensus which is both a new discovery for each participant and also an articulation of what they had pre-reflexively known before.

Report on a Socratic Dialogue on the topic: 'What, in the clinical setting, is human dignity?'

There were twelve participants in this Dialogue: namely, Irena, Isabel, John, Margaret, Tembi, Gwen, Rosie, Lynne, Terry, Laurinda, Ann and Jill. (These names have been changed to assure anonymity.) Most were nurses and some worked in other caring professions such as social work. The group was invited to bring forward incidents from each participant's professional practice which in some way raised the question of what human dignity was or illustrated human dignity in some way. The following examples were offered:

Terry (a social worker): I was given a referral of a released prisoner. He had been convicted of murder and there was a perceived risk that he might murder again. I was his case manager. I felt he had no human dignity. (He subsequently suicided.)

Laurinda (a nurse): I was involved in the resuscitation of a patient who had requested not to be resuscitated. He had collapsed while he was bathing. He was naked and soaking wet, in full view in the hallway. It turned out that he was a relative and I was deeply embarrassed for him. He died soon after.

Irena (a nurse educator): I was in an emergency ward (but not as a nurse on duty) when a young woman was brought in who was in extreme pain. She was thrashing about and exposing her nakedness (she was oblivious to this). Staff ignored her for a considerable time. I felt the patient's dignity was compromised.

Isabel (a postgraduate student nurse): An elderly gentleman who had had a hip replacement had had his prosthesis removed and was chairbound and in constant pain. I had gotten to know him as part of a research project I was engaged in. I was not part of the nursing staff of that nursing home. I was asked to assist him into a chair, when I saw him naked. He was clearly embarrassed and tried to cover himself.

Jill (a social worker): I was working with a group of young disabled adults and had to assist a young woman with a sanitary napkin.

It is interesting to reflect on this set of examples. It often happens that the participants will not have thought of examples before the Dialogue. It then happens that the offering of one example triggers memories in other participants of similar incidents in their own practices. This is the reason that nakedness and exposure of genitals became a theme in several of these examples. The further effect of this phenomenon is that there is a degree of prejudgement as to what human dignity is. While the dialogue process does not seek a definition of the Dialogue theme until quite late in the process, all the participants come to the Dialogue with some pre-existing conception of what, in this case, 'human dignity' is. Or perhaps they have not thought about it much and so are a little vague as to what it might be. If they then hear an example involving nakedness, they may limit their conception of what human dignity is (or what would compromise it) to cases involving nakedness. This involves the risk of limiting the scope of the discussion somewhat, but this is a risk which can be overcome in the later phases of the Dialogue.

Further, it often happens that in the course of discussing which example to focus upon, the group already begins to discuss the substantive question or will seek a definition of the key term, in this case that of 'human dignity'. It is important that such substantive issues not be explored at this stage since, without a discussion of the example, such exploration can only be too theoretical in form. My practice has been to note the questions that are raised during this stage of the Dialogue and 'park' them on the flip charts so that the group can return to them in the last phase of the Dialogue. If the group has achieved a consensus on what human dignity is in any clinical setting then it should be well equipped to answer the questions it will have raised earlier. On this occasion the following questions were raised:

> What is the relation between dignity and the power to exercise choice?
> What is the role in the preservation of the dignity of patients of the dignity shown by clinical staff?
> Is human dignity something that happens only in interaction with others or is it innate?
> How does dignity relate to privacy and gender (especially in relation to nakedness)?
> How can dignity be restored when it has been lost?

Most of these questions were answered in later stages of the Dialogue.

After some discussion, Isabel's example was chosen. The group then turned to the task of exploring the example. The objective of this phase of the Dialogue is to permit each participant to understand the incident in sufficient detail in order to imagine themselves in it. It would be a mistake for the group to explore Isabel's judgement about, and understanding of, human dignity, which are implicit in her offering the example. The task of this phase of the Dialogue is not to explore the example giver's thinking, but to explore the example. So it is important to ask the group to focus as much as possible on the facts of what happened and to be as descriptive as possible. It is especially important to avoid questions which are hypothetical in nature: questions which begin with, 'What would you have done if such and such had happened?' This is not a question about what actually happened and, moreover, it is seeking information about Isabel's attitudes and convictions rather than about the incident.

The following points were elicited by questioning Isabel about the incident:

1. I (Isabel) felt that the old gentleman deserved dignity.
2. He was very intelligent but could no longer read.
3. He was 91 years old.
4. He was a widower with three children.
5. His children were already fighting over his will.
6. He had been an aircraft mechanic and had worked on the railways.
7. He did not have may visitors.
8. He was of Anglo-Australian heritage and loved music.
9. He didn't like to be with the others in the nursing home. He seemed to find them boring.
10. He used to say that staff treated him like a child.
11. He had a bandaged and painful wound on his hip.
12. My research project involved exploring the lived experience of people in chronic pain. It involved in-depth interviews and participant observation (that is why I was helping out in an informal way in the nursing home).
13. We had interview session in the courtyard once a week for about twelve weeks.
14. I used to feed him in the courtyard.
15. He shared his room with dementia patients.
16. The incident occurred at about eleven in the morning.
17. There were six patients in the ward/cubicle. They were all very dependent and the nurse in charge was in a hurry and overworked.
18. I had asked to be present at his bathing as part of participant observation.
19. It was autumn and it was getting cooler.
20. No one else was there but the space was cluttered.
21. It was a bed bath and he was then to be moved to a perambulator chair.
22. I came in on the end of the bath.
23. In the incident he was completely exposed. The nursing assistant had drawn away the curtain without warning.
24. He was arthritic and flailed his arms about in an attempt to cover his private parts.
25. I tried to cover him by putting a crocheted rug that was lying nearby over him.
26. I helped put his pyjama top on.
27. After the incident he did not engage with me and said 'Just take me to the lounge room' (a place he had previously avoided because he hated the sing-alongs and other mindless games that took place there).
28. I seemed to him to have 'crossed over' to a nursing role by helping at this point.
29. He died about a week later.

Notice that the first of these points is more about Isabel's attitude than about the incident. It was when I pointed this out to the group and insisted that they gather just the facts of the case that the rest of the story unfolded. Point 28 is more an interpretation than a description also, but it seemed very significant in the story and everyone in the group understood and empathized with it, so it was deemed to be valid in the dialogue process.

Now that participants had a good grasp of the incident, the group turned to the question: What in Isabel's example did human dignity consist in? (The group decided to focus upon the dignity of the old gentleman in the example, rather than that of Isabel. This decision certainly accords with the intention with which the example was offered.)

There is also often an issue in the dialogue process about examples being positive or negative. A positive example is one that illustrates the presence of the concept or idea which is the theme of the Dialogue, whereas a negative example is one that illustrates the absence of the value or entity which is being explored. It may be absent because the incident is one in which it is destroyed, or it may be one in which a bad outcome results from its being absent. So, in this case, the incident could be seen as a negative example in that the sudden exposure of the patient resulted in his loss of dignity. But it could also be seen as a positive example if one focused upon his proud and somewhat surly silence in the face of the insult. By and large, a positive example is preferred in the dialogue process because it allows the group to focus more clearly upon the question. In this example, there was some ambiguity. This was clear when the following answers were offered to the question: What in Isabel's example did human dignity consist in?

1. Being known as a person: that is, not as an object. (This answer was judged to be a bit theory-driven rather than example-driven.)
2. His penis was exposed. (This was a negative way of indicating what dignity consisted in. This exposure constituted the loss of dignity.)
3. Isabel respected him. (a positive characterisation)
4. His feeling of self-worth was violated. (another negative characterisation)

Some questions that arose in this phase of the discussion were:

What is the difference between embarrassment and loss of dignity?
What gave the old gentleman dignity? And what took it away?

The point of the second question was that if dignity is innate, then no action on the part of others could take it away. On the other hand, it was countered, if this is so, then clinicians might be under less of an obligation to act in a way that supports the dignity of patients, since not acting in that way cannot rob patients of their dignity. This possibility suggests that dignity should be sought in the interaction between patient and clinician rather than being innate to the patient. But then again, even if dignity is innate, it can still be compromised by others and so we should not countenance behaviour that threatens dignity. These considerations led the group to agree that:

> Dignity is something an individual needs to maintain, and others can help or not by their actions in individuals' efforts to maintain their dignity.

While this formula does not capture what the essence of human dignity is, the suggestion did give rise to the following list of conditions that help individuals to maintain their dignity:

1. Their genitals should be covered (because nakedness makes one vulnerable).
2. They should enjoy meaningful communication with staff and with other patients. Patients should not be seen as strangers by staff.
3. Their choices should be respected.
4. They should be allowed enjoyable activities.
5. They should be known as an individual person.
6. They must be made to feel that they matter.
7. They should be touched gently.
8. Information about clinical procedures should be given and be understandable.
9. There should be warmth in all interactions between staff and patients.

Although the points above do not directly offer a definition of what dignity is in the example, they do display a considerable understanding of what is implied by the concept of dignity and what circumstances in the clinical setting are needed in order to preserve the dignity of this patient. Accordingly (and also because time was moving on), the group now turned to the general question: What, in the clinical setting, is human dignity?

Because there was not much time left in the discussion, the following points were sketched out only briefly (sometimes with a little too much input from the facilitator) and would require further time to explore thoroughly. It was suggested that dignity is something that all persons, including patients, seek to maintain for themselves. It is the object of an existential quest rather than an objective or socially constructed status. This gives nurses and clinicians the task of seeing what they can do to help the individual maintain their dignity. Human dignity is not a given, but a gift. It is a quality which arises both from within the patient and also from the way in which the patient is treated by the clinician. Once again, this conclusion does not specify an essence of what human dignity is and so does not offer a definition in the classical sense. However, it does operationalize the concept and indicate the practical implications of the implicit understanding of it that the group had. The group was clearest in being able to say what clinicians needed to do in order to preserve the dignity of patients rather than in being able to give a positive philosophical definition of human dignity.

Conclusion

It should be stressed that almost all of the content of this discussion was generated by the twelve participants. The discussion and its structure elicited from them knowledge that they already implicitly had. It was knowledge that allowed them to understand Isabel's judgement and to empathize with it. It was knowledge that allowed them to articulate a wide-ranging and sophisticated understanding of human dignity and of what it requires of clinicians, as illustrated by the experience that Isabel had undergone. I imagine that it would not be likely that each of these people individually would have come up with such an analysis of human dignity in a clinical setting. Yet it can still be claimed that each of them came to the discussion with enough of an inchoate understanding of human dignity in a clinical setting to be able to articulate and agree upon the analysis that was finally reached. In this sense it was implicit knowledge that they already had.

It is also worth highlighting the ethical content of the group's analysis. By seeing human dignity not as an inherent quality of human nature, grounded in metaphysical doctrines or in naturalistic theories, and by focusing on what practical measures are needed in order to preserve dignity, the group acknowledged the ethical challenge that was implicit in the thought that human dignity is something given, at least in part, by the caring approach of the clinician. The nature of the ethical norms here is personal and existential. These are norms concerning the attitudes that clinicians and patients should have towards each other and concerning the attitude or stances with which clinicians and patients should approach each other.

It seems clear from the report of this Socratic Dialogue that these twelve caring professionals were possessed of an everyday wisdom which guides their implicit micro-judgements and which can, with suitable dialogue techniques, be uncovered to display a relatively sophisticated understanding of morally deep issues. Everyday virtue, the ability of most people to act well most of the time, is based on an everyday wisdom which it is appropriate for philosophers to respect and which can, indeed, be a resource for philosophical exploration. While this knowledge can be expressed in general propositions or principles, its primary mode of presence in the moral being of its possessors is in the internally motivational micro-judgements that individuals make in concrete and particular situations in their lives. It lies in their everyday wisdom and is expressed in their everyday virtue.

PART 2
The Objects of Health Care

Chapter 7

The Body and Well-Being

The first clause in the Constitution of the World Health Organization reads as follows: 'Health is a state of complete physical, mental and social well-being and not merely the absence of disease or infirmity.'[1] This definition of health extends beyond the physical or bodily well-being of a person and includes the psychological and interpersonal dimensions, along with any other social circumstances that affect a person's happiness. Some health workers have been encouraged by this notion of health as an all-embracing state of well-being to think that their professional responsibilities and commitments extend to every aspect of the well-being of their clients. Others have argued against this implication of the holistic conception of health, saying that the exclusive focus of the health professions should be on the physical well-being of clients and that the mental and social well-being of those clients should be attended to by professionals in fields such as psychotherapy and social work. On this view, the proper and exclusive object of the efforts of health professionals should be the state of health of the client's body. Even in the areas of mental health where it is the psychological condition of the patient which is at issue, such thinkers will say that either the basic problem is neurological and therefore physical, or it is a matter for psychotherapy and in that case it is the adjustment and coping strategies of the patient that are at issue rather than their health. The conception of health is here unashamedly physical.

I will argue in this chapter that health professionals are indeed concerned primarily with clients' bodies. However, I will also argue that persons' bodies are central to their complete mental and social well-being and that, therefore, the efforts of health professionals have an impact on the whole and many-faceted aspects of the well-being of their clients. It is therefore both an appropriate and inevitable extension of the professional commitment of health professionals to be concerned about these wider ramifications of their body-centred practice.

---

[1]   Preamble to the Constitution of the World Health Organization as adopted by the International Health Conference, New York, 19–22 June 1946; signed on 22 July 1946 by the representatives of 61 states (Official Record of the World Health Organization, 2, p. 100) and entered into force on 7 April 1948. The definition has not been amended since 1948.

Against dualism

Before offering a positive argument for this position, I will offer a negative one to the effect that the debate between holists and 'corporalists' is frequently engaged in against the background of an erroneous metaphysical conception of the human person: namely, mind–body dualism. I do not mean to suggest that health workers explicitly hold to a set of metaphysical beliefs involving such technical concepts as *res cogitans* and *res extensa*. Rather, I am suggesting that part of the common-sense view of humanity which is current in our culture and which is therefore shared by most health workers is the view that human beings are made up of two kinds of reality which are marked by such dichotomies as body/mind, body/soul, or body/spirit.[2] That the term 'body' remains constant in these binary distinctions while the second term displays some variation indicates that this view of humanity does not have the status of a well-developed theory. Professional philosophers do have such theories of course, although it is fair to say that at this time, dualism does not enjoy wide support. Nevertheless, the metaphysics inherent in lay psychology has deep currents of dualism flowing through it. The relevance of this to our problem is that the distinction between the body and that mysterious entity which is thought to reside in it and which is the specific locus of the unique individuality and personality of the person allows health workers to define their task as being centred on the body alone. Without an implicit dualism, the exclusive focus upon the client's body would not be possible. If persons were understood from the very start in holistic terms, there could never be an ethos amongst health workers which stressed the client's body to the exclusion of the mind, soul or spirit.

It would follow from this that it would be a simple task to argue against this stress on the body. We would simply have to argue against dualism. But, while there are many such arguments in the philosophical literature,[3] they seem not to have had much impact upon lay conceptions of the human person. Even the holistic position, which has emerged as a kind of counter-movement to the exclusive stress on the body made possible by dualism, seems to be similarly infected with an implicit dualism. While the phrase 'whole person' is frequently repeated, especially in the literature associated with nurse education,[4] when you ask nurse educators what they mean by it, they will often answer that they mean

[2]   For a typical example, see Brent Q. Hafen, Keith J. Karren, Kathryn J. Frandsen and N. Lee Smith, *Mind/Body Health: The Effects of Attitudes, Emotions and Relationships* (Boston, Massachusetts, 1996).

[3]   For a useful overview of current philosophical thinking on this, see Peter Smith and O.R. Jones, *The Philosophy of Mind: An Introduction* (Cambridge, 1986).

[4]   For some examples, see Jean Watson, *Nursing: Human Science and Human Care: A Theory of Nursing* (Norwalk, Connecticut, 1985); Barbara Blattner, *Holistic Nursing* (Englewood Cliffs, New Jersey, 1981), and Madeline Leininger (ed.), *Care: The Essence of Nursing and Health* (Thorofare, New Jersey, 1984).

that a client is not only a body, but something else besides, and that it is the responsibility of the nurse to care for the needs of both aspects of the client. But what is this if not dualism once again? This explication refers to a body and to something else besides. Although there is seldom an explicit metaphysics to account for what this something else is, there is clearly a formal dualism involved. This creates the danger that, with a new and even vaguer form of dualism, the practical pressures of a health worker's responsibilities may well lead to a reduction of care to that which seems most concretely present in the therapeutic situation: namely, an entity which is taken to be nothing but a body.

What is needed is a new understanding of the body which makes it impossible to think of it as just a biological machine which houses a person's fuller self. Perhaps a solution to this problem may be sought in the phenomenological and existential strands of Continental European philosophy.[5] If I may engage in a gross simplification of this tradition and its questioning of metaphysical models of persons, I would propose that there arise from it two methodological strategies which will help us to proceed. First, there is the strategy of thinking about human beings in terms of verbs rather than nouns, and second, there is the strategy of thinking about being a human being as an essentially cultural phenomenon.

Let me begin with the first of these. We should not ask what sort of a thing a human being is, or what sort of thing the noun phrase 'human being' names, or what sorts of components a human being is made up of. We should take the phrase 'human being' to be a verbal phrase. In this way it will mean 'being human', or 'being in a human way'. What we need to understand is what it is to exist as a human being. It is this existing or being (notice that these are verbs) that we are interested in, not the thing that is. Another way of putting the point is to say that we are interested in the activity of being a human being.[6] But this sounds odd. Do we really engage in an activity called 'being a human being'? We engage in such activities as eating a meal, going to the grocer, helping a friend, caring for a patient, being with a lover, worshipping our God, and so forth. Is there an activity called 'being a human being' over and above all these particular activities? Surely not. What we should rather say is that the particular activities we have named, along with many others besides, are the sorts of activities that add up to being a human being. To be a human being is to engage in those sorts of activities. Yet it is not true that being a human being is simply the sum of these various particular activities. This is because, insofar as these activities are engaged in by human

---

[5]   I have in mind especially the work of Maurice Merleau-Ponty in his *The Phenomenology of Perception*, trans. Colin Smith (London, 1962), especially Part 1, Chapters 5 and 6. For a deep and far-ranging study of embodiment, see David Michael Levin, *The Body's Recollection of Being: Phenomenological Psychology and the Deconstruction of Nihilism* (London, 1985).

[6]   I am not making a distinction between the concepts of 'person' and 'human being', although such distinctions can be made. I use the phrase 'human being' because it admits of being read as a verbal noun, which the word 'person' does not.

beings, they are engaged in in a distinctive way. Particular activities of mine take their character from the fact that they are the activities of a human being, even as they partially constitute what it is to be a human being.

To illustrate this, let us take the case of eating a meal. It is clear that this is an activity that is importantly biological in nature. It is an activity that all animals engage in. But it is also clear that we engage in this activity in a way that is distinctly human. This is observationally obvious. We use knives and forks, or chopsticks, or whatever. (Some cultures do use their fingers, but in specified and approved ways.) We eat in restaurants as well as at home and we have a large number of rituals surrounding meals such as the dinner party or the wedding feast. In short, we have surrounded the act of eating with a framework of manners and norms which have made it a human cultural activity. This is true in a normative sense in that it is required by etiquette that eating be a cultured act, and in a descriptive sense in that eating is something which is meaningful beyond its being merely a matter of satisfying hunger. People who eat differently from the way their culture dictates are regarded as bad-mannered. And even when we do eat purely in response to hunger – something which might happen in desperate circumstances – this action will be given a cultural meaning both by myself and by any observer who may be present. No one denies that satisfying hunger is one of the purposes of eating, but eating has a social meaning as well. Through it we express ourselves in a way appropriate to the circumstances we are in. Whether we are eating a picnic lunch in a city park or sitting down at a formal dinner on a state occasion, we are doing more than just filling our bellies. We are behaving in a humanly meaningful way. To ask what it is to be a human being is to ask about the human meanings and contexts that transform our activities into something distinctively human.

Accordingly, being a human being is not something that I can achieve by myself. If being a human being means performing actions or thinking thoughts which are meaningful, and if such meanings derive from the culture of which I am a part, then my ability to perform meaningful actions and thus *be* in a human way, depends on my culture. To be a human being is not merely to be a member of a certain biological species. Neither is it to have a metaphysical component (such as a mind or soul) which is thought to be the origin of a range of meaning-giving thoughts and intentions. To be as a human being requires that you be an inducted member of a culture.[7]

Given that I am using the phrase 'human being' as a verbal gloss on the noun phrase 'whole person', we can now draw a first conclusion. To be a whole person is not simply a matter of having certain parts or functions. It is to behave in a socially and culturally developed way. It is to be educated in the deepest sense. Personal wholeness is an existential possibility that culture offers us, something

---

[7]   For the sake of simplicity I will leave out of account the important fact that today no one is a member of only one culture. You can be a member of a national culture, a local culture, a gender-specific culture, a religious culture, an ethnic culture, a professional culture, a scientific culture, and so on. And these may conflict on occasion.

that it allows us to enact as social beings, something that we enjoy when we are fully developed and shaped culturally. Whole persons or whole human beings are not defined metaphysically or biologically. Their being is constituted by the social formation and upbringing to which they are subject. We take the particular forms and contents of our being from the social and cultural contexts in which we exist.

These relations flow in two directions. Not only do human beings require the formation given them by their cultures, but they also actively contribute to those cultures as they live in a creative way. Individual persons cannot live as human beings, with all the experiences, aspirations and projects which that entails, unless they are formed within their cultures. Moreover, their pursuing their plans and projects adds to and changes culture and society, whether in small or significant ways. To be a human being, or to be in a human way, is to exist and act in relation to cultural and social realities which define our identity as well as to contribute to those realities and to our identities. To be a person is to exist and act in ways defined by our context while also being a contributor to that context.

And this leads to the second methodologial approach to understanding humanity which the Continental European tradition of philosophy has taught us. It is a mistake to ask the question of what it is to be a human being from an individualistic or atomistic viewpoint as traditional dualism does. For human beings (and, perhaps, for other animals), to be is to be social. It constitutes one of the great scientific breakthroughs of modern times for the social sciences to have established that our selves as persons are a product of social, cultural and historical formation. While traditional philosophers speak of an inner core to our being such as a soul or a mind, which is the kernel of our personhood and the ultimate origin of our actions and motivations, contemporary thinkers argue that social and cultural formation is necessary for the formation of a self so that it can become a person with an awareness of itself and able to act meaningfully in the world and to communicate with others.[8] We may conclude, then, that the question of what it is to be an actual and culturally formed historical human being, or a whole and integrated person, need not be answered by positing mind–body dualism. Rather, it is a question that will require us to investigate the contribution made by our social and cultural contexts.

Our bodies

However, I do not propose to engage in that exploration here. Rather, I want to explore the implications for our understanding of our bodies of the idea that our wholeness as persons is a function of social being. Being a whole person or being human is not a matter of being metaphysical and discrete entities having a non-

---

[8] For example, see George Herbert Mead, *Mind, Self and Society from the Standpoint of a Social Behaviorist* (Chicago, Illinois, 1934), and Rom Harré, *Social Being: A Theory for Social Psychology* (Oxford, 1979).

bodily component over and above our bodies, as dualists would maintain. Being human is something which our cultures and interpersonal circumstances allow us to achieve. It follows from this that whole persons enact a culturally structured comportment towards one another. Borrowing and adapting a term from Sartre, I will call this comportment, 'being-for-others'.[9] In the way I use the term, being-for-others involves a constantly present and implicit recognition that we are with others, either actually or potentially. It involves a readiness to express ourselves towards others, and to communicate with them. Even when I am alone, I am conscious of myself as a being which draws its identity from the way it might be seen and reacted to by others and from the way it addresses itself towards others. My being-for-others is a central modality of my being human. It is my claim that our bodies are centrally implicated in our being-for-others and are therefore essential and constitutive elements in our being social, communicative, expressive and human. It will follow from this that caring for our bodies will imply caring for our whole selves insofar as we are a being-for-others. In arguing for this claim, I will focus upon the role of the body without any reference to such 'inner' or 'mental' components or aspects of our being as intentions, wishes, beliefs or desires. To this end, I will concentrate on behaviours which are either completely involuntary or, if voluntary, not preceded by deliberation.

The first and most obvious way in which my body is central to my being-for-others is that it is through my body that I am present to the other. It is through my body that I am visible, audible, touchable and noticeable. Of course, all that is required for my body to be apprehensible by others in this way is that it be a physical object in the world. My body is an object in the crowded street just as yours is. However, at this level, is my body no more significant to others than a lamppost would be? Surely there are occasions when my body is present to the other in a sense that goes beyond this mere physicality? What needs to be the case for this richer presence to the other to be realized? I need to have some form of relationship with that other person. It is because the crowd contains only people with whom I have no relationship that we all seem like so many objects in the street together. Were I to see an acquaintance in that crowd and call or gesture to him, our bodies would immediately be present to each other in a new way. Even so minimal a relationship as acquaintanceship establishes our bodies as loci for our being-for-others.

And yet more needs to be said here. It does not seem correct to say that others in the crowd are equivalent to physical objects when they are not acquaintances of mine. If a stranger in the crowd is hurt in an accident or stumbles I will be inclined to assist and will feel sympathy, while if an object is damaged my reaction is typically more neutral. The other calls out to my sympathy because of a basic solidarity grounded in our mutual recognition of each other as fellow human beings. Even before we are acquaintances I recognize the other as a fellow human

---

9   Jean-Paul Sartre, *Being and Nothingness*, trans. Hazel E. Barnes (New York, 1956), Part Three.

being and I accord to the other's body a respect which I do not reserve for mere objects. We are present bodily to each other as beings-for-the-other. This is the reason why I and many other writers use the term 'bodily' rather than 'physical' in connection with human beings. The lampposts of my example are physical. Were we physical, our bodies would be like these lampposts to those who have no personal relation to us. But the phenomenon of a primordial form of mutuality in human co-presence shows that our bodies are not just physical entities, but the loci of our being-for-others. To speak of our existence as 'bodily' is to signal a richer form of presence in the world than can be enjoyed by a merely physical object.

While a thorough exploration of my body as a being-for-others would address the role of my body in a variety of human relationships which could be arranged on a spectrum ranging from the most impersonal to the most intimate, limitations of space will necessitate our moving towards the latter end of this spectrum immediately. The sexual attraction between two adults, which leads to physical love, is an instance of an intensely intimate form of presence to the other as a bodily being-for-others. In what way is the body implicated in physical love? Many layers of cultural meaning and learnt expectation separate bodily love from the purely biological level of human existence. The coupling of lovers is not just a congress of two bodies considered as physical objects. Yet neither is it a pure meeting of minds. My presence to the other is importantly bodily. Reflection does discover a bodily feeling of desire for, and self-offering to, the other. Parts of the culturally formed rituals and practices surrounding sex, whether at the stage of selecting a partner or at the stage of giving physical expression to the liaison, have as their purpose precisely the production of this feeling of bodily abandonment to the other. And the word 'abandonment' is revealing in this context. What seems to be conveyed by it is the stripping away of all the cultural and social identities and self-images that constitute our self-possession as a fully formed person. In moments of sexual abandon we seem to return to a primaeval selfhood which is purely biological.

I say 'seem' because this point is not uncontentious. There are some who say that no matter how abandoned the love-making becomes, we never do, or never should, revert to a biological or animal level of existence.[10] The dimensions of meaning which arise from the cultural levels of our existence as human beings are never absent, and our love-making will always have a human meaning. Where two lovers are fully formed human beings there will be communication and fellow-feeling of some sort in any loving exchange. Love-making must never be just physical or biological. But this objection conflates the idea of being biological with that of being animal. The biological level of human existence is not the same thing as being 'merely animal'. (I will not comment on the denigration of the animal kingdom implied in this formulation.) To suggest that it were would be to suggest an almost automatic or driven form of coupling which was devoid of significance

---

[10]   For an example, see Thomas Nagel, 'Sexual Perversion', in Alan Soble (ed.), *The Philosophy of Sex: Contemporary Readings* (Totowa, New Jersey, 1980), pp. 76–88.

for the participants. Against this, I argue that we can understand human sex as 'bodily' as opposed to 'physical' or 'purely biological' provided that we see the human body as communicative from the very first. When all self-consciousness is stripped away and we abandon ourselves to sex, we are becoming communicative through the most direct bodily form of fellow-feeling which is available to us. Our being-for-others is then purely and directly bodily. We are not conscious of ourselves as whole persons. It is as if we direct our entire self as a whole person into our bodies and towards the body of the other. While the completeness of our embodiment at such a time may lead us to suppose that we cut ourselves off from others by retreating into a pre-conscious self, in fact the quality of that embodiment is communicative and expressive in that it arises from my sexual being-for-others. At such moments, my closeness to the other is as complete as it is unencumbered by a consciousness of self. The intimate physical contact of lovers is not lived at a purely biological level even though it is centrally bodily. It is meaningful in a way that is a function of the culture in which the lovers have their being. But this meaning is completely realized in the body. In the context of love, my body is intensely invested with meaning as my direct being-for-the-other. It is not a mere vehicle for a 'mental' passion, as dualists would argue. In stripping away self-consciousness, I do not lessen the fullness of my being.

I can continue to build up a case for the role of the body as an expressive and communicative locus of our being human by discussing the cries, gestures or expletives which I utter when I am in pain, in fear, or in any other of the states of distress that seem to wring cries from the deepest core of my being. I might be hammering a nail and hit my thumb or I might be undergoing deep emotional trauma when I give expression to the state of my being with some such involuntary cry. In instances such as these I most resemble animals that cry out or bark in response to a variety of stimuli. However, insofar as such events are involuntary and seem to be caused by that which stimulates them, we might ask whether they are genuine cases of communication. I do not standardly seek to communicate with anyone when I cry out in such ways. I do so whether there is someone within earshot or not. Of course, given that I am self-conscious and purposive, I might allow such cries to escape me in an attempt to manipulate the emotions of another but, in such a case, it can no longer be said that the event is purely involuntary. There seems to be a difference between an infant's cries of hunger and those same hungry cries when uttered by the infant in an attempt to manipulate its mother. The ability to manipulate others in this way indicates a degree of self-consciousness which, even if it is not yet so full as to allow explicit deliberation, does bespeak a certain distancing between the child and its expressive gestures. Such distancing is necessary for the self-control that is required to elevate the act into purposive behaviour.

But this talk of a 'distance between a child and its expressive gestures' is implicitly dualistic. If my bodily being is already a being-for-others, then it is inherently communicative and its every gesture, whether voluntary or involuntary, is communicative in meaning if not intent. Therefore, in order both to continue my critique of dualism and to press my case for the fullness of our bodily being, I need to argue that groans and involuntary gestures are inherently communicative. We see such direct communicativeness when we note an important difference between direct expressions of pain, for example, and the reports and descriptions of my pain which I might offer a health worker in the course of therapy or care. I do not directly express my pain when I tell the nurse about it in the way that I do when I groan because of it. The groan is caused by the pain, while the report is offered intentionally. A dualist might explain this difference by saying that such groans are not owned by me as a conscious agent, but are events which are causally linked to my body. My body seems to be operative in these spontaneous cries without reference to my intentions. Indeed, there might be cases where the intensity of the pain or distress (or of pleasure, for that matter) are such that the cry is wrung from my body despite my attempts to suppress it. This would seem to indicate that it is my body rather than my conscious self which is the origin of these events. However, it is not true that I do not own these gestures. If it were, it would have to follow that I do not own my body. Rather, what we have here are events which are mine in a bodily and primaeval sense. They are instances where I am pressed back, as it were, to the least culturally formed locus of my being. These cries are extensions of my bodily being. They are as intimate to my own being as is the rest of my body. But this does not mean that they are purely biological or pre-cultural. Rather they are a form of nakedness. And nakedness is a cultural phenomenon. There is often some embarrassment involved in certain cultures in allowing cries to become public. They not only take place within the public sphere, but they have a public meaning. They are more than just physical symptoms which convey information about my condition. Without explicit intentions on my part, they are a way in which I am meaningfully present to the other. As such, they are an expression of my being-for-others.

However intimate, involuntary and purely bodily they are, our cries and groans have a communicative meaning. Like the rest of our bodies, they are expressive in and of themselves. In order to explain this, it might be suggested that the processes of natural selection will have favoured those species of animals which accompanied their undergoing of pain or fear with cries and yelps because other members of the group would thereby be warned of danger. If this is right then animals with an instinctual tendency towards externalizing their intense feelings would have greater chances of survival and reproduction. In the absence of any communicative intentions, their gestures would still have communicative significance and be of help to others. However, this significance is entirely general in form. At the fundamental biological level of spontaneous bodily gesture, such events lack any direction towards a specifiable other. There is no intended terminus for the communication. They are wrung from the body in the intensity of experience and thrown into the world without a direction. Our bodies and the gestures and sounds that they generate in response to a variety of stimuli are not yet formative of specific relationships even if they do express the relational nature of our being. These gestures are inherently communicative even if we do not intend to communicate anything to anyone through them. No 'mental' event such as an intention needs to lie behind them in order to make them communicative.

These various examples, ranging from the wave of recognition in the crowd and the intimacies of sex to our involuntary expressive utterances, demonstrate that our bodies allow us to be social. That we are a being-for-others, that we are present to the other as a person, and that this very presence to the other is spontaneously expressive and communicative, is grounded in our bodies. But it is not true that our bodies are vehicles for our communications separable from those communications. Although they are biological entities, our bodies are expressive and meaningful in and of themselves. Certainly this expressiveness depends upon the movements and sounds that the body can make and upon the fact that our bodies are sensorily present to the other. But there is more to it than that. Insofar as our being social, or our being a being-for-others, is constitutive of our being complete as human beings, our bodies are the incarnations of our being as whole persons. Our being whole persons or social beings is not just grounded in our being bodily; it is the form which our bodily being takes in our cultural context. Our thoughts and aspirations are as much a function of our cultural context as they are of our brains. They are certainly not to be attributed to a metaphysically distinct entity called mind, soul or spirit residing in our bodies. Whereas dualism accounts for the emergence of a self or of a person in terms of there being a metaphysical entity called 'mind' or 'soul' present in a body, the tradition of thought I am relying upon suggests that the self or being of a person emerges from that body's location in a cultural and interpersonal context.

To establish this, I argue that expression and communication are not cases of using our bodies as material means for the conveying of a message generated from inside of our selves. On the dualist view of human beings, communication would be analysed as a contact between minds which makes use of the bodies in which those minds are housed as instruments for such communication. So, in analysing how a gesture or an utterance is expressive or meaningful, it might be suggested that it becomes so because the person intended that it be so; that the person had a thought or an emotional flush which he then sought to express with some bodily or physical means. The problem with this view, of course, is that it presupposes that persons can recognize their thoughts and emotional experiences for what they are apart from the expressions that they give to them. On this view, persons have to choose an expressive gesture or word which suits the content which they wish to convey. They must, therefore, have a full cognitive grasp of this content before they can give expression to it. But this is impossible. To have such a cognitive grasp requires that the thought or feeling be given some form whereby it can be cognized. And this imparting of a form is already expression. It may take place privately, 'in our heads' as we say, but it is still an expression given a communicative form. Moreover, as Ludwig Wittgenstein was at pains to point out, this expressive form has to be learnt from others in the public arena for it to be cognizable, let alone communicable.[11] Both gestures and words, therefore, are already-constituted publicly meaningful items. They do not derive their meanings from the thoughts that might be taken to lie behind them. Rather, it is because of the meanings that communicative gestures and words in fact have that we are able to express ourselves through them.

The meanings of our gestures and words are not things which can be separately identified as if they were mental artefacts. Thoughts are not items in our minds or brains which are the internal counterpart of the meaning which our activities and utterances have for us, as if thinking about the meaning of what we are doing is enough to establish that meaning. Does my intention to say 'Hello' make my arm movement meaningful as a wave? Or is it the cultural conventions which define waves and the appropriate social contexts in which we might wave to our acquaintances which turn my gesture into a wave? If it is the latter then my acquaintance can take me to have greeted him even when I wave absent-mindedly, something that does happen on occasion. Again, what turns our communal eating into a dinner party? Is it our intention to create a friendly ambience around a meal, or is it the culturally defined form of the dinner party into which we insert ourselves for the evening so as to enjoy the friendly ambience which that form creates? The point about these questions is to argue that the human and cultural meanings which our bodily activities have are not given them by us individually in our minds or by way of our intentions. Rather, our bodies are defined as humanly expressive and communicative by the way their movements and gestures participate in the meanings which arise from our culture and society. It is our induction into our cultures which make available to us those meaningful words, actions and gestures which go beyond the small repertoire of direct bodily reflexes with which we are born. It follows that for culturally formed persons, bodies are fundamentally meaningful social realities. My being-for-others does not make use of my body to express itself through that body towards you; my being-for-others is my body. In order to achieve wholeness as a person, I must exist in bodily form so as to become a meaningful and expressive presence within an interpersonal world.

I could return to my example of love to reinforce this point. The fact that our bodies are expressive of our human existence is evidenced not only by how we live our own bodies as our being-for-others, but also by the way in which we relate to the bodies of others. When we love someone, the expressiveness of our bodies in the context of the giving and receiving of sensual pleasure is a direct expressive act. We do not embrace another in order thereby to convey a separate, inner state of affection. Our affection is present in the embrace as its immediate meaning. We are not removed from our bodies as we would be if we were using them as a mere medium of communication. Our whole selves are given forth in the embrace without remainder. And similarly, we do not embrace the other in order thereby to receive a bodily indication of their love. It is their love we receive. Lovers express

---

[11] Ludwig Wittgenstein, *Philosophical Investigations*, trans. G.E.M. Anscombe (Oxford, 1963).

their caring for each other and their communicating with each other in an intensely intimate form of being present to the other; of being-for-the-other in a direct and mutual way. It is in the way that lovers touch each other, in the way one holds the other's arm, or in the way one embraces the other, that their solidarity of emotion is realized. In this we see the wholeness of our being human. Our deepest and most intimate communications – namely, those which involve both our most significant commitments and our being intensely present to significant others – return us to our bodily being. It is in our bodily comportment that our deepest selves are manifest.

There are two implications to be drawn from this point. First, our deepest selves are nothing aside from this manifestation. Protestations of love (as 'inner' emotions or feelings) are empty if the body does not enact that love. And second, without the engagement of our deepest concerns, without the involvement of our beliefs and our loves, our gestures are but heartless manipulations of the other. The wholeness of our being must be and can only be present in our body as it comports itself towards the other, for without this we would not be present to the other with any authenticity. And the mutual presence of lovers is but the most intense instance of a wider phenomenon. Even acquaintances clasp each other's hands on meeting each other in the street. Our various modes of being present for the other are behaviourally realized in the bodily touch and gesture. There is in any culture a large repertoire of expressive gestures and bodily touches through which mutual emotions are shared and conveyed, ranging from the formal to the intimate, from the public bow at state occasions to the private embrace of lovers. And these gestures can either be empty rituals or authentic modes of being present to the other depending on the degree of commitment with which I comport myself through my body. It is not necessary to postulate, as the dualist does, a separable and inner mental intention which would give my bodily gesture its meaning.

In such ways as this our bodies take on a human cultural existence. We have body language, expressive gesture and bodily adornment. We have physical love, the eating of meals in a context of sociability, and the myriad of meaningful movements that constitute ritual and social forms of communication and celebration. As well, we have health and illness, pain and pleasure and birth and death as events of a bodily nature which are given a profound meaning in the context of human existence and culture. For mature human beings, there is no separately identifiable purely physical level of existence. Rather, the bodies that constitute our biological selves are social and expressive forms of our existence as a being-for-others.

Implications

There are practical implications for health work in this argument. A rather obvious point is that, wherever health workers care for clients, there is a need for observing those clients' bodily movements as well as for listening to any words that might be spoken. Body language often tells us more about what a person is feeling than the things that that person says.

But it may be more interesting to direct our attention upon the health worker's own body. The wholeness of the person as bodily and cultural being is a fact which we need to recognize not only in the person of the client in health work, but also in that of the health worker. Only if health workers act as whole persons themselves will their care be genuinely felt and their actions truly expressive. The way a nurse or doctor touches a patient can, in itself, convey a sense of being present to the other. But it follows from my arguments that health workers do not need to fabricate caring feelings or motivations understood in dualistic terms as grounding such bodily behaviour in order to achieve this. If a person is authentically present in their bodily comportment and if that person has the professional commitment appropriate to a health worker, then that bodily comportment will be an expressive presence for the other which conveys the authenticity of the health worker's care. Because our bodies are the locus of our social and cultural being, nurses do not need to be deliberate and strategic so as to express caring. They do not need to inspect their inner lives to see if they feel the required sorts of caring emotions. If there is professional commitment, and if the objects of that commitment in terms of health and the whole person are understood, then those health workers will express care in their bodily comportment. Such health workers will be fully present to their clients. Unless they are prevented by fatigue or particular negative feelings, they will express their commitment towards the client. Nurse educators who seek to inculcate caring attitudes separately from such a bodily comportment or professional commitment are still thinking in a dualistic manner. It is enough to teach nurses caring behaviours carefully performed. The attention that is given to a task is a better indication of the authenticity with which a worker is present to the patient than is the emotion or intention that might be present as an inner aspect of that action.[12]

But let us return to the matter of the definition of health with which we started. My central point is that the expressiveness of the body in an interpersonal world grounds the significance of health and illness. Persons exist in and through their bodies. They have no 'inner' existence apart from their bodies such that they use their bodies to externalize that existence. This would be the dualistic view. Rather, the social and interpersonal relationships of persons define them as the persons they are, and the necessary locus of these relationships is the body. My illustrative argument against dualism – an argument that highlights the bodily being-for-others of the whole person – leaves us metaphysically with a body, but without leaving out anything of the rich existential reality of being human. It follows that to be healthy in the biological sense of having a body that is functioning well is as central a part of a person's identity and existential well-being as is experiencing states of satisfaction and contentment. But this is not true in the way that having a

---

[12] For a non-dualistic account of attention, see Alan R. White, *Attention* (Oxford, 1964).

car that runs well might be important to our well-being. Having instruments and tools that work well certainly increases our effectiveness in our social environment and so enhances our self-esteem and success or gives us experiences of satisfaction. But we do not relate to our bodies as to tools or instruments that we own and through which we act in the world. We *are* our bodies. We do not value health just as we value a well-oiled machine. We value it because it constitutes, in bodily form, our ability to be whole and human in the world. Accordingly, to care for the body is to care, inevitably, for the well-being of the whole person.

And this leads us to the last of the implications for health care which I want to draw attention to. It is not uncommon today to detect an attitude being evinced towards patients in which they are treated as objects with purely physical problems that need to be solved. This attitude is akin to that which might be evinced by mechanics as they service car engines to correct their faults. The transformation of the therapeutic situation into an objective problem-solving one in which the body of the patient becomes the exclusive focus of attention is an example of the dualist error of seeing the body as nothing more than a physical object. In this context the person being treated evokes no sense of responsibility or care in the medical practitioner other than a concern to solve that person's physical problem. The proliferation of advanced medical technologies in our hospitals constitutes a continuing force towards the depersonalization of patients in this way. This tendency joins those which arise from the ever increasing demands being made upon the health service sector by an ageing population, by increasing road trauma, by the spread of new and little understood viruses, and by an increasing tendency to seek medical solutions to life-style problems. These tendencies have the collective effect of placing health work ever more under the twin demands of efficiency and effectiveness and thereby reducing the amount of interpersonal care and communication that can be involved in it. It will be seen as a relief from such pressures if the patient's body can be taken to be the sole object of medical attention. The upshot of my argument in this chapter has been that, with commitment and authentic presence, the caring exercised by a health worker may indeed focus upon the body, because such commitment and authentic presence will imply a recognition that that body is, in its turn, the authentic presence of the patient.

Chapter 8

Health and Subjectivity

It is doubtful whether the world needs any more theories or descriptions of health. The nursing theory literature and the literature of philosophy and medicine contain many discussions of what health is and how it should be theorized.[1] They give us the subtle distinctions needed to understand health phenomena and to express our understanding of them. They also allow us to understand more fully and in richer conceptual terms the problems which our patients might be having. But the key to a caring health care practice is sensitivity to the particular life situation of the patient and a relationship with that patient which acknowledges the patient's experience of their own health status. What is required for such a sensitivity and acknowledgement is more than an objective and theoretical description of health. It requires a subjective and reflective understanding of the experience of health. Such an understanding is more than the ability to apply sophisticated theoretical categories to objectified health phenomena. It is an understanding based upon the articulation of our own experience of health and of how this is important and valuable. In this chapter I will move from an objective description of health to such a subjective understanding.

Models of health

It is remarkable that a concept which we use so often, like that of health, is so difficult to define. The editors of a seminal collection of studies of health and disease say that 'health is different from pleasure, happiness, civil peace and order, virtue, wisdom, and truth'.[2] But this tells us what it is not, rather than what it is. Health is a strangely hidden topic. Most discussions of health in the literature turn quickly from that positive state to discuss disease and illness and other negative states. In contrast, one nursing writer, Judith Smith, engages in a sustained

---

[1]   For example, see Arthur L. Caplan, Tristram H. Engelhardt Jr and James J. McCartney (eds), *Concepts of Health and Disease: Interdisciplinary Perspectives* (Reading, Massachusetts, 1981).

[2]   Ibid., p. 9.

discussion of the concept and distils four models of health from the literature.[3] In her words, these are:

Clinical Model
Health-extreme: absence of signs or symptoms of disease or disability as identified by medical science; illness-extreme: conspicuous presence of these signs or symptoms.
Role-Performance Model
Health-extreme: performance of social roles with maximum expected output; illness-extreme: failure in performance of role.
Adaptive Model
Health-extreme: the organism maintains flexible adaptation to the environment, interacts with environment with maximum advantage; illness-extreme: alienation of the organism from environment, failure of self-corrective responses.
Eudaimonistic Model
Health-extreme: exuberant well-being; illness-extreme: enervation, languishing debility.

We can see in the first of these models an expression of the modern biomedical model of health and disease in which cures are effected by medical procedures which target hypothesized disease entities. In this model, the focus is upon the individual patient as an isolated individual with a problem.[4] The task of medicine is to find the physical causes of these problems and to counter them with therapeutic agents or procedures. This conception received a great impetus from Descartes' separation of mind from body so that the body could be conceived of as a biological machine which could be repaired by suitable techniques.[5]

---

[3]   Judith A. Smith, *The Idea of Health: Implications for the Nursing Professional* (New York, 1983), p. 31.

[4]   The first of these models seems to correspond to what Harris Coulter has called the Rationalist tradition in medical thought and has characterised as follows:

The internal processes of the body are knowable *a priori*; the functioning of the organism as well as its relations with the environment are analyzable in terms of chains of causes passing from the external exciting causes to the internal (proximate) causes and ultimately to the symptoms; medical doctrine is a body of logically coherent theory reflecting the essentially logical structure of the human organism; the aim of medical diagnosis is to discover the disease 'cause', and the aim of therapeutics is to counteract or oppose this cause by the appropriate 'contrary' medicine; the emphasis on 'contrariety' leads to an interpretation of symptoms as harmful, morbific phenomena.

Harris L. Coulter, *Divided Legacy: A History of the Schism in Medical Thought*, in three volumes (Washington, DC, 1977), p. 89, cited by William J. Lyddon, 'Emerging Views of Health: A Challenge to Rationalist Doctrines of Medical Thought', *The Journal of Mind and Behavior*, 8/3 (Summer 1987): 365–94.

[5]   George L. Engel, in 'The Need for a New Medical Model: A Challenge for Biomedicine', in Caplan, Englehardt and McCartney, pp. 589–607, argues that as a legacy of Cartesian dualism, the biomedical model stresses the body as machine while ignoring the psychological dimensions of illness.

The second model takes a more social view and focuses on the individual as an occupier of social roles and as a working contributor to the common good. This model owes much to the sociological descriptions of Talcott Parsons,[6] who defined illness as a social role which permits the person adopting that role to opt out of socially productive activities provided that they seek medical help. It is within this model that there occur discussions as to whether health is a socially relative norm defined by the average state of operational well-being that obtains in a given society, or an ideal (which might still be defined relative to a given culture) to which all should aspire,[7] and further, whether the ideal is simply a matter of the organism functioning in accordance with its biologically ordained specifications, or whether it is something more than this. Is health optimal functioning or merely adequate functioning in a given pragmatic context?

Smith's third model owes much to the Hippocratic tradition and is more recently associated with the work of René Dubos.[8] According to William Lyddon, this tradition:

> emphasized the importance of a dynamic equilibrium among the bodily humors and underscored the establishment of a harmonious relationship between the body, the individual's living habits, and the totality of environmental influences (for example, quality of air, water, and food). Within this perspective, illness represented a disruption of this intricate interplay of factors.[9]

This tradition is variously characterized as holistic, homeopathic, and even vitalistic. It focuses on the physical and social environment as a contributor to the health status of individuals and populations.[10] Also, in this tradition, the healer enters into empathic relationship with the diseased and effects a cure through

---

[6]   Talcott Parsons, 'Definitions of Health and Illness in the Light of American Values and Social Structures', in Caplan, Englehardt and McCartney, pp. 57–81.

[7]   Mervyn Susser, 'Ethical Components in the Definition of Health', in Caplan, Englehardt and McCartney, pp. 93–105, p. 95.

[8]   René Dubos, *Mirage of Health: Utopias, Progress and Biological Change* (New York, 1959), and his *Man, Medicine and Environment* (Harmondsworth, 1970).

[9]   Lyddon finds the following quotation from Castiglioni on page xi of Coulter's text:

This Hippocratic conception considers man as an indestructible part of the Cosmos, bound to it and subject to its laws: it may be called, therefore, a universal, cosmical, unitarian, conception. Disease, according to it, is a general fact which strikes the whole organism and has its origins in a perturbation of natural harmony.

'Emerging Views of Health: A Challenge to Rationalist Doctrines of Medical Thought', p. 368.

[10]   On page 112 of 'What is Disease?', in Caplan, Englehardt and McCartney, pp. 107–18, Lester S. King says: 'Environmental states (both external and internal) which are intimately connected with the ideals and norms, are parts of health, even though the general public is unaware of them, while environmental states intimately connected with disease are similarly parts of disease.'

emotionally charged rituals and a deep understanding of the individuality of the patient.

The dichotomy between Smith's first and third models, despite the dominance of the biomedical model, continues to influence debates about health today, especially as they relate to privatized, interventionist health care on the one hand, and public health and preventative medicine on the other.

The fourth model takes its name from the writings of Aristotle, who defined *eudaimonia* (an ancient Greek term which literally means 'good-spiritedness') as a state of being fulfilled through doing well those noble things that you were expected to do or which you undertook to do for yourself. Developed in more modern times by Abraham Maslow,[11] the concept of health in this model refers to an individual or group reaching its potential. The famous World Health Organization definition of health as 'a state of complete physical, mental and social well-being and not merely the absence of disease or infirmity' which I discussed in Chapter 1 would be an instance of this conception. This idea extends the notion of health beyond that which would be functional in a given society in order to appeal to an ideal embracing all the potentialities, both physical and psychological, possessed by human beings.

All four of these models are described by Smith in terms that suggest she wants them to be objective descriptions of health states. They are presented as alternative frameworks for understanding what is objectively the case. Yet it is clear that health is a subjectively experienced condition. Many physicians report that their judgements as to the health status of their patients can differ from those patients' own judgements.[12] Health is not just an objective condition of the person considered as an observable state of that person in the world, but, as I will explain presently, a condition of subjectivity itself.

Smith proposes that nurses should adopt not one or other of these models, but all four of them on a progressive scale of concern. Nurses should be professionally engaged with the enhancement of health at all four levels of this scale. This is a laudable ideal, albeit one that I called into question in Chapter 1. Nevertheless, I believe a more sophisticated form of this thesis can be argued for. One way of arguing for it would be to show that the four models are intimately connected to each other and can only be delineated with some degree of artificiality. As experienced in the subjective states of persons, health constitutes a single totality embracing the experience of all four of Smith's models. So the argument that nurses should concern themselves with all four ways of conceiving health only needs to show that adopting the perspective of the subjectivity of the patient

---

[11] Abraham H. Maslow, 'Health as Transcendence of Environment', *Journal of Humanistic Psychology*, 1 (1961): 1–7.

[12] See, for example, Benjamin F. Fuller, *Physician or Magician: The Myths and Realities of Patient Care* (New York, 1978), pp. 57–67, and Michael Calnan, *Health & Illness: The Lay Perspective* (London, 1987).

inevitably involves embracing these four models. In order to elaborate on this point, we will need to embark on a major theoretical excursion.

A fourfold model of subjectivity

Smith's four models of health can be brought into alignment with a model of human subjectivity which I have developed elsewhere.[13] The theoretical advantage of such an alignment would be to show that these varying conceptions of health cannot be separated from each other, but rather constitute partial descriptions of a complex whole. In this way a professional concern for health cannot but be a concern for health as conceived on all four of Smith's models. I argued in Chapter 1 that health, rather than the general welfare of patients, is the appropriate object of the caring of clinicians. In this chapter we will begin to see that health embraces more than just the biological functioning of the body. A further advantage of such an alignment is that it would allow us to use philosophical descriptions of subjectivity in accordance with my model to develop this richer conception of what health might be.

What do I mean by subjectivity? Subjectivity is the pre-intentional activity of constituting ourselves as a self. It is a dynamic, innate and autonomous process of which the goal is becoming a person capable of constituting our own identity and of forming rich relationships with others. This is not a conscious goal, but a pre-intentional purpose inherent in our very mode of being. It is a natural striving to be which, in the human person, culminates in selfhood. To be a person or a self and to encounter others as persons are achievements which, I will suggest, require the exercise of at least four modes of subjectivity.

My model of human subjectivity comprises four kinds of functioning. Although it is inspired by Aristotle's distinction between four parts of the 'soul',[14] my model does not postulate entities of any kind. Rather, it suggests that the rich and complex set of activities, functionings and reactions of human subjectivity might be understood a little more easily if at least four kinds of such functioning were distinguished. My use of the word 'functioning' highlights this in that it refers to events or actions rather than substantive parts of the person. Again, there is no suggestion that these kinds of functioning are to be thought of hierarchically as if they constituted a gradation of excellence, or a sequence of developmental steps, or a set in which one kind of functioning controls another.

---

[13] Stan van Hooft, *Caring: An Essay in the Philosophy of Ethics* (Niwot, Colorado, 1995). The terminology and order in which aspects of subjectivity are presented in this chapter differ from those developed in that book, but the present chapter constitutes a further development of the model.

[14] I draw on Aristotle's conception of the soul as articulated in Book One of his *Nicomachean Ethics*, in Richard McKeon (ed.), *The Basic Works of Aristotle* (New York, Random House, 1941).

The four kinds of functioning that I want to distinguish are the material, the pragmatic, the conative and the integrative. It is my thesis that no person is complete as a person unless they function in all four of these ways.

The notion of material functioning refers to the processes of the organism which are necessary for biological life. They include respiration, metabolism, growth and the myriad of internal physiological processes which are studied by biology and in which health care workers are expert. Many of these processes will not be uniquely human in that other animals undergo them also, while others will be specific to the species *Homo sapiens*. About the only time that human beings function exclusively in the material mode is when they are asleep and not dreaming. These processes are not usually thought of as having anything more than bodily equilibrium as their goal, but think of a weed breaking its way through the concrete of a roadway and you will have a primitive image of this material mode of subjectivity and of its dynamism. The goals of the striving of subjectivity at this level include survival, growth and the propagation of its genes. There are also goals or functions of parts of the organism which would consist in their contribution to the goals inherent in the whole.[15]

The second mode of our subjectivity in my model is the pragmatic. This is the sphere of our lives which includes our deliberating about and purposively doing the things that we do. It includes the everyday practical concerns and activities that we engage in. It is rational, purposive and self-conscious. Because it is what our self-awareness usually focuses upon, it leads us to suppose that it is all that our mental lives consist in. Even the things that we do which are not obviously purposive, like stamp collecting or playing sport, tend to be subsumed under its rubrics so that we think of these activities as recreations whose purpose is to refresh us for more serious practical tasks. They are certainly activities that involve us in deliberation and planning. The goals of this kind of subjectivity are efficiency and effectiveness in the pursuit of whatever goals self-conscious subjectivity finds itself with as a result of the other modes of subjectivity, including survival, growth, and so forth. If we are going to be effective in our practical lives, then we must deliberate and plan effectively. The ideal of rationality operates in this mode of subjectivity.

The conative kind of functioning of subjectivity is difficult to describe because it is largely absent from our self-awareness. One of the legacies of Descartes is that

---

[15] Horacio Fabrega Jr, 'Concepts of Disease: Logical Features and Social Implications', in Caplan, Englehardt and McCartney, pp. 493–522, argues that the respiratory system is part of the atmosphere system. Reproduction is part of the evolutionary process with imperatives of its own, for example. Citing Dubos, Fabrega says that man is always struggling with nature at various levels and with varying success and so is always 'diseased'. As he puts it, 'health and disease, rather than representing discrete "states" or conditions, need to be seen as phases of the continuously changing multilevel set of processes (for example, cellular, chemical, physiological, behavioural) that at any one moment constitute human striving'. (p. 513).

we are apt to think of all human functioning that is not physical as being mental. And insofar as the mental is equated with the conscious, we are left with a dualism in which an unconscious body and a fully self-conscious mind work in tandem to constitute the whole person. Freud was not the only theorist to question this image. Many thinkers have pointed to an unconscious or subconscious mode of functioning which could not be adequately described by referring to the workings of the body or any parts of it.[16] This mode of functioning of subjectivity seems to occupy a space between the purely bodily and the mental. It is that functioning which Plato described as *thumos* or spirit. It links with desire, emotion and inclination and seems to well up from deep and pre-conscious levels of our subjectivity. It is motivational. Think of a wild and free animal, a spirited horse or a playful pet dog and you will have images of a kind of functioning which seems more than merely physical and yet not rational in a self-conscious or deliberative sense.

The central concepts that characterize the conative mode of our subjectivity are desire and care. Desire is the reaching out of subjectivity towards the world and others in it with a view to possession and absorption. Subjectivity cannot attain selfhood without absorbing and taking possession of parts of the world. We need the satisfaction that sustenance brings as well as the sustenance. Care, on the other hand, is the reaching out of subjectivity towards the world and others in it with a view to enhancing those things. Once again, subjectivity cannot attain selfhood without developing a concern for others and for things. Love is a constitutive part of our being.

The goals of the conative mode of subjectivity are hard to define. Some may say that equanimity in the form of the satisfaction of desire is that goal. Certainly this was Freud's view. However, I think it more suggestive to say that the goal is stimulation rather than contentment. One of the things we want is to feel that we are alive and dealing with the challenges of living. To be merely content is an inadequate goal for living in a human way.

The fourth mode of subjectivity which I want to describe is the integrative. This is the striving for meaning in our lives. It is not enough that we survive, succeed in our pragmatic tasks, and experience positive emotions and stimulation. We also need to feel that these achievements and experiences form part of a meaningful life. We need to feel that there is a point to it. It is not enough that the things that happen to us follow one another in a merely temporal sequence. We need to feel that they add up to a coherent life. We need to give our lives a structure analogous to the narrative form of a history. Our activities now must seem to lead to some future goal or accomplishment, and the things that have happened to me in the past or which I have done in the past need to be embraced into a coherent life story such that a unity or meaningfulness is established. To regret things that have happened or have been done is to think that they cannot be integrated into the narrative of my life in this way. And to suppose that there is no overarching meaning to the things

---

[16] For example, see Drew Leder, *The Absent Body* (Chicago, Illinois, 1990).

that we do is to live from day to day without a sense of depth in my life. Various cultures might seek to give meaning to life in different ways – for example, by aligning a life with the cycles of the seasons or of destiny, or by referring to the exemplary lives of ancestors or of a God – but each of these cultural forms can be understood as an expression of the integrative function of human subjectivity. Moreover, in a multicultural society, various integrative forms may coexist and may even simultaneously shape the lives of particular individuals.

The goal of the integrative mode of subjectivity is to unify our lives, give them meaning and establish an articulated form of selfhood through which we can define our fulfilment as human beings. Using the term in a somewhat unusual sense, I call this fulfilment 'integrity'. In order to give meaning and integrity to our lives we need something to believe in. Whatever that may be, and whether we devise it for ourselves or acquire it from our cultural context, these beliefs will be articulations of our faith in life itself. It is in the fourth integrative mode of subjectivity that we can, in the words of Nietzsche, say 'yes' to life.

It should be clear that the four modes of subjectivity that I have described constitute a unity. The material mode is required to make persons real as functioning entities in the world, while the practical mode constitutes the substance and content of much of our lives. Without the conative dimension, we would be driven only by biological instincts without motivations or intentions that we could own as expressing our desires and concerns. And without the integrative dimension, our commitments and concerns would seem shallow and lose the motivational force which meaningfulness gives to them. Without these latter dimensions, our practical lives would lack overarching purpose and our relationships with others would lack commitment.

What is health in the context of each of these four kinds of human subjective functioning? I will attempt to align the four models of health described by Smith with my four modes of subjectivity in order to answer this question.

Health in the material and pragmatic modes of existence

The material mode of subjectivity accords with Smith's clinical model. On this level health would consist just in the absence of disease or disease symptoms. More positively, we might say that health consists in the effective functioning of the organs so as to conduce to a trouble-free physical existence. We are healthy if all parts of the body are working well and performing their biologically ordained functions or able to do so adequately when required. The irony is that, from the point of view of subjectivity, this state is absent from consciousness. In this mode, what the drive of subjectivity consists in is pure process; the sheer urging of biological functions producing survival and growth. But in the purely bodily mode of subjectivity, this effective process is an absence: a non-conscious event. So from the point of view of subjectivity, this cannot be what health is in its entirety. And it follows that, just as the material mode of subjectivity is not the whole of human subjectivity, so clinical health is not the whole of health.

Smith's role-performance model of health accords with the second mode of subjectivity which I have described: namely, the pragmatic mode. In this mode we are concerned with the achievement of our tasks, whether these are self-imposed or arise from the role we occupy in society. Any failure to perform our roles or to achieve our goals will be experienced as illness if it is involuntary and not due to lack of skill or to an identifiable failure of executive virtue such as courage or persistence.[17] More positively, health will be experienced as success and efficiency in fulfilling our practical goals. Once again, however, we seldom allude to health defined in this way. Insofar as we are living our lives more or less successfully, our health is not an issue for us and it is not directly experienced as a state of our being. In this way, in the practical mode of subjectivity, health as successful role-performance is largely implicit in our lives. It is not experienced as a state of our being, but as the absence of hindrance in our activities or of pain and discomfort in the functioning of our bodies.

However, health can be understood theoretically in the pragmatic mode of our subjectivity as the *sine qua non* of success and achievement in our practical lives. As part of our deliberative understanding of our practical lives, we can know that health is a necessary condition for our being successful in our projects. As such, health can enter consciousness as the object of understanding and planning. The rational organization of our lives will include provision for health by way of diet, exercise and the control of environmental conditions. We will consult relevant experts and make provision for our needs in regards to health. In short, health will be a practical project for a rational agent. To be unmindful of the needs of health will be one of the ways that agents can be seen to be irrational within the pragmatic mode of subjectivity. In this mode, then, health is not so much a qualitative experience as the object of a practical project with a defined place in the scheme of practical projects that arise from our social roles and other responsibilities.

Health in the conative mode

But is there an experience of health? Can this absence of debilitating conditions be given a positive description, and can health as the goal of our practical projects be given experiential content? In order to explore these questions we need to turn to the third mode of subjectivity which I have described and also to what Smith has called the adaptive model. In Smith's description, this model of health involves the adaptation of the organism to its environment, and perhaps also the internal harmony and balance of organismic functionings within the body. From Smith's perspective this is a description of organismic functioning offered from outside of

---

[17]   This is the definition of illness offered by K.W.M. Fulford in *Moral Theory and Medical Practice* (Cambridge, 1989), Chapter 5.

that organism. As such it can be interpreted as offering a more complex and system-theoretic description of the material mode of our subjectivity. On this interpretation, the adaptive model is still biological. It simply offers a richer and more Hippocratic conception of what the biological functions consist in. What my concept of a conative mode of subjectivity allows us to do is to describe this model of health from the point of view of the subject. Although health is an absence rather than an explicit experience, and although the conative mode of subjectivity is largely pre-conscious, a form of phenomenological description can be given of health understood as a modality of the conative mode of our subjectivity. In order to do so I will allude to some ideas developed by Emmanuel Levinas in his book *Totality and Infinity*.[18]

Levinas' primary philosophical concern in this book is with the relationship between subjectivity and the world, or between 'interiority' and 'exteriority'. He seeks to describe a 'metaphysical relationship' with the world which is not one of 'grasping' or 'action', but rather one of 'living from ...' or 'enjoyment'.[19] I interpret this to mean that a pragmatic or technocratic approach to the world in which the world is used as a resource should be secondary to one in which the agent is in harmony with the world. For Levinas, the structures of our knowledge as expounded by Kant involve a relationship of mastery of the world. Levinas suggests that, prior to such relationships to things, there is a relationship of rapport and of being at home in the world. It is my thesis that the primary mode of subjectivity in which this loving relationship to the world is lived out is the conative mode.

To illustrate this intimate relation of 'living from ...' or 'enjoyment', Levinas says, 'We live from "good soup", air, light, spectacles, work, ideas, sleep, etc. ... These are not objects of representations. We live *from* them.'[20] Objects of representation or things that we experience within the rational, pragmatic mode of being are things of which we are self-consciously aware and in relation to which we deliberate and plan our lives. They are things that we take to be exterior to us so that they can be objects to which we relate in a pragmatic way. To make them into representations is to take hold of them in some way and this implies some previous distance between us and them.[21] The pragmatic mode of our subjectivity is a comportment *to* them. The things we live *from*, on the other hand, are not distant from us. They are not objects of our self-conscious awareness. They are, like our own bodies, a basis from which we reach out into the world. They are the implicit content of the conative element in our living. What this means is that things like the ones Levinas mentions in the quotation are givens within the pre-

---

    [18]   Emmanuel Levinas, *Totality and Infinity: An Essay on Exteriority*, trans. Alphonso Lingis (Pittsburgh, Pennsylvania, 1969), Section II.
    [19]   Ibid., p. 110.
    [20]   Ibid., p. 110 (emphasis added).
    [21]   Emmanuel Levinas, 'Ethics as First Philosophy', in *The Levinas Reader*, ed. Seán Hand (Oxford, 1989): pp. 75–87.

conscious conative mode of our being. They are not things we think about or represent to ourselves, but are things which are taken for granted and constitute a kind of platform from which we act out our concerns in the world. They are not things that we consciously use or even seek. They are the form and basis of our reaching into the world as subjectivity.

This is especially clear with Levinas' example of spectacles. The spectacles we wear are not things that we own in the way that we might own a stamp collection. The point is not just to *have* spectacles in the way that the point of a stamp collection is just to have it. Moreover, we do not look *at* our spectacles as we would at our possessions. The point of spectacles is to look *through* them at the world so that we can experience our world as a clear visual field. Spectacles not only give us our clear visual world, they also provide the form that that world takes for us. Whereas the visual field might be blurred and vague, when we live *from* our spectacles, our world becomes clear and sharp. Moreover, most of the time we do not notice our spectacles. They structure our visual field without themselves being a content of that field. They are useful things insofar as they disappear as objects. In this they differ from tools which are useful things that become objects within the pragmatic mode of our subjectivity. (Although tools, too, tend to 'disappear' as we use them. In use, we live *from* them towards the things that we are working on *through* them.)

Useful things belong to the pragmatic mode of our subjectivity. In contrast, the contents of the conative mode of our being 'are always in a certain measure – and even the hammers, needles and machines are – objects of enjoyment, presenting themselves to "taste", already adorned, embellished'.[22] They do not only already have a meaning of utility as an objective counterpart of our pragmatic mode of subjectivity (as in Martin Heidegger's notion of things 'ready-to-hand'); they also already have a quality corresponding to taste – an aesthetic quality or a quality that responds to our enthusiasm or enjoyment of them. They constitute an environment for our living, but an environment that is so intimate as to constitute the very elements in which we exist and from which we live towards objects. There is more here than a recognition of the subject's interaction with the environment as stressed in Smith's adaptive model of health. This environmental interaction is lived and experienced in an inchoate way. Think of a swimmer. When she first enters the water she will experience it as an object of awareness, but as she moves through the water with grace and ease, and as her awareness moves to other things or begins to lose any focus, the water will become an enveloping element through which the body moves without feeling itself separate from it. Indeed, most of the time, most of us relate to the air around us in just this way. Levinas' point is that our world can be such an environment. It is not just a collection of objects that we

---

[22] Levinas, *Totality and Infinity*, p. 110. Levinas goes on to say: 'Moreover, whereas the recourse to the instrument implies finality and indicates a dependence with regard to the other, living from ... delineates independence itself, the independence of enjoyment and of its happiness, which is the original pattern of all independence.'

might use or own. It is the very element *from* which we live towards the objects of our specific projects.

But the elements from which we live are not just hidden and neutral substances of which we have no awareness and, consequently, towards which we have no comportment. We can enjoy these elements. Our living our lives with ease, interest and stimulation, and without internal hindrance, constitutes a relation with the elements around us which is a direct extension of our embodiment. Levinas' words 'taste' and 'enjoyment' capture very well the operation of the conative dimension of our subjectivity. We do not decide to enjoy something or to find it to our taste. Our pragmatic subjectivity is not involved here. To enjoy something is a state of restfulness and acceptance in relation to it. Our existential striving need not concern itself with that which we enjoy. Even as we pursue our conscious goals and plans, we 'enjoy', in Levinas' sense, the elements which make that striving possible. This is more than just a material process of effective bodily functioning and interaction with the world. There is a subjective quality to it which goes beyond the material well-functioning of the body and which is not reducible to the satisfactions that might arise from the successful completion of our tasks.

Levinas refers metaphorically to this relation with the environing elements as 'nourishment':

> Nourishment, as a means of invigoration, is the transmutation of the other into the same, which is in the essence of enjoyment: an energy that is other, recognized as other, recognized, we will see, as sustaining the very act that is directed upon it, becomes, in enjoyment, my own energy, my strength, me. All enjoyment is in this sense alimentation.[23]

The phrase 'transmutation of the other into the same' is Levinas' technical way of describing the process of absorbing the world into ourselves. ('The same' refers to our own identity here.) Eating would be a literal example of this in that the food that we eat is largely absorbed into the body in the form of nutrients. But the notion of nourishment has a metaphorical meaning here as well. Whatever elements in our environing world become part of our project of living – including the tools we use – become a part of our body as it acts in the world, and hence a part of us. Think of a blind man's stick. Insofar as he reaches into the world and finds his way in it through that stick, it is a part of his existential being. The stick is absorbed into him and becomes a part of his operational body. The dividing line – never sharp – between the person and the world is here drawn on the outside of the stick rather than at his hand. In a metaphorical sense, his stick is nourishment to his being. He enjoys the stick. The stick is expressive of the conative dimension of his subjectivity rather than being an object used by him. In the same way a musical instrument in the hands of a competent performer is not just an objective

---

[23]   Ibid., p. 111.

instrument for making music, but a means of personal expression, expression of the conative dimension of subjectivity:

> One lives one's life: to live is a sort of transitive verb, and the contents of life are its direct objects. ... One does not only exist one's pain or one's joy; one exists from pains and joys. Enjoyment is precisely this way the act nourishes itself with its own activity.[24]

What Levinas is saying here is that, understood in its conative mode, subjectivity seizes life, seeks it and forges it. It does not just undergo life. But at the same time, the life that we live and the experiences that we have are the necessary springboard from which we reach out to further living and further experiences. The enjoyment of life provides the impetus for the further affirmation of life. But this is not a conscious act of using, as if we lived our lives in order to derive the nourishment necessary to go on living it. Rather, it is the innate structure of our relationship with the world and of the very activity and reality of our own being. We are constantly in a process of absorbing and exchanging material from our environments. Much of this is processing in the material mode of our subjectivity and much of it comprises the pragmatic engagement that we have with the world of work and responsibilities. But much of it also constitutes the tone of our comportment to the world. This brings it into the conative mode. When these processes and activities go well, we are in good spirits and things are to our taste, while when they do not go well, life is a struggle and we are out of sorts – even if we do not know what the problem is. And so, when things go well, we are in a state that enlivens us, a state that is a form of nourishment for us and from which we are invigorated to go on with the struggle of living. In this way, life nourishes itself. We live towards life and also from it. It is as if living were an action that needed a motivation; and the best motivation is living, when that living is marked by enjoyment. Living is the nourishment of life.

All of this reflects on how we think about our practical lives of work as well. Work is not just a means of maintaining the material level of our existence, our survival, and our bodily functioning. At its best, it is also a means of enjoying our existence. 'We live from our labour which ensures our subsistence; but we also live from our labour because it fills (delights or saddens) life.'[25] My life does not only consist in my pursuing the things I need, it also consists in the experience and enjoyment of that pursuing. This pursuing is the content of my life and I live *from* that too. This does not imply an act of reflection which discovers that enjoyment as an explicit content of consciousness, but a quality of enjoyment that accompanies experience implicitly; a quality that consists in more than the absence of pain or hindrance. Nor does it imply an overarching value which might give meaning to the work I do. Such values and ideals may arise from the integrative mode of our subjectivity and they may enhance the quality of my life, but the enjoyment of

---

[24] Ibid., p. 111.
[25] Ibid., p. 112.

which Levinas speaks is a stimulation and enthusiasm that comes from worldly existence itself.

The key point here is that even though the quality of our living and the elements we enjoy by absorbing them into our lives and taking nourishment from them are not objects of consciousness, enjoyment of them is something of which we can be inchoately aware as a modality of our being. It is like a mood. What we are vaguely aware of is our living joyfully and our nourishment from the environing elements and from our own living. My suggestion is that this modality or tone of being is the pre-conscious experience of health. As Levinas puts it:

> Life is *love of life*, a relation with contents that are not my being but more dear than my being: thinking, eating, sleeping, reading, working, warming oneself in the sun. Distinct from my substance but constituting it, these contents make up the worth of my life.[26]

While most of the activities Levinas mentions here have intentional objects of their own so that our attention is focused on their objects rather than upon the fact of our being engaged in them, the sense of well-being and worth that we gain from living arises not just from the successful attainment of the goals of these activities, but also from the enjoyment of being engaged in them. My thesis is that this 'love of life', this inchoate feeling that the living of life is enjoyment and nourishment, is the pre-articulated experience of health. Health, in this sense, is when things go well with us in the conative mode of our subjectivity.

If this is right, then health has an importance for us that is much deeper than its being the hidden material wherewithal for effective pragmatic existence or feelings of personal well-being. Levinas gives us a clue as to the nature of this importance when he says: 'Subjectivity originates in the independence and sovereignty of enjoyment.'[27] What Levinas is suggesting here is that enjoyment (or health in the conative mode of our existence) is not just a qualitative state of subjectivity, but a state that makes subjectivity possible. Let us recall that subjectivity is the striving to be through which we achieve being a person. This striving needs positive feedback and encouragement. Well-being and the joy of existence contribute to providing this encouragement (along with faith in ideals which arises at the integrative level of our being). As Levinas puts it: 'Enjoyment, in relation with nourishment, which is the *other* of life, is an independence *sui generis*, the independence of happiness. The life that is life *from* something is happiness.'[28]

Moreover, there is a suggestion in Levinas that full awareness of self is generated in part by this joy of existence. It is when we enjoy living that we gain a

---

[26]　Ibid., p. 112 (italics in original). This point is implicitly critical of Nietzsche and of Heidegger. For them, life is striving and anxiety and, while there are modes of our existence about which this might be true, the conative mode (in the case where the subject is in health) is one of harmony and enjoyment. We settle into this mode as our hand fits a glove.

[27]　Ibid., p. 114.

[28]　Ibid., p. 115.

sense of our own being as independent. When we struggle unsuccessfully and suffer, we feel ourselves subject to 'the slings and arrows of outrageous fortune'. The world seems to oppose us and to reinforce our dependence upon it. It is in this context that we seek the grasping and controlling form of relationship with the world that separates us from it. We seem to be in conflict with it. Enjoyment, on the other hand, involves a sense of wholeness with the world. In enjoyment, my reaching out towards the world in order to gain nourishment is successful and the world is absorbed into my being. In this way I gain an innate sense of fulfilment and support, and the self begins to experience itself as a self that is cosseted by the world rather than separate from it. As Levinas puts it:

> Whereas the recourse to the instrument implies finality and indicates a dependence with regard to the other, living from ... delineates independence itself, the independence of enjoyment and of its happiness, which is the original pattern of all independence.[29]

At the material level of our existence, of course, this is a fiction, but at the conative level, it is a necessity if we are to achieve the selfhood which subjectivity seeks. At this level, enjoyment and health are constitutive of our very being as persons.

Levinas goes on to deepen this point when he says: 'Happiness is a condition for activity.'[30] Happiness can here be taken to mean enjoyment, and thus, following my thesis, it connotes health as a constituent of the conative mode of our subjectivity. Levinas is not just saying that enjoyment or health is a condition for activity in the way that a problem-free body is a condition for success at the pragmatic level of our existence. Rather, he is alluding to the philosophical thesis that selfhood comprises a certain kind of experience of time. Life is not lived as just a series of events flowing causally together into a meaningless sequence. Life is a series of episodes or experiences having beginnings and completions marked by the enjoyment of accomplishment.[31] These episodes are not discrete events, but experienced as accomplishments stemming from previous plans and efforts and from which new beginnings can be made and new episodes embarked upon. Such episodes are 'activities' in Levinas' sense of the term. A life acquires a narrative structure with an internal unity through the coherence of such activities. This structure is delineated by the sense of completion that constitutes happiness. It is in this sense that enjoyment is necessary for the creation of a lived life as a narrative comprising complete experiences or activities. In this way, health or enjoyment, being constitutive of happiness, is the very precondition of our continuing selfhood through the narrative of our lives. It provides the meaningful structure of our subjectivity.

---

[29] Ibid., p. 110.
[30] Ibid., p. 113.
[31] This is a thesis also developed by John Dewey in his *Art as Experience* (New York, 1934).

In terms of my own model of subjectivity, this last point begins to allude to the integrative mode. The goal of creating a unified life narrative and a personal integrity belongs to this mode of subjectivity. Yet our reading of Levinas is now suggesting that the unity of the self is already constituted by enjoyment at the conative level. What this suggests, of course, is that subjectivity is a single whole in which the modes I have identified are but theoretical abstractions. Insofar as I am arguing for the integration of Smith's four models of health by way of the integration of the four modes of subjectivity that I am mapping onto those models, I welcome the way in which Levinas' deep analysis inevitably moves us to the integrative mode of subjectivity.

Before we move to that mode, however, we should consider our relationship to our needs. Needs such as hunger are usually thought of as lacks within the material mode of our being, and traditional philosophy takes them to be an aspect of our unfortunate mortal existence. Rather than seeking to integrate them into our lives, this approach wishes that we could be like disembodied angels with no physical needs and a destiny only of contemplating the higher realities of Goodness, Truth, Beauty or God. From this perspective, needs are states that we seek to escape from. In contrast, Levinas says: 'What we live from does not enslave us; we enjoy it. Need cannot be interpreted as a simple lack. ... The human being thrives on his needs; he is happy for his needs.'[32] This quotation can be understood adequately only if we bear in mind my distinction between the material mode of our subjectivity and the conative mode. At the conative level, there is felt to be a degree of independence from the material dimension of subjectivity even though, materially, there is also dependence upon it. At the material level, need is indeed constituted by the lack of something. The body's need for food becomes operative as hunger or food-seeking behaviour when the body lacks food. Here the dependence of subjectivity is the operation of the material mode, where we draw vital energy from the world, but:

> *Living from* ... is the dependency that turns into sovereignty, into happiness. ... Physiology, from the exterior, teaches us that need is a lack. That man could be happy for his needs indicates that in human need the physiological place is transcended.[33]

This quotation reinforces the point that the material mode of our subjectivity is but one aspect of our subjectivity. Taken just in that mode, need can only be understood as productive of stress and anxiety. So in what way could 'man be happy for his needs'? Levinas seems to be saying that the cycle of need-motivated action followed by successful need fulfilment gives us that feeling of accomplishment and satisfaction which is the basis of our enjoyment of life, of our sense of independence as selves in symbiotic interaction with the world, and of the episodic meaningfulness of our activities. The conative mode of our existence and,

---

[32]   Levinas, *Totality and Infinity*, p. 114.
[33]   Ibid., p. 115.

at the more self-conscious level, the pragmatic mode are essential to the existence of this kind of enjoyment and health. And this enjoyment or experience of health could not be had if we did not have needs. Needs are the challenge the overcoming of which yields our joy of living. Were we to exist only in the material mode, a need would only be a material lack and thus something that our bodies would seek to overcome or escape. But, given the further modes of our existence, needs provide the occasion for enjoyment and health to manifest themselves to us. Happiness is not just the absence of need. It is the satisfaction of need. As such, it is accomplishment and satisfaction, not the enervated state of having no desires, achieving equilibrium or suppressing desire. As such, it is the fulfilment of the conative dimension of our being rather than its overcoming.

For classical philosophers like Plato, need is a lack and a negativity illustrated, for example, in sickness. And insofar as the material, pragmatic and conative dimensions of our existence are so bound up with needs, Plato urged us to overcome these dimensions in favour of his conception of the integrative dimension: namely, a life of pure intellectual contemplation. But his notion of need was that of an animal's need understood just at the material level of existence. This is need as experienced by one term in a metabolic relationship marked by a flow of matter and energy to maintain equilibrium and growth. Need is here like a vacuum into which things flow, or like a stimulus for need-fulfilling behaviour in the world. For such a creature, needs mark its integration into the material world. In contrast, for creatures like us with our various modes of subjectivity, needs define our separation from the world. They define that which we need as *other* and hence ourselves as independent. To be needful is one state of being, while to be the object of need is another. The world is defined as other than ourselves through its being an object of need. But it must not be thought that this is because subjectivity is disembodied or a pure consciousness able to define itself as separate from the world and the world as other than the subject. Needs are located in the body and constitute a modality of our material bodily existence. They are the basis of the conative mode of our being. If we were a pure mind, our separation from the world that we need would become a spiritual isolation from the world. That we are embodied ensures that subjectivity continues to be intimately related to the world. As Levinas puts it, 'The body is the very self-possession by which the I, liberated from the world of need, succeeds in overcoming the very destitution of this liberation.'[34]

As I have noted, Levinas' analysis is gradually moving us towards the integrative mode of our subjectivity. Health as enjoyment establishes the narrative unity of the self over time. But Levinas also argues that it establishes the particular and unique nature of the self. The self is not an instance of a kind. It falls under no genus. It is not the individuation of a concept. It is not graspable with the kinds of categories of knowledge with which we apprehend the world. The making real of subjectivity is not achieved by naming or classification. It is achieved by the

---

[34]   Ibid., p. 117.

happiness or enjoyment that comes from the fulfilment of the conative mode of our being: that is, by health. This fulfilment of needs gives us our internal sense of independence and uniqueness as selves. As Levinas puts it:

> This logically absurd structure of unicity, this non-participation in genus, is the very egoism of happiness. Happiness, in its relation with the 'other' of nutriments, suffices to itself; it even suffices to itself *because* of this relation with the other: it consists in satisfying its needs and not in suppressing them.[35]

So the self comes to itself in enjoyment. The function of the conative mode of existence, like that of the other modes, is to constitute the self. The satisfaction, independence and self-possession of enjoyment make the self real to itself. The biological fact of our existence belongs to the material mode of our subjectivity, purposive and self-conscious action belongs to the pragmatic mode, while, in between as it were, is the conative mode of our being which, in the healthy individual, is marked by enjoyment and happiness.

The insights from Levinas which I used to articulate health as experienced at the conative level of our existence also gave us intimations of how health might be involved in the integrative mode of our being. Indeed, they were giving us intimations of what might be involved in Smith's *eudaimonistic* model of health as well. Insofar as this model involves the fulfilment of our potentialities as individuals, it would certainly need to begin from the establishment of our selves as unique and particular beings with aspirations and goals that we can fully own as contributing to the meaning and integrity of our lives. Levinas' use of the term 'happiness' points to this further relevance of his discussion to my thesis.

Health in the integrative mode

How, then, does the implicit operation of conative subjectivity lead to the operation of the integrative mode of subjectivity? How can the happiness that arises from my gaining nourishment from the environing element become constitutive of my integrity, my fulfilment or the meaningfulness of my life? One way might be through myth. Levinas suggests that the element does contain intimations of a beyond and a future. As he puts it, 'To be affected by a side of being while its whole depth remains undetermined and comes upon me from nowhere is to be bent toward the insecurity of the morrow.'[36] What this means is that the conative level of existence, even as it experiences enjoyment and happiness, is also dimly aware of the possibility of frustration and denial. This is because it does not know the element as an object and hence cannot feel itself in control of it, as it would in the pragmatic mode of existence. At the conative level,

---

[35]   Ibid., p. 118.
[36]   Ibid., p. 142.

health is accompanied by the vague fear of illness and unsatisfiable need. Insofar as these are not objectified, says Levinas, they are expressed as myth, as faceless gods. In enjoyment, the self depends biologically on the non-self. Therefore, it is vulnerable. Health and happiness are an achievement of luck.

This has two consequences. In the pragmatic mode of subjectivity it motivates a desire for control which gives rise to magic and science, and in the integrative mode it gives rise to myth and religion. Levinas does not explore these suggestions further, but we will return to them presently in the light of remarks made by Paul Tillich.

Notice first that religion and magic are not seen as identical. Magic is a functional system for achieving certain results which we designate as magic because it is based on a different theory of how the world works from that of modern science. As such, magic belongs to the pragmatic mode of our subjectivity. The theory on which it is based refers to sympathetic powers in the universe so that illness occurs when these cosmic powers are out of sorts. Health is then seen as a microcosmic parallel of macrocosmic harmonies.[37] For its part, religion is an expression of the integrative mode of our subjectivity in that it seeks meaning by relating personal events to a redemptive narrative or system of metaphysical beliefs.

In what way might health be understood in the integrative mode of our subjectivity? And how do we relate the integrative mode of subjectivity to Smith's eudaimonistic model of health in which the extreme of health is said to be 'exuberant well-being'? What we have said so far suggests that Smith's four models no longer map so neatly onto my four modes of subjectivity at this point. The conative mode already grounds the creation and fulfilment of self which is central to the eudaimonistic model. Smith's notion of 'exuberant well-being' might well be the happiness and enjoyment of which Levinas speaks and which I have called the innate experience of health in the conative mode of our subjectivity. What the integrative mode might add to our account of the role of health in our fulfilment is articulateness. The conative mode is inarticulate because it is pre-conscious. But as human beings, we think about our lives and how to attain meaning, happiness and the fulfilment of our potentialities. Hence the mode of

---

[37] Some modern holistic writings on health tend to be magical in this way. For example, Margaret A. Newman, in her *Health as Expanding Consciousness* (St Louis, Missouri, 1986), argues for a new paradigm of health in which the duality of health and disease should be replaced by a perspective in which the state of the individual becomes secondary to the state of a system of which that individual is a part. From such a perspective the travails of the individual dissolve into insignificance, and disease and non-disease are but aspects of the system that inevitably co-exist in a fluid way. This would seem to be a modern scientifically formulated version of the macrocosmic harmonies to which magical beliefs appealed in their accounts of health and disease. For another example, see Larry Dossey, *Beyond Illness: Discovering the Experience of Health* (Boston, Massachusetts, 1984).

subjectivity that is concerned with meaning and integration must be articulate. While it might be possible to achieve fulfilment in a pre-conscious and naïve manner, Socrates' dictum that 'the unexamined life is not worth living' remains true. We need a mode of thinking through which we can find meaning in our lives and which is not just oriented to need or driven pragmatically. And this mode of thinking or being must include a notion of health as an ideal which we can draw upon so as to include our physical and mental well-being in the articulation of what it is for our lives to be meaningful.

The integrative mode of our subjectivity is given articulate form in our commitments (which are expressed in relevant actions), our faiths and our ideals. Amongst these ideals is health. What I mean by this is that health is not just something we enjoy, hope and strive for or fear the loss of, it is also an encapsulation of what we consider fine and noble about humanity and about ourselves. Along with Truth, Justice, Beauty and other ideals, health is a concept that articulates the best ways of being human. It is one of the potentialities which we seek to fulfil in ourselves. Achieving these ideals in our own lives and circumstances is one way that we have of making our lives meaningful. These are the ideals against which we measure ourselves so as to establish our self-worth and eudaimonia.

The ideal of health can be given a number of different forms in different historical and cultural contexts. Some of these forms are present in popular culture. The images of musclebound men and slender women that occur in our entertainments and advertising present images or ideals of health even when it is not their purpose to do so. Moreover, they are images which are often unrealistic or even harmful. Sport and its heroes present better images. Here we see a vitality and level of fitness which we can all aspire to within our physical limits. Such a representation of the ideal of health, however, has a tendency to turn health into a commodity. Sport equipment, sports clothes, health club memberships and dietary programmes are all commodity forms related to the ideal of health. In the terms of my analysis, thinking of health as a commodity would be to make health into a goal of our practical concerns. It would be something that we can achieve by suitable practical and rational means. As such it would become a goal of the pragmatic mode of our subjectivity. This would place health on a par with the other goals of our practical lives, whether as a means for attaining other goals or as a hobby with goals particular to itself. But either way there would be a tendency to devalue it as an ideal inherent in the integrative mode of subjectivity.

To be the latter, health needs to have the significance of something that can give meaning to our lives. While I do not deny that this can happen in fields such as sport, I want to explore more traditional expressions of the health ideal first. One way in which health could acquire integrative significance is when it is given certain mythical meanings. To explore this more thoroughly I turn to the writings of Paul Tillich.[38]

For Tillich, religious myth presents health and healing as forms of salvation through which an individual or humankind as a whole is reconciled to the powers of the cosmos or the god that those people believe in. Tillich explores philological connections between such words as 'health', 'hale' (as in 'hale and hearty') and 'holy' to indicate that health has an integrative meaning expressive of man's relation to the ultimate. Further, he indicates that, as in the Hippocratic tradition, some religious traditions consider that unhealth or lack of salvation do not occur at the individual level, but are states of the cosmos. Achieving our own health therefore requires that the cosmos be put right. Disease is the result of forces of evil, and cosmic disease is 'cosmic guilt'.[39] Accordingly, the task of healers was not just to cure or comfort the sick, but also to restore the harmony of the cosmos. The connection of healers with gods in many religious narratives shows this. For example, the healing actions of Jesus in the Gospels are taken to be emblems of his salvific power. The ancient Greeks revered the great ancient healer Asclepius as a god. Many religious and cultural traditions make these connections between health and various form of salvation. This demonstrates that health can have a role in the integrative mode of our subjectivity and that health can be a part of what makes our lives meaningful in an ultimate way.

But what form might this concept of health as an integrative ideal take in a modern secular culture such as ours? Some key words which we would expect to use in answering this question are 'purity', 'harmony', 'vitality' and 'strength'. The opposite of purity here includes both dirt and decadence. Ever since the formation of the germ theory of disease and the consequent stress on hygiene, dirt has been thought of as the opposite of health. Even in ancient times, as Hippocrates' stress on clean air and pure water shows, there had been a correlation between cleanliness and health. All of this has given rise to a set of attitudes which has given an almost moral connotation to cleanliness. 'Cleanliness is next to godliness', as the saying has it. This, in turn, has given to health the metaphorical meaning of virtue. The ancient link between a healthy mind and a healthy body bears this out. This in turn explains why decadence can be thought of as an opposite of health. A life of luxuriance and excess, of course, often does lead to ill health at the material level of our existence. Excessive eating is linked to obesity and heart disease and so forth. But at the metaphorical level of discourse characteristic of the integrative mode of our subjectivity, we often characterize the life of those we judge as decadent to be 'unhealthy' in a moral sense as well as a medical one. The connotative links in this integrative mode of discourse place the notion of health at a centre of a chain of concepts that have moral implications. As

---

[38]   Paul Tillich, 'The Relation of Religion and Health' (1946), in his *The Meaning of Health: Essays in Existentialism, Psychoanalysis, and Religion*, ed. Perry LeFevre (Chicago, Illinois, 1984), pp. 16–52.

[39]   Tillich, p. 18

an ideal of the integrative mode of our subjectivity, health comes to acquire the meaning of moral probity.

There are dangers in this, of course. The tendency to 'blame the victim' which often exists in relation to social deviances such as poverty and disease is linked to this feeling that a healthy lifestyle is a morally upright lifestyle and that those who live a healthy lifestyle will not suffer from ill health. It would follow from these premises that those who do suffer from ill health must have not lived a healthy lifestyle and thus must be morally decadent, and hence have only themselves to blame. It is obvious that this is fallacious reasoning since ill health can strike even the most diligent and hygienic persons. But the links in the reasoning still have a rhetorical power because of the connotative links between the concepts as they operate at the meaning-giving integrative mode of our subjectivity.

Moreover, it was not only the modern discovery of hygiene which gave the notion of cleanliness the rhetorical power of an ideal of health. In ancient times and in our own biblical tradition the notion of uncleanness and the need for ritual purification are associated with menstruating women and other forms of blood-letting. As modern psychoanalysis indicates, there are fears of the unknown involved in such practices as well as rational provisions for hygiene. The unknown in these cases might include the feminine, or the powers of life that were thought to inhere in blood. To our modern sensibility, these beliefs seem both erroneous and prejudicial to the status of women in society. However, the concepts that operate in the discourses that express the integrative mode of our subjectivity must not be judged by the same standards of rationality as operate in the pragmatic mode. The kind of associations and links that are made when we articulate our faiths and ideals depend as much on analogy and metaphor as they do on modern logic and scientific knowledge of causality. They articulate our fears and anxieties as much as our hopes and aspirations. Nevertheless, given the unity or integrity of our modes of being, superstition and rationality are not as distinct as we children of the European Enlightenment might like to think.

The notions of harmony and balance operate in a similar way to that of purity. While the Hippocratic tradition was right to suggest that appropriate and balanced interaction with the physical environment is a material component of health, the metaphorical extension of this idea to the notion that a balanced and harmonious lifestyle is healthy draws its rhetorical force from the integrative mode of our subjectivity. It can become part of our meaningful sense of ourselves as worthwhile individuals that we have a balanced diet, that we engage in a range of activities that engage different aspects of our being, and that we maintain harmonious relationships with our environment and our social world. It is undeniably true that these ways of living conduce to health at the material level. But my point here is that this set of health notions also takes on a quasi-moral connotation so as to enhance our sense of personal integrity and worth. To think of myself as a healthy person is not only to consider myself as free of physical or mental disease and as being able to operate effectively in the practical world. It is more even than having an implicit sense of enjoyment of life. It is a moral reassurance that I am living well from which I derive a sense of self-worth and meaning in life.

A further avenue of inquiry to help us answer the question as to how health figures as an integrative concept for subjectivity in modern times would be to think again about the appeal of sport. Both from the point of view of those who engage in sport as a weekend activity[40] and from the point of view of those many more who watch sport as spectators, sport represents something more than just a recreation or a means of getting fit. As we have seen, the ideal of health as fitness is one that reduces the integrative mode to the pragmatic. I think of fitness as a functional matter. In contrast to this, there are several ideals present in sport. One is that of competitiveness. To compete against others, or to identify ourselves with others who do so, gives meaning to our lives not just because we like to win. We admire the courageous loser as well. It is competitiveness itself which constitutes the ideal in question. However, this is not the ideal on which I want to focus because it is not an ideal of health. Rather, the ideal of health that is present in sport is that of 'vitality'.

Vitality or vigour is a health ideal which gives meaning and integrity to a life because it is the articulated form given to the happiness and enjoyment of which Levinas spoke. When we seek to articulate the feelings of enjoyment of life that arises from our existing in the elements that nourish us, we do so by describing feelings of strength. We feel that we are able to do what we want. We feel we have the vitality and the power to achieve what we aim for. Not only will our bodies not let us down but they also provide the vigour and spirit with which we approach what we do.

As an ideal of health, vitality can be understood with reference to the writings of Friedrich Nietzsche and his concept of 'will-to-power'.[41] And this connects it once again with the ideal of competitiveness which inheres in sport. As I interpret Nietzsche, will-to-power is the impetus to distinguish ourselves and differentiate ourselves from the common and the average. It is, in effect, another term for subjectivity itself since subjectivity too is the struggle to become ourselves and create our identities. Vitality and vigour are not just physical or material means that will allow us to pursue this existential struggle, they are also the spiritual or integrative feelings that accompany our success in it. We feel ourselves strong and vigorous to the extent that we are independent and differentiated from the crowd.

Classical and Renaissance art provides evidence for the presence in our culture of these ideals. The classical nude frequently portrays a health ideal. Nakedness and the beauty of the human body are symbols of the pure and unadulterated form that health can take as an integrative ideal. They are also, frequently, symbols of

---

[40] The case of professional sports persons is different. They are largely operating at the pragmatic level of existence when they play.

[41] Friedrich Wilhelm Nietzsche, *The Will to Power*, trans. W. Kaufmann and R.J. Hollingdale (New York, 1967).

the strength and vitality which are aspects of the ideal of health and which can give meaning to our individual lives and cultural expression to our social ideals.

My stress on vitality might remind us that we should not expect to find a single or simple answer to the question of what the integrative ideal of health is in our contemporary culture. Our post-modern culture is marked by pluralism, and the refusal of overarching theories which would relate all meanings together into a single system of truth. One clear difference which will mark our modern ideals of health, for example, is that between men and women. Health ideals are gendered. The form that vitality takes for men derives from the warrior tradition. For warriors, vitality implies strength, competitiveness and courage. It also involves independence and not needing the assistance of others. Think, for example, of Franklin D. Roosevelt who went to great lengths to hide from the American electorate the fact that he could not walk because of his having suffered polio. In modern Western societies, when the warrior traditions are largely irrelevant, they have been translated into the ideal of the sports hero. Again, for men, the ability to provide for their families is part of their feeling of self-worth. Many men take pride in their being able to work despite injury or ill health. Studies of working-class men show that the ability to 'soldier on' is highly prized.[42] This may seem to be the same ideal as that of fitness, but the presence of the integrative factor of pride in oneself elevates it to that further mode of our subjectivity. It becomes one of the several expressions of the masculine health ideal of vitality.

For women, in contrast, the traditional forms of vitality are the ideals of the mother: namely, fecundity and nurturing. In this set of ideals there is less stress on power and competitiveness and more on community and sharing. Health, once again, is more than the material ability to perform our roles. It is the very impetus to want to do so. Caring and nurturing are signs of health as well as of the right moral stance towards children and towards others. The woman who fails to evince these behaviours is deemed unhealthy where that term includes the connotations of immoral and deviant. And this might not only be thought of as a case of mental ill health. Infertility is clearly a physiological problem and yet it is described as 'barrenness' and then linked with mean-spiritedness and other departures from the ideal of healthy womanhood. Of course, these ideals are being contested today. Feminism has questioned these traditional connotative links. But the fact that this questioning requires the undoing of conceptual links that have been built up over many generations shows that we are dealing with concepts that are not just objective beliefs, but also structures of our understanding of ourselves and articulations of the meanings which we give our lives.

The key point in all this is that the concept of health operates as an ideal which gives meaning to our lives in the integrative mode of our subjectivity. It is part of our self-image as worthwhile persons. Health contributes to our well-being not just through being the material wherewithal for our physical functioning and social effectiveness, and not just through being the inchoate basis of our enjoyment of

---

[42]   Michael Calnan, *Health & Illness: The Lay Perspective* (London, 1987).

living. It also does so through being one of the forms given to our search for a meaningful selfhood and integrity. Smith's notion of 'exuberant well-being' must mean more than just physical strength and vitality. It extends to the spiritual well-being that comes from feeling good about ourselves in moral and existential terms.

Conclusion

Individual persons experience their own state of health in all four modes of subjectivity. A professional concern for health must therefore also extend to all four modes of subjectivity in which health is experienced. While the everyday tasks of health workers should be focused upon the material mode, sensitivity to the patient as a unique and particular person requires an awareness of the depth to which health is experienced and the meanings that it can have in an individual's life. This depth points to the nature of health as a self-constituting, inchoate and joyful rapport with the environing world. It follows that the loss of health through injury or disease is a personal trauma more profound than just the experience of pain or disability. It threatens our very existential being.

Chapter 9

Disease and Subjectivity

There has been considerable debate in recent years surrounding the concept of disease. There has been debate about what this concept refers to, with some arguing that it is an entity that, in paradigm cases, invades the body, whereas others have argued that it is a holistic state of an organism involving internal disharmony or a dysfunctional mode of interaction with the biological and lived environment.[1] As a result, there is an ontological (an invasion by a disease entity) and a physiological (an upsetting of internal balances) concept of disease. Writers have also disagreed on the classificatory criteria for diseases, asking whether they should be based on symptoms or causes, and whether the concept should embrace injuries and wounds as well as other pathological conditions. Some have wondered whether the notion designates naturally occurring types of entity or event, or whether we have invented the concept for pragmatic purposes.[2] This has been called the problem of 'taxonomic scepticism versus taxonomic realism'.[3] There has been debate as to whether the concept is a descriptive concept designating a dysfunctional state of the organism,[4] or an evaluative concept partly expressing attitudes to that state.[5] There has also been debate regarding the extension of the concept: whether it covers only physiological conditions or whether it is used, without change in meaning, to describe psychological conditions as well.[6] Are

---

[1] See René Dubos, *Mirage of Health: Utopias, Progress and Biological Change* (New York, 1959), Chapter V, for an interesting discussion of the history of this debate. See also Chapter 1 of Eric J. Cassell, *The Nature of Suffering and the Goals of Medicine* (New York, 1991).

[2] Lester S. King, 'What is Disease?', in Arthur L. Caplan, Tristram H. Engelhardt Jr and James J. McCartney (eds), *Concepts of Health and Disease: Interdisciplinary Perspectives* (Reading, Massachusetts, 1981), pp. 107–18. King argues that disease is a classification that alters with knowledge and interest.

[3] Lawrie Reznek, *The Nature of Disease* (London, 1987), p. 25.

[4] Christopher Boorse, 'On the Distinction between Disease and Illness', in Caplan, Englehardt and McCartney, pp. 545–60. For Boorse, disease is a deviation from the natural functional organization of the species: 'In general, deficiencies in the functional efficiency of the body are diseases when they are unnatural, and they may be unnatural either by being untypical or by being attributable mainly to the action of a hostile environment' (pp. 552–3).

[5] Joseph Margolis, 'The Concept of Disease', in Caplan, Englehardt and McCartney, pp. 561–77.

[6] Anthony Flew, *Crime or Disease?* (New York, 1973).

stuttering, hyperactivity, homosexuality or drunkenness cases of disease? Further, there have been suggestions that disease is one of a set of concepts used for social labelling and that it can thus have repressive implications, as when Soviet dissidents were confined in mental asylums on the grounds that they suffered from mental disease.[7] The concept of disease raises the issue of the scope of medicine. Insofar as medicine deals with disease, the definition of disease will set the boundaries of what it is appropriate for medicine to concern itself with.[8] And underlying many of these debates has been a concern about the close connection perceived to exist between some concepts of disease and a dehumanizing biomedical model of treatment.[9]

The dispute that I want to focus on in this chapter is that between those who see the concept of disease as neutral or objective and those who see it as value-laden; the dispute between 'naturalism' on the one hand, and 'normativism' on the other. I support normativism, but, rather than adjudicate this dispute, I want to suggest that the meaning of the concept of disease, as it is used in the clinical setting of health care, is value-laden in a richer way than writers on either side of this debate have recognized.

I mention the clinical setting because this highlights the perspectives of those who care for patients with disease and of those patients themselves. This is important because the meaning of a term depends in part upon the context in which it is used. Some of the debates about whether the concept of disease is descriptive or evaluative seem to suppose that this matter can be decided in the abstract. However, it may well be true that a medical researcher in a laboratory appropriately uses the notion of disease in a purely descriptive way, whereas a general practitioner is more aware of the evaluative connotations that the term carries when she uses it in her professional context. Again, in the debate between the ontological concept and the physiological, public health officials and pharmaceutical workers will use the ontological concept, while the physiological approach with its case histories and attention to the individual sickness will be appropriate to the clinical setting.[10]

What makes the caring context significant is that it has ethical implications for health care workers, who are frequently called upon to make ethically sensitive decisions. The conventional approach of medical ethics and bioethics is to posit fundamental ethical principles or norms which can be used as the bases for deriving moral imperatives which will apply to the particular situation with which

---

[7]   Michel Foucault develops this idea in *The Birth of the Clinic: An Archaeology of Medical Perception*, trans. A.M. Sheridan Smith (London, 1973).

[8]   Raanan Gillon, 'On Sickness and on Health', *British Medical Journal*, 292/1 (February 1986): 318–20.

[9]   George L. Engel, 'The Need for a New Medical Model: A Challenge for Biomedicine', in Caplan, Englehardt and McCartney, pp. 589–607.

[10]   Owsei Temkin, 'The Scientific Approach to Disease: Specific Entity and Individual Sickness', in Caplan, Englehardt and McCartney, pp. 247–63, p. 262.

the health worker is confronted. As one author has put it, ethicists take themselves to provide an algorithm by which decisions can be deduced syllogistically from uncontentious principles and norms.[11] I have argued in Chapter 2 that this is not a productive way of approaching morally complex situations, and the apparent intractability of bioethical debates would seem to bear this out. My suggestion would be that what is required for ethical decision-making is a sensitive awareness of what is at issue in the situation at hand. My ethical theory is particularist, virtue-based and Aristotelian in its insistence on the importance of being aware of the moral demands that a situation contains. In the context of health care, morally difficult situations frequently involve disease. As such, sensitivity to the moral demands inherent in those situations will require a deep understanding of what disease is and what its significance is within human life.

Much of the literature agrees on the following points about the concept of disease. The first is that disease is involuntary. We are victims of it. Drunkenness is not a disease, but alcoholism is. Second, as K.W.M. Fulford argues, it renders us incapable of doing things we want to do and could otherwise do.[12] Third, it is unpleasant (though it can save me from something worse, as when my asthma gets me out of military service). However, there are exceptions. Not all unpleasant, debilitating experiences are diseases (for example, childbirth), and it is also possible to be the victim of an asymptomatic disease which involves no unpleasantness because the victim is not aware of it (for example, undiagnosed or asymptomatic HIV infection). So, in more formal terms, I would say that disease is harmful to its victims.[13] Fourth, disease is distinct from many congenital defects and from wounds and injuries. I will be following Lawrie Reznek in using the notion of disease to designate those pathological conditions of which the cause is not obvious, so as to differentiate them from wounds and injuries which are pathological conditions of which the cause is patent.[14] Fifth, disease is a process with an onset, a typical course, and an outcome. Sixth, disease is not the contrary of health. There are other contraries of health, such as being unfit, which are not equivalent to disease. Lastly, we should not assume that disease is by definition physiological since such an assumption would beg the question concerning whether mental illness is genuine disease.

---

[11] Anne MacLean, *The Elimination of Morality: Reflections on Utilitarianism and Bioethics* (London and New York, 1993).

[12] K.W.M. Fulford, *Moral Theory and Medical Practice* (Cambridge, 1989).

[13] Even here there can be exceptions in that a person may become morally better as a result of suffering a disease.

[14] Historically, 'there was a need to explain suffering in the absence of an obvious cause' (Reznek, p. 77). Even now, Reznek argues, when we do understand the causes of many diseases, we continue to preserve the distinction between diseases and other pathological conditions. The distinction between medicine and surgery would have preserved the distinction also.

Further, much of the literature on the concept of disease agrees that there is a structured set of distinctions to be drawn between the concepts of illness, disease and the sick role.[15] In the context of such a set, the concept of disease is often seen as more objective and as more closely related to the physiological. As one writer puts it, 'Disease is something an organ has: illness is something a man has.'[16] So it is often suggested that disease is the pathological condition that causes negatively valued physiological or other changes. In this aetiological form the concept seems to be both value-free and universal.[17] In contrast to this, illness is said to be the subjective state that responds to the changes caused by disease. Illness has a phenomenology that includes such states as pain, discomfort and curtailment of the ability to do things.[18] Given this, it is clear that illness is a value term. It designates an unpleasant or painful state of partial or whole debility that people usually seek to avoid or seek relief from. Talcott Parsons has developed the notion of a social role that people who are affected by illness may fit into and which involves permission to not contribute to work and an obligation to seek cure and assistance. He called it the 'sick role', with the result that cognates of the term 'sick' are now most frequently used in this sociological sense.[19] Sociologists have also described 'illness behaviour' and the factors (apart from actual disease) that contribute to it.[20]

---

[15]   This three-way classification is also accepted by Alan Radley in his *Making Sense of Illness: The Social Psychology of Health and Disease* (London, 1994). See also Cecil G. Helman, 'Disease versus Illness in General Practice', *Journal of the Royal College of General Practitioners*, 31 (September 1981): 548–52, and Jeremiah A. Barondess, 'Disease and Illness – a Crucial Distinction', *The American Journal of Medicine*, 66 (March 1979): 375–6.

[16]   Helman, quoted in Michael Calnan, *Health and Illness: The Lay Perspective* (London, 1987), p. 134.

[17]   As Horacio Fabrega Jr, puts it: 'It should be clear that a consequence of applying or using this essentially biologistic framework regarding disease is that specific diseases can then be said to be *universal* or transcultural occurrences' ('Concepts of Disease: Logical Features and Social Implications', in Caplan, Englehardt and McCartney, pp. 493–522, p. 497).

[18]   Peter Sedgwick, 'Illness – Mental and Otherwise', in Caplan, Englehardt and McCartney, pp. 119–29, and Fulford.

[19]   Talcott Parsons, 'Definitions of Health and Illness in the Light of American Values and Social Structures', in Caplan, Englehardt and McCartney, pp. 57–81. See also Robert M. Veatch, 'The Medical Model: Its Nature & Problems', in Caplan, Englehardt and McCartney, pp. 523–44, who says: 'To be sick is to have aberrant characteristics of a certain sort which society as a whole evaluates as being bad and for which that society assigns the sick role' (p. 526). Various other concepts are linked to this three-part distinction, though not always systematically. So we describe a physiological pathological condition as a disease if it is a process, but as an impairment if it is a static and persistent condition such as a malformed limb. Again, the notion of illness as a description of a subjective experience is confined to experienced processes, while if the experience is of a state which is static and persistent, it might be referred to as a disability. In a similar way sickness as a social role that results from a pathological process might have its static and persistent counterpart in the

In this chapter I will be arguing that in settings of patient care, the concept of disease does not belong at the lower, reductionist end of this three-level schema, but is evaluative in a very strong sense. In order to develop this argument, let us revisit some recent contributions to the debate on that issue.

Naturalism and normativism

Christopher Boorse has argued that disease is a purely descriptive concept. He has argued that disease is the theoretical concept, while illnesses are 'those diseases that have certain normative features reflected in the institutions of medical practice'.[21] For Boorse, disease consists of a dysfunction afflicting a bodily process, whereas health is simply a case of each part of the organism fulfilling its natural function. Boorse offers the analogy of a Volkswagen that is in perfect working order when it fulfils its designer's specifications. To say this is not a value judgement, because it may still not be a very good car as compared to a Mercedes, for example. To say that it is in perfect working order is simply to describe a fact about it. In this way Boorse offers a purely descriptive analysis of health in terms of a well-functioning organism, and of disease as the equally value-free matter of the organism not being in perfect working order. Of course the Volkswagen analogy has limitations. Science assumes that organisms do not have a designer in the way a car has, but that science can discover the functions of our organs empirically (though not of the whole organism). As Boorse puts it, 'A function in the biologist's sense is nothing but a standard causal contribution to a goal actually pursued by the organism.'[22] Disease is a deviation from the natural functional organization of the species. Again, the notion of a deviation can be grounded on a non-evaluative description. Not all deviations are diseases, but 'in general, deficiencies in the functional efficiency of the body are diseases when they are unnatural, and they may be unnatural either by being untypical or by being attributable mainly to the action of a hostile environment'.[23]

---

social role of being handicapped (Mervyn Susser, 'Ethical Components in the Definition of Health', in Caplan, Englehardt and McCartney, pp. 93–105). Given that these latter terms have a degree of unacceptable social stigma attached to them, however, they are frequently changed in order to avoid the negative connotations that come to apply to them. So disability and being handicapped are now sometimes referred to as 'being challenged' or 'being differently abled'. Similar attempts to overcome the stigma attached to the sick role are represented by the tendency to replace the word 'patient' with that of 'client' or even 'health care services consumer'.

[20]   David Mechanic, 'The Concept of Illness Behaviour', in Caplan, Englehardt and McCartney, pp. 485–92.

[21]   Boorse, p. 550

[22]   Ibid., p. 551.

[23]   Ibid., p. 552–3.

Admittedly, the function of an organ or process can only be discerned in the context of an understanding of the wider goal-directed or teleological processes of the organism of which that organ or process is a part. After all, the disease entities may be functioning perfectly well and doing so in conjunction with relevant parts of the body. It is just that they are incipiently forming a different system and a different set of system interactions from that which would be functional within the host system. Once the operation and goals of the host organismic context is understood, functions can be attributed objectively and the failure of functions likewise described without appeal to values. It does not make sense, nor is it necessary, to say that the liver *wants* to purify blood, which is what we would have to say if we maintained that it was a frustration of value if it did not successfully purify the blood. For Boorse, it is simply objectively the case that the function of the liver within the organism is to purify the blood, and if it fails to do so, this is likewise an objective fact about it. It is diseased.

Boorse allows that disease is often undesirable, but this is a further and separate matter depending upon a still larger context of human purposes and goals. That a person with a diseased liver will suffer frustration of her life goals does not imply that the dysfunctional state of the liver is inherently bad. It is made so by the further and non-inherent fact that she has certain goals and desires. That it is undesirable for its victim is one of the reasons that we would describe the disease as an illness.[24]

Reznek, in contrast, endorses normativism. As he puts it:

Disease is to be understood in terms of the evaluative notion of being harmed. It also requires a reference to some norm – not all conditions that we would be better off without are diseases. The Normativist theory commits us to Normativism – the thesis that the concept of disease is value-laden.[25]

In the course of his discussion, he points out some difficulties with the notion of a function as defined with reference to goals, as it is by Boorse. Some things may contribute accidentally to my goals. Asthma may help me achieve my goal of getting out of the army, but it is not an instance of health. Again, some things, like chairs, have functions but are not part of any goal-directed system. So there does not seem to be the logical link between functions and goals that Boorse requires. Reznek prefers an aetiological theory which defines a function thus:

The function of X (in Y) is Z if and only if (a) X does Z, and (b) X's doing Z makes a causal contribution to X's continued presence in Y in the right sort of way (by human intervention or via the mechanism of natural selection).[26]

---

[24] In a footnote, Boorse says he ceded too much to normativism in saying that illness is disease laden with values: 'Illness is better analysed simply as systemically incapacitating disease, hence as no more normative than disease itself' (Boorse, p. 560).

[25] Reznek, p. 170

[26] Ibid., pp. 116–17. (My formulation combines several points that Reznek makes.)

On this account, the context of a goal given by a designer or by the process of evolution is needed to specify what the causal process is which explains X's occurrence. Reznek admits that the notion of dysfunction in this account will be value-free in that the goals and values of the organism are extrinsic to its functioning.

However, this is no comfort for the naturalist because Reznek goes on to argue against the view that 'being a process productive of a malfunction is a necessary condition for being a disease, and a sufficient condition for being pathological'.[27] To make this point, he imagines a malevolent dictator who programs our genetic makeup so that we will self-destruct when we have outlived our usefulness. If this succeeded, then this process would fulfil the function it was given by its designer. It would not malfunction. Yet what the dictator had given us would still be regarded as a disease. Again, Reznek points to some processes which, in an evolutionary context, have no function (for example, female orgasm, or the appendix) yet when they regularly fail to occur, or if they malfunction, we speak of disease. Indeed, from an evolutionary perspective, after reproduction has ceased, an organism has no further function, and so it cannot malfunction. Yet it can have a disease. In this way Reznek breaks the nexus between disease and dysfunction completely, tying the concept rather to the evaluative notion of harm, as we had noted earlier.

However, the notion of harm can only be explicated with reference to interests or goods the frustration of which constitutes harm. As Reznek puts it, 'someone is worse off, if and only if, his interests are impaired. But here someone's interests are impaired if and only if, his leading a good or worthwhile life is interfered with.'[28] Yet Reznek admits that it is not easy to say what makes a life worthwhile except to say that it '*does* seem to have something to do with the satisfaction of desires, and the achievement of happiness'.[29] On this account, then, human goods or those values that can make a human life worthwhile provide the necessary context for understanding disease as a negative value. The disvalue that attaches to disease would seem not to be inherent in it but to arise from the fact that it frustrates the victim's pursuit of happiness and the goods of life.

William Fulford argues differently from Reznek. For him both dysfunction and disease are value concepts.[30] He takes non-biological functional objects to be the paradigm cases in which the meaning of the concept 'function' is established. Such a non-biological purposive context implies a designer such that the purpose of this designer is frustrated when there is dysfunction. This makes the value component of the notion of function depend upon the purposes of the designer. And it also places limits on the valuations that may be imposed on a thing. It would be

---

27 Ibid., p. 126.
28 Ibid., p. 150.
29 Ibid., p. 151.
30 Fulford, pp. 36–56

appropriate to say that this was not a good watch if it did not keep time, but not if it failed to serve as a paperweight. That a limited range of valuations are appropriate is argued for by Fulford when he suggests that purposefully designed things (and their parts) are capable of 'functional doing'.[31] Not everything that a watch can do – like be a paperweight – is what it functionally does. Keeping time (along with the relevant movements of the mechanism) is, and this licenses a move from 'is' to 'ought'. If a thing is designed in a certain way for a certain purpose, then it *ought* to functionally do what it is designed to do. Dysfunction is a failure to do what it functionally ought to do and, as such, is a negative value.

I would add that this point also allows us to understand the notions of intrinsic value and extraneous value. It may happen to be true that a particular watch serves as a paperweight, but this would be an extraneous value. The watch's intrinsic value is that for which it was designed. It is the value that attaches to its doing what it functionally ought to do: namely, keep time. It follows that it would only be an intrinsic disvalue if it fails to keep time.

How does all this apply to biological organisms and to persons? Fulford says that 'biological functional objects – hands, hearts and so on – do not have designers. Yet they have "designed-for" purposes.'[32] These purposes arise from biological needs such that an organism's fulfilling these needs in normal ways is a case of 'functional doing' in the context of evolutionary teleology. It would follow that there would be intrinsic disvalue in any organismic dysfunction. But Fulford's crucial point is that human beings are capable of a richer form of functional doing: namely, 'intentional doing', in which the agents themselves set the purposes and goals that are being pursued. This form of doing can also be frustrated in a variety of ways. Where these frustrations are internal to the agent (so that they do not seem to have been done *to* one by someone or something else) and are not desired or under the agent's control, and where there is no apparent obstruction or opposition, we will have a case of illness.[33] Illness is related to intentional doing (or 'ordinary doing', as Fulford describes simple actions) as dysfunction is related to functional doing. Illness is therefore a value concept just as dysfunction is. In illness, something fails to happen which ought to happen: namely, an agent's doing what he normally could do.

This also explains a difference in the use of the concepts of disease and illness. Only human beings and higher animals can be described as doing things intentionally.[34] As others have also noted, illness is more frequently attributed to human beings and higher animals, as opposed to disease, which can be attributed even to plants. This is because human beings and higher animals do things in a richer sense than plants (or watches).

---

[31] Reznek, p. 93
[32] Ibid., p. 107.
[33] Ibid., p. 119.
[34] Ibid., p. 123.

A crucial point in Fulford's argument is that the structure of concepts which I described earlier, which makes disease the fundamental concept because it is the physiological concept, is in error. For Fulford, the fundamental concept is that of illness. The experience of not being able to do what we normally can do, and the concomitant experience of pain and discomfort, provide the basis for the concept of illness. Because it has the experience of frustration built into it, and because that which ought to happen fails to happen, this concept is clearly a valuational one. The concept of disease, in contrast, designates a subcategory of illness distinguished from other cases of illness simply in being regarded as disease, thereby directing attention to causes. The foundational idea is that disease is causally implicated in 'failure of action' rather than its necessarily being physiological. (Fulford is concerned to argue this case because he wants to defend mental illness from the scepticism that would arise from taking physical disease to be paradigmatic. For Fulford, any action failure can be thought of as disease, whether its symptoms and aetiology are physical or psychological.) Insofar as disease is a subcategory of illness, it too is a value concept.

But does this mean that the disvalue involved in the valuational concept of disease is simply that something fails to happen which ought to happen, as it is in the case of dysfunction? Yes, but there is something more. The purposes that I pursue in my everyday intentional actions will gain their importance for me from the values that I hold. So values are the matrix of my actions, and of my action failures due to illness. In this way, illness will be a disvalue to me that goes beyond its merely being a frustration of my agency. It will also prevent me from attaining the goals and values in pursuit of which I act.

However, this raises a question as to whether the disvalue of illness or disease is intrinsic to it. Even Boorse agrees that disease is seen as a disvalue, but he denies that that disvalue is intrinsic. And Reznek attributes the disvalue of disease to its frustrating the victim's good rather than to its being intrinsically dysfunctional. Fulford can make good sense of the idea that something ought to functionally do what it is designed to do and that it is therefore a disvalue if it fails. However, this merely describes what ought to happen given the teleological matrix in which the item functions. This is not yet to say that when that happens which ought to happen, it is a value pure and simple. A gun may fire perfectly well and in that sense functionally do what it ought to do, but if it kills an innocent victim, its doing so is not to be valued. What this shows is that there is a value which can attach to functional doing but which is distinct from its success in functionally doing just what it ought to do. 'Success' in this sense is an intrinsic value derived from the function the item is given by its designer or teleological context, whereas the further value is a value derived from a wider valuational framework in which the item is used. This further value is, in my sense of the term, extraneous. Something's succeeding in functionally doing what it ought to do is not valuable in the same way that the consequences of that functional doing might be.

Human intentional actions are similar. I may go to do something and succeed in doing it. This success counts as a value in that my action has not been frustrated.

But there are further values or disvalues that might attach to the action. A criminal who fires the gun at an innocent victim will judge (if he has reason to think about it) that that which ought to have happened has happened when he shoots. Moreover, he will value this in the light of his own criminal goals. In a larger context of social values, however, others may judge that action negatively. In this context, an illness that prevents the criminal from firing the gun would be a value to society, even though it is a disvalue to the agent in that it frustrates his intentional action and prevents him from achieving his goal. So it seems that there is scope to go beyond the value of successful intentional action and find a further value in the action; a value that goes beyond the fact that the action came off successfully, and which derives from broader personal and social frameworks of evaluation. We can distinguish the disvalue of dysfunction or action failure from the broader disvalue which would be typically attributed to such failures, but might not be. This latter disvalue is clearly extraneous, and it might be this kind of broader value which Boorse is referring to when he says that the value component in the idea of illness or disease is an extraneous one arising from people's attitudes rather than an intrinsic one belonging to the concept of disease as such.

How do the notions of intrinsic and extraneous value, which I have analysed in terms of 'functional doing', apply to 'intentional doing' abstracted from the broader social context? My discussion of Fulford shows that illness can be a disvalue in a number of ways. It is an intrinsic disvalue in that it involves action failure. The body will not do what it ought. Second, there is typically a further and less intrinsic disvalue in that the agent's goals are frustrated. (That this is less intrinsic is shown by the possibility that the agent might be relieved to find that an illness – a sudden paralysis, say – has prevented him from doing something which he had only decided unwillingly to do.) Third, there is the social disvalue or value of the action's not taking place. That this last can be an extraneous value so far as the agent is concerned is shown by the possibility that the agent, like the criminal, does not share those social values. In each case the valuation depends upon differing teleological contexts. First, there is the inherent functional doing of the body. Second, there are the intentions of the agent. And third, there are the moral and cultural values of a society. Even if we leave aside the broader extraneous social values, there seems to be a question as to the extent to which the agent's intended values are intrinsic or extraneous to the action. They are certainly not as intrinsic as is the value of the action occurring successfully.

Fulford needs an account of values which ties them to actions intrinsically, rather than extraneously, while being more than the value of the absence of action failure. For him, there is an analogy between functional doing and intentional doing. In my analysis, the value of a thing's successfully doing what it is designed to functionally do is intrinsic to it (and derives from the thing's designer). In the case of organisms, we assume no such designer but the analogy is still said to hold. However, the case of organisms who are human agents seems to introduce a new element. We give ourselves our goals in the way that a designer gives a functional item its goals. This would now seem to be a case of our imposing goals upon our bodies understood as teleological systems that already have goals so that they are capable of functional doing. There seems to be a dualism here in which there are both functional values inherent in the body and intentional values arising from human agency.

The reconciliation of 'is' and 'ought' which Fulford espouses involves the notion of an 'ought' which is less intrinsic to the agent than the 'ought' which applies to the functioning of her body. If a car engine is designed to propel the car then it is a true description of it to say that it ought to propel the car, but there is no sense in which the engine intends or 'owns' this obligation as a part of its being. For organisms, including human organisms, the biological need to avoid harm grounds a prudential 'ought'. But this is intrinsic to the agent because it belongs to the body. For Fulford, this value is a function of the biological teleological framework in which the agent exists. The goals which an agent intentionally pursues seem not to belong to the agent in this intrinsic manner. If dualism is to be overcome, then the intentional values of agents must be fully intrinsic to them also. I will argue that the values that frame intentional action are the kind to which agents can be committed and which are fully owned by them because they are not reducible to biological needs. These values constitute the good of the agent as that term is used by Reznek.

I would propose that the values in pursuit of which an agent acts intentionally are adopted or accepted so that they become intrinsic to the agent. It is not the case that agents ought to act in this way or that because this would fulfil some goal which is less intrinsic than the value of their own bodily functioning, but rather that agents find it important to be able to act in certain ways given the values that they hold. Only an intrinsic value of this kind is a value that can make a life worthwhile. Only such an intrinsic value could be described as a 'good' for the agent. And only such a value would be so intrinsic to the agent that its frustration by illness or disease would be a disvalue in a richer sense than would be the failure of a bodily function. The notion of value that is needed to understand disease is therefore not a richer version of that of a goal or purpose as applied to functional objects or organisms. There are limits to the analogy between the functional doing of an object that is designed for a purpose and the intentional doing of an agent who pursues purposes.

I would argue that value in the rich sense that we need is a property of subjectivity as such. Therefore, in order to understand value and its relation to illness and disease, we now need to explore the notion of subjectivity.

Subjectivity

Subjectivity is best understood by us (who are subjects) as exemplified by human beings. (I leave open the question as to whether there are other beings who evince subjectivity. Human subjectivity is the only instance of subjectivity that we can know of directly through phenomenological reflection.) As Martin Heidegger has put it, we are beings for whom being is an issue.[35] If we read the first instance of the word 'being' in this phrase as a noun and the second as a verb, we will glimpse what Martin Heidegger is getting at. The fundamental, primordial and innate impetus that undergirds human life is the drive towards being, towards 'real-izing' ourselves and our possibilities. Subjectivity is this impetus. The mode of being that we participate in as human beings is that of striving and seeking, of struggling and willing. We have an innate goal of being: namely, of realizing and distinguishing ourselves and of fulfilling our potential. I call this an innate goal because we do not become aware of it in this abstract and primordial form. We become aware of it in terms of the specific things we actually pursue in life, whether it be high academic grades, successful careers, loving relationships, respect of peers, health, or peaceful death. These are the particular goals and values, shaped by our culture and personal history, which we actually pursue. But our pursuing them is an expression of our primordial concern just to *be* in the way that a human being is. They are not values to be explained as arising just from evolutionary goals or social demands, or as if they were designed by the extraneous purposive frameworks in which we live.

While it is internal to the person, it would be an error to suppose that this existential struggle to be was a purely mental or emotional phenomenon which did not involve our bodies. Indeed, Maurice Merleau-Ponty has famously argued that our bodies are the very expression of this quest.[36] In the previous chapter I elaborated this dynamic picture of human subjectivity as comprising four modes of functioning. I do so again now, using a slightly different terminology that refers to 'levels' of functioning. The first of these is the level of the organism. At this level the biological functions operate which are necessary for the continuance of life and the propagation of our species. We can gain an image of what this level would be like in its pure form by considering plants. The weed that breaks its way through the concrete of a carpark is evincing the sort of will to live that, in us, provides the basic level of our subjectivity. In us, this level comprises all the metabolic, visceral, and instinctive processes that keep us alive.[37] The existence of this level is what makes sociobiology relevant to, but not exhaustive of, a description of our subjectivity. The simplest value that arises at this first level of our subjectivity is the intrinsic value of survival. But it would be misleading to call this a value in any complete sense since, at this level, subjectivity is blind to itself. At this level we evince little more than functional doing.

The second level is that of cognitive and affective reaction to the world around us. Lower animals display this level in its pure form when they respond instinctively to stimuli and display the kinds of affective stimulation which leads to

---

[35]   Martin Heidegger, *Being and Time*, trans. John Macquarie and Edward Robinson (Oxford, 1962), Section 9.

[36]   Maurice Merleau-Ponty, *The Phenomenology of Perception*, trans. Colin Smith (London, 1962).

[37]   That these processes are both hidden and central to our lives as conscious beings has been argued by Drew Leder in his *The Absent Body* (Chicago, 1990), Chapter 2.

appropriate action (such as hunger leading to feeding, or fear leading to flight). In the case of human beings, many of our pre-conscious, immediate responses and desires will be either instinctive or learnt as part of our acculturation. The most basic of these is our ability to recognize things for what they are and respond appropriately to them; an ability to which our having language is central. Our immediate aesthetic reactions, whether they be disgust at something repulsive, or delight in something beautiful, also belong at this level, as do the kinds of unconscious association which advertisers rely upon to make their products seem attractive to us. Jean-Paul Sartre's understanding of emotion as a way of colouring our experience of the world which is not in our full self-conscious control would be an example of a level two phenomenon in that it is a pre-conscious structuring of our world which is functional within our affective life.[38] What traditional philosophy calls the transcendental level of human existence should be located at this level also. For example, Kant's transcendental ego is driven by a pre-conscious purposiveness which gives us useful knowledge, and the knowledge-constitutive interests that Jürgen Habermas describes operate at this hidden level of our being.[39] As I explained in the previous chapter with reference to Emmanuel Levinas, the values that arise at this level include the intrinsic and inchoate values of joy at being alive and of desire-satisfaction, and the value that the world has for us insofar as it allows us to live our lives in it and through it.

The third level of subjectivity involves consciousness in the full self-aware form in which humans experience it. It is the level of functioning that involves thinking, planning and deliberating about how we will meet our needs and fulfil our desires. Most of our everyday practical lives are focused on this level. It is the level that is most obvious and most present to consciousness on an everyday basis. It is the level at which we seek and find explanations for phenomena so that we can solve our practical problems, work, help those who are in need, and do the myriad of things that make up our daily lives. The notion of happiness as a fulfilment of our desires (as opposed to the notion of *eudaimonia* as a fulfilment of our whole being as persons) would be a third-level concept.[40] The values that operate at the third level of our being are prudential values as well as those extraneous values, such as efficiency and wealth, which society might urge upon us and which a given agent might adopt for prudential reasons.

---

[38] Jean-Paul Sartre, *Sketch for a Theory of the Emotions*, trans. Philip Mairet (London, 1962).

[39] Jürgen Habermas, *Knowledge and Human Interests*, trans. J.J. Shapiro (London, 1972). Habermas identifies a technological interest in the control of nature, a communicative interest in mutual understanding, and an emancipatory interest in overcoming material and social forces that prevent us from fulfilling our being. These interests are not present to consciousness while they operate to constitute knowledge.

[40] From which it would follow that utilitarianism is a third-level moral theory and therefore inadequate to the fulness of human existence.

The fourth level of subjectivity is the most distinctive and the most frequently neglected. It is the level at which our primordial need to find meaning in our lives is expressed in beliefs and commitments which are central to our integrity and our sense of ourselves. Our religious faiths, our moral principles, our search for pure knowledge, and our aesthetic values are just some of the cultural constructs that arise from, and structure, this level of our being. It is at this level that we express our commitments and at which we invest ourselves in that which gives significance to our lives – something that was most frequently done collectively through a shared culture in traditional societies, rather than individually as in modern societies such as ours. It is at this level that we can find our lives worthwhile and establish the values to which we find ourselves committed or to which we commit ourselves explicitly, and which it would jeopardize our integrity to flout. As such, these are values that are intrinsic to us, not in the sense that they represent our 'designed-for' purposes, but in the new and richer sense that we fully 'own' these values and invest ourselves in them.

Because it is our own integrity and sense of ourselves that is achieved by subjectivity at this level, there will be no psychological room for doubt and scepticism about the concepts and ideas that belong to this level. Concepts that operate at this level will be thought of as objective and as having an air of ultimacy attached to them. Plato's Theory of Forms was only the first in a long line of conceptualizations to posit objective, universal and eternal realities as a counterpart to this level of our being. In the same way, believers in God think of Him as objectively real, and believers in morality think of its tenets as objectively binding.[41]

A full and rich human life will involve an integration and consonance of all four of these levels of our subjectivity so that whatever we do or experience will have some positive significance at all four levels. A simple act like eating will have organismic significance at level one, will satisfy desires at level two, will be the solution of a needs-based or scheduling problem at level three, and very often will have the significance of a social ritual that cements loves, friendships or social relationships at level four. All these levels give eating its intrinsic value. Again, whereas the world will be a functional environment for us at level one of our being, and will appear intelligible and fascinating to us at level two, and useful to us at level three, it appears as having importance and value at level four. The hidden and inchoate proto-values which arise from the lower levels of the model will provide the impetus and motivational power of the values which are thematized at higher levels.

Despite my talk of levels, this model of subjectivity is not hierarchical. There is no suggestion that the level at which the significance of our lives is established is more valuable or more important than the organic level. After all, it is clear that

---

[41]   See Immanuel Kant, *Religion within the Limits of Reason Alone*, trans. Theodore M Greene and Hoyt H. Hudson (New York, 1934), for a rigorous example of this kind of thinking.

our functioning as an organism is a prerequisite for subjectivity at the other levels. We are not angels. Neither are we mere animals content with nothing more than the satisfaction of our desires, or *Homo Economicus* or *Homo Faber* content with nothing more than the successful completion of our projects. We need meaning in our lives. The model is holistic because the meaningfulness of our lives depends upon the integration of the four levels of subjectivity that I have identified. A person's values should be an integrated set arising from all four levels of subjectivity, and the good of a person is constituted by the fulfilment of her subjectivity at all four levels of her being.

This model of subjectivity can provide the basis for the notion of human good, and thus harm, which Reznek needs, for the teleological structure which both Boorse and Fulford require for the concept of disease, and for the notion of intrinsic values which I have argued is needed to understand disease adequately. This model overcomes the dualism suggested by attributing value to functional doing on the basis of a biological teleology and then to intentional doing on the basis of self-imposed goals. On this model, an agent's ideals, practical goals, comforts and successful bodily functionings are all equally intrinsic values. Indeed, insofar as these values are interdependent, they constitute a single holistic intrinsic value. How might this help us understand the disvalue of disease?

The model applied

The concept of disease and its cognate concepts might be mapped onto my model of subjectivity in a fairly straightforward way. If we regard disease as a bodily condition or invasion, then we would be apt to put it on level one. Organic dysfunctions occur at this level. It may be that our good at level one is our biological survival. Then again, it may be that, as individual organisms, we have no good of our own at level one. Perhaps at this level there is only evolutionary good. At this level, dysfunction may well just be failure to propagate our genes. If this were true, dysfunction would be an objective notion in Boorse's sense. But it is an error to separate out one level of human subjectivity from the rest. Take Reznek's example of a physiologically grounded failure of orgasm. This is hardly likely to be experienced just and only as a biological dysfunction. Indeed, the harm that is suffered in this case has no organismic significance at all.

The notion of illness would seem to belong on level two. Illness is an affective state because it is an alteration in the way that the body operates such that its ability to act in certain ways is frustrated. This is experienced only after it has had an impact upon how the organism reacts to, and moves within, its world. The inability to do certain things which marks illness in Fulford's account is a pre-conscious state. Although we, as conscious beings, can be aware of it and can respond in deliberate ways to it at level three, our state of well-being is already affected and our feelings and emotions are already elicited. In illness we present ourselves to ourselves in a different way. Whereas in health our awareness flows through our body, as it were, without hindrance and on to the things and people in the world with which we are practically concerned,[42] in illness, the flow of our agency is interrupted and hindered, if not stopped altogether, by our bodily condition.[43] This produces immediate reactions that structure our state of being. Among these will be suffering, discomfort, and the pursuit of compensatory means of acting. Pain will also be a direct bodily response to lesions of many kinds which structures our affective being. As self-conscious beings, we will be aware of many of these responses as a complex of feelings and emotions.

At the third level of our being we will respond to this suffering by deciding what to do. We may ignore it, we may self-medicate or rest if we think the problem is not too serious, or we may seek medical help. With any of these responses we enter onto the third level of our being where our illness has become a practical problem for us such that we engage in illness behaviour. In the broader social context, this is the level at which we make provision for health care, establish hospitals and clinics, and develop the professions of medicine, nursing and other forms of therapeutic practice. It is at this level too that Talcott Parsons's notion of the sick role belongs, since this is defined as a functional social role which emerges as a practical response to the disablement for everyday tasks which illness (or injury) brings.

Among the prudential values that operate at this third level of our subjectivity are those relating to health and illness. As Joseph Margolis puts it:

> Human beings, viewed in a sense that is relatively neutral to their condition as animals or persons, subscribe to a characteristic set of (what may be called) prudential values – avoidance of death, prolongation of life, restriction of pain, gratification of desires, insuring security of person and body and property and associates, and the like.[44]

Medicine is a means for managing some of these prudential interests and, as such, it belongs at the third level of our being. Moreover, this level is where I locate what I have called extraneous values of illness and disease. There may be a prudential reason (like avoiding military service) for valuing being in a sick-role, but this does not mean that the illness is intrinsically valuable. In this example, the possibility of differing extraneous prudential evaluations pertains to the sick-role, not to the presence of disease. Nevertheless, this distinction between prudential evaluation and intrinsic worth is what allows us to explain why Boorse could say that the concept of disease is intrinsically value-free. Taken just as a level-three

---

[42] The way in which the body 'disappears' in ordinary life and re-emerges as a problem in illness is described by Leder.

[43] A graphic description of this is given by Kay Toombs, 'The Body in Multiple Sclerosis: A Patient's Perspective', in Drew Leder (ed.), *The Body in Medical Thought and Practice* (Dordrecht, 1992), pp. 127–37.

[44] Joseph Margolis, 'The Concept of Disease', in Caplan, Englehardt and McCartney, pp. 561–77, p. 574.

phenomenon, disease and its consequences might indeed attract differing kinds of prudential evaluation in differing circumstances. However, this says nothing about the intrinsic value or disvalue of disease for a human subject taken as a whole.

But whereas it may seem illuminating to map disease, illness and the sick role onto the first three levels of my model of subjectivity in this way, does this mapping do justice to the concept of disease and to the phenomenon of human subjectivity? It seems to leave us with two problems. First, because it makes the concept of disease seem fundamental (insofar as our bodily existence is fundamental to our subjectivity), it is at variance with Fulford's point that illness is the more fundamental concept in the set. Second, it seems to leave no role for the fourth level of our being even though it is precisely this level which grounds the intrinsic nature of the values by which we live. Without this level we would have intrinsic values at levels one and two and extraneous values at level three. But this would leave a human subject without an integration of values and without a sense that life was worthwhile. It follows that the notion of disease needs to obtain its negative value through its connection with my holistic notion of the human good.[45] In order for its disvalue to be intrinsic to it, it needs to be analysed in a way that includes the fourth level of our subjectivity.

I would suggest, therefore, a new way of mapping the relevant concepts onto my model of subjectivity. I propose that the concept that belongs with the organic level of our subjectivity is that of 'pathological condition'. This concept will include those of injury and wound as well as disease, although this need not concern us. The key point about this concept is that it designates a condition of the body that is counter to the proper functioning of the body. It is, in short, the concept of dysfunction on which Boorse places so much stress. If Boorse thinks that this concept is value-free, it is simply because it is so impoverished. It relates to only one level of human subjectivity. Yet, against Boorse, I would now say that, while it may be a value-free concept when applied to plants, it is not when applied to human beings, since human beings have intrinsic goals by virtue of their subjectivity, even at the organismic level. Incidentally, another way in which the concept of dysfunction is impoverished in the context of caring for patients, is that it is typically used to refer to bodily parts. It is the heart, or the liver, or a limb which is said to be in a pathological condition rather than the body as a whole. In scientific settings the word 'disease' may be appropriately used for pathological conditions or agents, but in clinical settings the word is not rich enough.

I would leave illness and the sick role on levels two and three respectively so as to explain what Fulford is saying when he argues that 'illness' is the more

---

[45] As Reznek puts it, 'I have argued that causing a biological malfunction is neither necessary nor sufficient for being a disease (or pathological). It is not necessary because interference with some non-functional systems count as diseases. It is not sufficient because interference with self-destruct systems with functions do not count as diseases. What explains why these are counterexamples is that these process either have or lack a connection to harm' (*The Nature of Disease*, p. 155).

fundamental concept of the set. There is something important going on when our immediate reactions are deformed and curtailed by a pathological condition such that our ability to do what we normally can do is frustrated. The pathological condition issues in an affective reaction that flows onto the other levels of our being such that, at the third level, we display the reactions of a sick person as defined within our culture if the illness is of an appropriate kind (that is, sufficiently serious, debilitating, unusual or threatening to others). We refer to the whole organism as suffering an illness, rather than just an organ within the organism. Indeed, for Fulford, it is important that the notion of illness is applied to persons rather than just to organisms, because for him, the concept is used to report the action failure that a person is aware of themselves as experiencing. In this way, the notion of illness spills over onto the third, self-conscious and pragmatic level of our subjectivity.

I would further suggest that, rather than belonging on level one of my model, the concept of disease takes a distinctive connotation from the fourth level of our being. Disease is typically thought of as an evil. What I mean by this is that it is an experience or presence (either actual or potential) in a person's life which that person needs to assimilate into a structure of meaning and which is understood by our culture, not just as a harm, but as an evil. Most cultures think of disease as an attack upon the bodily or personal well-being of a person which is to be feared and hated, which approaches us mysteriously, and which has the potential to cause suffering and death. It can come from outside of the person, or it can originate within. It can be a curse imposed by enemies, a punishment from the gods,[46] or it can be a deliverance of fate. In each of these conceptions, the meaning that is given to disease derives from a faith or a cosmology which is the form that the ultimate commitments of subjectivity are given in those cultures.

A clue to what is being said here is provided by Reznek, who argues that we have retained the disease concept, despite a reductionist tendency driven by science that would favour the concept of a pathological condition, because of an ancient tradition in which disease was associated with mystery. A disease – as opposed to an injury – was something the cause of which was not obvious.[47] As such it was apt to be understood holistically rather than physiologically in terms of strange and malevolent powers beyond our knowledge. Disease (unlike injuries, which were treated as bodily problems to be solved with bandages and the like) was an event that called for the intervention of priests, shamans or witch doctors.[48]

---

[46] Loretta Kopelman gives a modern, secular critique of such views in 'The Punishment Concept of Disease', in Christine Pierce and Donald VanDeVeer (eds), *Aids: Ethics and Public Policy* (Belmont, California, 1988), pp. 49–55.

[47] Reznek, *The Nature of Disease,* p. 77. Support for this idea is also found in E.J.M. Campbell, J.G. Scadding and R.S. Roberts, 'The Concept of Disease', *British Medical Journal*, 29 (September 1979): 757–62.

[48] Horacio Fabrega Jr, speaks of a phenomenological framework for describing disease: 'The defining characteristics of a disease formulated within this framework would

For me, this signals that we are talking about a level-four event: an event or process that is to be structured by subjectivity as part of the complex of ideas that expresses our pursuit of meaning.

As reported by medical anthropologist G. Lewis,[49] the Gnau people of Papua New Guinea think of disease not as instances of a general type of ailment which might strike anyone, but as personal, unique and individual events that occur to them in response to some event which is a part of their own personal history. He describes a case of a person with a bad headache who attributed this to the cutting down of a tree that had significance in the kin structure of his tribe. In another case, a woman fell ill (without there seeming to be a physiological cause) and attributed the illness to arguing with relatives. In cases such as these, not only the significance of disease, but its very identification is tied to the meaning that the episode has in the context of the victim's life and relationships. However, not all meaning-conferring constructions of disease refer to taboos, magic, supernatural agencies or powers. For example, L. Hammer argues that:

Chinese medicine views illness as an expression of the personal violation of a person's own nature and calls upon the person to become aware of how he or she is interfering with the flow of nature, both within and without.[50]

It might be objected that such examples are not relevant to our modern Western understanding of the notion of disease. For us, science has displaced such apparent superstitions. But it should not be thought that modern scientific thinking has countered the tendency to think of disease in these ways. After all, we are subjects in the same way that pre-literate people were subjects, and we have the same need to give meaning to our lives and to the things that happen to us. Although a great many people no longer believe in curses, divine punishments or the benevolent influence of providence (though there are still many who do), the question 'Why me?' still resounds in wards and sick rooms. This question, whether or not it receives a coherent answer in these secular times, expresses subjectivity's need to find meaning in what happens to it. Disease is still experienced by most people as

---

include changes in the *states-of-being* (for example, feeling, thought, self-definition, impulses, etc.) which are (*a*) seen as discontinuous with everyday affairs, and (*b*) believed to be caused by socioculturally defined agents or circumstances' (p. 505). Folk beliefs and symbol systems would structure these beliefs, for example, disease as punishment. Again, these beliefs will ground a distinction between defining characteristics of disease (it is a punishment) and its indicators (the symptoms). But Fabrega seems to confine this analysis largely to pre-literate societies. My claim is that it should also apply to our own societies.

[49]   G. Lewis, 'Some Studies of Social Causes of and Cultural Response to Disease', in C.G.N. Mascie-Taylor (ed.), *The Anthropology of Disease* (Oxford, 1993), p. 104. For other interesting examples, see Kathryn V. Staiano, *Interpreting Signs of Illness: A Case Study in Medical Semiotics* (Berlin, 1986).

[50]   Leon Hammer, *Dragon Rises, Red Bird Flies: Psychology, Energy & Chinese Medicine* (New York, 1990), p. 389.

an undeserved affliction challenging their sense of justice,[51] and justice is a level-four concept. As well, it seems to be a threat to our faith in the progress of science in that it is a personal disaster that modernity has not been able to prevent, and our faith in science belongs on the fourth level of our subjectivity. Moreover, even in modern English, the word 'disease' continues to carry connotations of rottenness and corruption, which are concepts with a deeper resonance than is found in the practicalities of everyday life.

It follows that the concept of disease is a bearer of meaning that is richer than that of a bodily pathological condition, illness as reaction to action failure, or the sick role as practical social construct. It is the stuff of metaphor and myth. The essays of Susan Sontag on cancer and AIDS bear witness to this.[52] She argues that diseases of these kinds (where once again, significantly, the causes are not well understood) play a cultural role continuous with the notions of demonic possession and sin, as well as those of ennobling affliction and victimhood. These are ways of structuring the experience of disease (especially fatal and wasting disease) so as to give it meaning. As Sontag puts it:

> TB was a disease in the service of a romantic view of the world. Cancer is now in the service of a simplistic view of the world that can turn paranoid. ... For the more sophisticated, cancer signifies the rebellion of the injured ecosphere: nature taking revenge on the wicked technocratic world.[53]

Leaving aside the details of her thesis, it is clear that this quote is redolent with the sort of language which bespeaks the fourth level of our subjectivity. Crucially, what Sontag highlights, in contrast to understanding diseases in terms of their specific physiological causes (which would be level one thinking), is an attempt to attribute blame for their occurrence in the lifestyle of the victim, the levels of daily stress imposed by social arrangements, or in the environmental conditions which obtain. But this attempt to apportion blame is an attempt to give meaning to the disease. It is an attempt to answer the question 'Why me?' and to place it into a context of cosmic justice. This means that disease is a disvalue that belongs at the fourth level of our subjectivity. It is not just that our third-level goals are frustrated

---

[51]   Richard M. Zaner, in 'Chance and Morality: The Dialysis Phenomenon', in Victor Kestenbaum (ed.), *The Humanity of the Ill: Phenomenological Perspectives* (Knoxville, Tennessee, 1982), pp. 38–68, has argued that this undeserved nature of affliction is the basis of the moral imperative to assist those who suffer from disease.

[52]   Susan Sontag, *Illness as Metaphor* (New York, 1978), and *Aids and its Metaphors* (New York, 1989).

[53]   Sontag, *Illness as Metaphor,* p. 73. Horacio Fabrega Jr makes the following point on page 139 of his 'The Scientific Usefulness of the Idea of Illness', in Caplan, Englehardt and McCartney, pp. 131–42: 'The formal theory of illness of a group, together with folk understanding, gives a distinctive ideological cast to what can be termed the group's medical care system.'

by action failure, but also that a threatening, disempowering and evil fourth-level reality has entered into our lives.

At the fourth level of our being, health and disease are contraries. Health is a good which we all strive for as an ideal and attribute to ourselves as part of our meaning-conferring construct of self-identity (even, sometimes, when we are suffering disability or disease),[54] while disease is an evil which we need to accommodate ourselves to while preserving a sense that our lives are worthwhile. The ideal of health can be manifest as a cult of vitality celebrated in art and sport, while the sense of evil that attaches to disease is manifest in the preventative significance given to practices of hygiene and in the isolation of its victims in sterile institutions (although the latter practice has pragmatic import as well). The representation of disease in art and literature that Sontag and others have explored provides evidence of this. There is very little poetry in pathological conditions, but disease can be a subject for art because it is a concept to which connotations of human significance readily attach. The notions of defilement, corruption, deformity and suffering are notions with an aura of significance that more clinical categories do not have. The fact that our relation to disease is normally one of fear and loathing does not negate this point. After all, we define ourselves not only by what we love and commit ourselves to, but also by what we contrast ourselves with as our 'Other'. At the fourth level of our being, disease is part of that which is alien to us and defines our being by difference from it. Health is that which we absorb into our ideal being, while disease is that which is foreign to our ideal being. This explains the significance of both Reznek's point that the concept is retained in order to designate illnesses with mysterious causes and also the lasting attraction of an ontological concept of disease as an invader of the body.

What is needed to apply these insights to our own modern situation is an exploration of the kind of myths and metaphors that are available in a multicultural secular society such as ours to enable people to make sense of their diseased condition. Such an exploration will be empirical in the way that sociology and anthropology are empirical. That is, it will require empathy with, and *Verstehen* of, the meaning-giving life beliefs of others. It is likely that such an exploration will disclose that, for many people, the concept of disease will take on meaning-giving power from the religious faiths that those people have. The notions of providence and the will of a benevolent God will provide many victims with the basis for maintaining the meaning and worth of their lives. For others, in a modern 'disenchanted' culture such as ours, the meaning of disease will arise from its association with science. Insofar as the concept is used in the context of the biomedical model it will acquire its aura and its connotations from that model. The germ theory of disease, amplified in terms of bacteria and viruses, and the notion

---

[54] Calnan, p. 139, gives the following quote from an interview:

Q: How has your health been over the last few years?

A: ... apart from the fact that I am a disabled person, and apart from my aches due to an accident, it is excellent.

of medical science as the designer of magic bullets to destroy these invaders can become an icon in the faith of modern secular humanity.

Ironically, understanding disease as a bodily dysfunction on analogy with a dysfunctional machine is precisely the kind of metaphor which would be needed to understand disease in secular terms, rather than as a punishment, or a curse, or an expression of the will of God. Perhaps the impetus behind Boorse's insistence that the concept of disease is value-free is that only such a concept escapes the false comforts of a mythical conception. A thoroughly modern secularism loves fate. It believes that things can go wrong and that material processes are subject to failure and breakdown. This love of fate would be a Stoic determination to go with the flow of nature and to accept whatever it delivers.[55] This meaning may be austere, but it can be comforting in the way that a sense of tragedy is comforting. Like bushfires, earthquakes, the sinking of ships and other accidents, disease is just something that happens. And it is to be accepted honestly and bravely when it does happen. Attributing it to non-natural powers would be, for this attitude, a form of escapism. However, even if this were what Boorse was getting at, it would still be the case that the concept of disease which carries this connotation of accepted tragedy would be a construct of subjectivity designed to give meaning and worth to the life of the victim. Along with the various religious frameworks that are available in our culture for giving such tragedies as disease a meaning in human life, there is the secular faith that disease is just something that happens and that we must make the best of. Like any faith, this allows us to affirm the event, to own it, and to not blame anyone or anything else for it. On this view the question 'Why me?' has no answer. Accepting this is also a meaning-giving faith expressing our subjectivity at the fourth level of our being.

It might be objected that my thesis seems to leave the concept of disease hopelessly subjective and relative to mythical and metaphorical construction. Health workers need an objective concept. The burden of Susan Sontag's essays was to show the harmfulness of the metaphors that are applied to diseases such as cancer, syphilis, AIDS and others; for example, in the way the metaphors of plague and scourge allow blame to be attached to the victims.

Now it is true that, in diagnostic and treatment settings, disease concepts will assimilate themselves to descriptions of bodily pathological conditions so as to have the kind of objectivity needed for scientific practice, whereas at the fourth level the connotations of the concept of disease might seem subjective and relativistic. However, I have argued that the faith and commitment concepts which

---

[55]   Epictetus said the following: 'Ask not what events should happen as you will, but let your will be that events should happen as they do, and you shall have peace.' And he follows this aphorism immediately with: 'Sickness is a hindrance to the body, but not to the will, unless the will consent. Lameness is a hindrance to the leg, but not to the will. Say this to yourself at each event that happens, for you shall find that though it hinders something else it will not hinder you.' Paragraphs 8 and 9 of 'The Manual of Epictetus', in J.L. Saunders (ed.), *Greek and Roman Philosophy after Aristotle* (New York, 1966), p. 135.

subjectivity develops will seem objective to it. Disease will be understood as objective even at the level of meaning. The believer in myth sees himself really affected by the curse of another, and the HIV-positive person might see himself as really a victim of a plague. Disease may be a myth, but that will be a form given to its experienced reality.

However, the objector will not be satisfied with this answer since it merely restates the problem in more acute terms. A further answer that I could give is that no matter how much the cultural constructs that shape the meaning of disease are challenged and undermined, subjectivity will seek some new construct. The key point is that disease is always going to be the sort of thing to which metaphorical and mythical meanings can attach themselves. This shows that it is a fourth-level phenomenon. The meanings that it is given can be altered, and many of them ought to be, but the crucial point is that some meaning or other must be given to it. Disease is not experienced just as a pathological condition, as illness, or as the sick role.

Implications

The implications of this for health care are clear. A health care worker when confronted with a diseased patient is not confronted just with a body with a pathological condition, a being whose reactions are curtailed, or a person whose social and practical life is in turmoil. These descriptions are all true of the patient, but they are not complete. The crucial point is that the patient is one the meaning of whose life has changed. The patient's subjectivity is not just frustrated and redirected into a new social role: namely, that of being a patient. The patient's subjectivity suffers a diseased embodiment. Her life must and will achieve a new integration by the application of a disease concept that will give meaning to her new existence. It is not true that this will be a purely descriptive concept. It is true but shallow to say that this will be a valuational concept. It is a concept of deep value or, in my sense, a concept that belongs to the fourth level of our subjectivity; a concept that shapes our commitment to life itself. Even without knowledge of what patients might believe in particular cases, this clearly implies that health care workers need to understand the concept of disease as a form available to give expression to the subjectivity of patients when under threat from something alien, rather than as the name of a class of pathological conditions or illnesses of which the only implication is the nature of the prognosis and treatment that should be given.

That the concept of disease is a value-laden concept constituted by the fourth level of our subjectivity has immediate moral implications for health care workers (and for others, such as the family of the patient). A diseased patient is one who calls upon our moral response in a direct way, through the shared understanding of the significance of their situation (which differs from that of an injured patient). It is not enough to say with Arthur Caplan, 'Choosing to call a set of phenomena a disease involves a commitment to medical intervention, the assignment of the sick role, and the enlistment in action of health professionals.'[56] There is more: namely, the acknowledgement that patients now have or need a new structure of meaning for their lives, at least for the time being. The sick role by itself does not provide this meaning because, through the experience of action failure and loss of control over their own lives, it militates against finding their lives worthwhile.

What is the form of the ethical response which health professionals are called upon to make? I have already indicated in the first section of this chapter that sensitivity is the first requirement. Knowing that disease is not just a bodily pathological condition, but also a new structure of meaning in the life of the patient, is the key to avoiding the dehumanizing effect often attributed to the routinized application of the biomedical model. Treating the patient as a person involves being aware of each of the four levels of subjectivity that constitute that personhood. As well, health care workers need to acknowledge the role that the concept of disease plays in their own lives. The notion of professional commitment includes that of an understanding of the central ideals and values in a professional life. Insofar as health care work involves a commitment to the promotion and restoration of health and to the eradication of disease and relief of its symptoms, health care workers ought to have a deep understanding of the values involved. This will ground not only their caring for patients, but their own sense of worth and dedication to the everyday tasks that belong to their profession.

---

[56]   Caplan, Englehardt and McCartney, p. 41

Chapter 10

Suffering and the Goals of Medicine

In its issue of November–December 1996, the Hastings Center Report published a special supplement setting out the findings of an international consultative group into the goals of medicine. Faced with new pressures including those arising from new technologies, the needs of developing nations and ageing populations, it was felt that the basic objectives of medicine needed to be rethought. After months of painstaking consultations and discussions, the four goals that were identified by the group were:

1. the prevention of disease and injury and the promotion and maintenance of health
2. the relief of pain and suffering caused by maladies
3. the cure and care of those with a malady, and the care of those who cannot be cured
4. the avoidance of premature death and the pursuit of a peaceful death.[1]

The second goal identified by the Hastings Center mentions both pain and suffering. It distinguishes them as follows:

> Pain refers to extreme physical distress and comes in many varieties: throbbing, piercing, burning. Suffering, by contrast, refers to a state of psychological burden or oppression, typically marked by fear, dread, or anxiety.[2]

And the authors go on to point out that pain and suffering are not always associated; we can experience pain without suffering, and we can suffer without feeling pain. We might have a toothache but not be distressed or disturbed by it, especially if we understand its origin and have a plan for dealing with it, or we can be suffering from mental distress or anxiety related to illness without actually experiencing pain. The authors go on to castigate the medical profession for often failing to take seriously the psychological suffering and anxiety that can accompany disease and which can, indeed, be present even when disease is not. But the research group was not of one mind as to the extent to which medicine should pursue the relief of suffering. It recognized that suffering can be related to such 'spiritual or philosophical'[3] questions as the meaning which the patient

---

[1] Daniel Callahan et al., *The Goals of Medicine: Setting New Priorities,* Special Supplement to *The Hastings Center Report,* (November–December 1996): S9–S13.

[2] Ibid., p. S11

[3] Ibid., p. S12

attributes to their pain and illness. But it urged doctors to exercise empathy and sensitivity as one human being in the presence of another in dealing with such suffering. While palliation can be offered for pain, in the presence of psychological suffering, medicine as such would seem to have reached a limit.

This is wise counsel, but it does raise the philosophical problem of dualism. Pain is understood to be associated with physiological insult, while suffering is the mental distress occasioned by this pain. This distinction between pain and suffering corresponds to the distinction between body and mind which has been challenged in recent times on the ground that it discourages a holistic conception of the patient and encourages clinicians to think of the body in reductive terms. The so-called biomedical model is dualistic in that it focuses on the body conceived of just as a physiological system and isolates it from the psychological distress of the patient (and thereby threatens to ignore the latter). Eric Cassell has argued that medicine falls short of its mission when it focuses just on pain conceived of physiologically while neglecting the suffering which the patient is undergoing.[4] This contrasts with the Hastings Center document's reticence as to how far medicine should go in addressing the problem of suffering. Could it be that this disagreement arises from making the pain/suffering distinction in the first place and of seeing suffering in purely psychological terms?

In this chapter, my hypothesis is that suffering is the more fundamental concept of the two, and that pain is one of several possible forms of suffering. I will also argue that malady is a form of suffering and that being sick is a form of suffering. I will then argue that, understood in this way, it becomes self-evident that the relief of suffering should be one of the goals of medicine. However, I will qualify this thesis by arguing that not all kinds of suffering should be the explicit object of medical interventions. In order to argue my case I will need to challenge the way that pain and suffering are often distinguished.

The conventional view of suffering

A great deal of contemporary discussion of pain and suffering is inherently dualistic. It distinguishes pain from suffering by saying that pain is a bodily sensation while suffering is a psychological reaction to such pain. On the face of it this seems to parallel the distinction between body and mind and to suggest that pain belongs to the body while suffering belongs to the mind. However, I think it would be naïve to see the matter in this way. First, it is clear that, even if we see pain as a bodily phenomenon, it would need to be experienced. This would make it in some sense mental. It is a hurtful sensation and, as such, it is an experience with a negative psychological quality. It is not just a bodily event. Again, suffering is often manifested in physiological ways. Listlessness, fatigue, various physical

---

[4]   Eric J. Cassell 'The Nature of Suffering', in *The Nature of Suffering and the Goals of Medicine* (New York, 1991), pp. 30–47.

manifestations of stress, as well as an increased vulnerability to certain diseases can come in its wake, as has been shown by the emerging discipline of psychoneuroimmunology.[5] It follows that suffering is bodily in some sense. However, these are only preliminary remarks to show how difficult it is to theorize this matter adequately if we maintain a dualistic framework of thinking.

There is a widely quoted definition of suffering offered by Eric Cassell. On the grounds that the two can occur separately from each other, he says that suffering is distinct from pain, and goes on say that 'suffering is the state of distress induced by the threat of the loss of intactness or the disintegration of personhood – bodies do not suffer, persons do'.[6] One virtue of this definition is that it locates suffering in the person. The concept of 'person' advances our discussion in that it is a non-dualistic concept. By attributing suffering to the person, Cassell invites us to think holistically and with reference to the relationships that a person maintains with others, with the world and with society. But a striking feature of this definition is its cognitive nature. In order to suffer, according to this definition, persons have to apprehend a threat to their personhood. This implies that suffering depends upon a cognitive grasp of the threat which the person is subject to. Even if we allow that a fear of such a threat or an anxiety that it may exist (when it is not yet established whether it actually does) might be included in this definition, it is still clear that suffering depends on a form of cognition. It involves an anticipation of the future and the foreshadowed loss of the central relationships and experiences that give a person's life its meaning. In contrast, I want to suggest that this is only one aspect of suffering, and that suffering can include rather more innate or inarticulate elements.

We can call Cassell's view into question by noting that on his definition no being that is incapable of cognition would be able to suffer. Animals that could not anticipate their own futures and cognitively apprehend threats to their integrity or survival would not suffer. They could, of course, feel pain, but they would not suffer since they lacked the higher cognitive functions in which suffering is based. Now, there is a tradition of thought (once again stemming from Descartes, just as dualism did) that would espouse this view. But it is denied by our ordinary usage of the verb 'to suffer', and it could justify callousness in the face of the suffering of animals. Cassell's contribution to this discussion has been profound and important, but it lacks a sound basis in philosophical anthropology. He fails to give us an account of what 'personal intactness' is.

In this chapter I want to argue that suffering is not just an epiphenomenon that supervenes on pain, and nor is it a cognitive reaction to such pain. Rather, it is a comportment or mode of being which colours the entire being of the person in pain

---

[5]   David Michael Levin and George F. Solomon, 'The discursive formation of the body in the history of medicine', *Journal of Medicine and Philosophy*, 15 (1990): 515–37.

[6]   Eric J. Cassell, 'The Nature of Suffering: Physical, Psychological, Social, and Spiritual Aspects', in Patricia L. Starck and John P. McGovern (eds), *The Hidden Dimension of Illness: Human Suffering* (New York, 1992), p. 3.

including the pain itself. The pain of a person that does not suffer may not be physiologically different from the pain of the person who does suffer, and yet the quality of that pain for the person will be different in either case. In what does this difference consist? In the fear or apprehension of the disease that is causing the pain, in the distress at the unbearable intensity of the pain, or in the sorrow at the loss of former life possibilities and relationships that the pain and the malady that is causing it are bringing to the sufferer? Or is it the anguish of knowing that our loved ones are in grief and distress at our pain? It can be any of these and more. No one of them should be taken, as it is by Cassell, as the defining feature. My thesis will be that suffering is not a phenomenon separable from pain. It is not a psychological effect of it, and it is not a cognitive grasp of its significance on the part of the sufferer.

An Aristotelian framework

In order to see this more clearly, we need to engage in some philosophical theorizing. Let us understand persons and their suffering along Aristotelian lines. Aristotle identified four 'parts of the soul' as making up a full human being. These were the vegetative, the appetitive, the deliberative and the contemplative.[7] While it may seem like an irrelevant exercise in classical scholarship to explore these concepts, I believe that much can be learnt from this description of the human person. Albeit for the simple reason that it describes four levels of human being, Aristotle's model is at least not dualistic.

More importantly, these levels of our being, or parts of our souls, are not separate substances as dualism would suggest. The best way to understand the relationship between these four aspects of our being is with an image. Imagine a large sphere made of white glass and with a hole in the bottom. Now imagine that a yellow light globe is inserted into the sphere and turned on. The glass of the sphere will now glow with a yellow light. Imagine further that a blue light globe is inserted into the sphere and turned on. The sphere will now glow with a green light. Third, a red light globe is inserted. The colour of the sphere will now be a muddy or brown sort of colour. Fourth, let us imagine a white globe being inserted and switched on. The colour of the sphere will now become lighter. Let this sphere represent a person, and let each of the four coloured globes represent the functioning of a 'part of the soul' or an aspect of that person's being. What emerges as life is lived is a new colour or mode of being as each part of the soul becomes operative. It is no longer possible to identify the functions of each level of our being separately, and their expressions are always combined into a whole. Moreover, this image shows us that the parts of the soul or functions of our being project themselves outwards into the world and form the dynamic wholeness of a

---

[7]   Aristotle, *Nicomachean Ethics*, 1102b4–1103a10, in Richard McKeon (ed.), *The Basic Works of Aristotle* (New York, 1941).

person as they do so. Each aspect of our being colours and modifies the whole. We create our own wholeness or self as we project ourselves into the world and into relationships with others. As we will see, our sense of the well-functioning of our bodies infuses our whole being, as do our desires, our practical tasks, and our ultimate commitments.

The vegetative level

The vegetative level of our existence is what we would describe today as the biological functioning of our bodies. It consists in those many processes of growth, metabolism, blood circulation and so forth that make up the dynamic of our bodily existence. None of this would be difficult for health care workers to understand. It is what Edmund Pellegrino and David Thomasma call the 'living body'.[8] The vegetative aspect of our being is the body as conceived by the biomedical model in health care. It is the body as machine. Do note, however, that while the body as machine was conceived by post-Cartesian modernism as an objectified and even dead body – a body without personality or subjectivity – Aristotle does not theorize the body in this abstracted way. His pre-modern terminology of 'parts of the soul' makes it clear that he is talking about an aspect of a whole. The soul is the whole, single and distinctive animating principle of the person, and to delineate a 'part' of it is not to identify an entity which constitutes a portion of a larger whole in the way that an engine is a part of a car – the part that makes it move. Rather, we should think of Aristotle as identifying different kinds of functioning that make up the whole living, active and thoughtful person. The vegetative 'part of the soul', or the living body, comprises those aspects of the dynamic existence of the human person which centrally involve her body. These aspects cannot be distinguished clearly or definitively from other aspects of human existence, even though, by virtue of the specializations that have emerged in human affairs – specializations such as medical science and health care, for example, as opposed to those of psychiatry or priesthood – we can focus on these aspects in various practical settings and for various practical purposes. In health care, the non-exclusive focus is often on the body understood as the vegetative aspect of a person's existence.

Aristotle's conception of various aspects of the human person is thoroughly teleological. This means not only that he understands the vegetative part of the soul as an aspect of the human person which is ontologically inextricable from the whole, but also as a mode of functioning of the person which aims at a specific goal. To illustrate this, we might say that the goal of the vegetative part of the soul is the survival of the organism or its systemic homeostasis at the physiological level.[9] Seeing the biological body as a dynamic and teleological system is not new,

---

[8] Edmund D. Pellegrino and David C. Thomasma, *A Philosophical Basis of Medical Practice: Toward a Philosophy and Ethics of the Healing Professions* (New York, 1981), p. 107.

[9] Lawrie Reznek, *The Nature of Disease* (London, 1987).

but it has been questioned by the modernist scientific paradigm of linear causal explanation in the light of necessary and sufficient conditions rather than final causes. For the purposes of this chapter we can leave aside the deep metaphysical questions that this raises about the nature of the causal processes that hold the universe together. It is enough to note that teleological thinking is a profoundly necessary heuristic form of thinking in the health sciences and in biology more generally. There could be no understanding of bodily existence without it. What this means in concrete terms is that we need to think of bodily processes as having a goal. The immune system, for example, can only be adequately understood if we see it as having as its purpose the defence of the body against viral invaders. Breathing can only be adequately understood as a system for providing the body with necessary oxygen. The skin can only be adequately understood as protecting the body against externally based insults, and so forth. Teleological or purposive thinking is inseparable from our understanding of the body or of the vegetative part of the soul.

But there is more to the notion of teleology than just that of being directed upon a purpose or goal. A simple implement would be teleological in this sense. Aristotle's notion is richer than this. It is a structural notion in that it understands things in terms of what would fulfil them. For Aristotle, all of the parts of the soul have a tendency or internal goal which is distinctive of them and which they seek to fulfil. To put it rather abstractly, this goal or *telos* is the perfection or excellence of our being given by the nature of the relevant part of the soul. To use a simple implement such as a knife as an example, we could see this as teleological in the sense of having an external goal in that it is made for the purpose of cutting things. But Aristotle's richer notion of an internal goal or *telos* would also apply to it, albeit metaphorically. This notion would suggest that it would achieve its own fulfilment only to the extent that it is sharp enough to cut things well. This is metaphorical in the case of the knife because we do not imagine a knife wanting to be sharp or taking pride in its achievement when it cuts well. But a living creature might. It can produce a kind of 'vital satisfaction' when the vegetative aspect of a person or animal fulfils its functions well, and it is this satisfaction which is the internal goal, as it were, of the organism. So if breathing is a function of the organism, then that organism gains a fulfilment or satisfaction from breathing well. This can be illustrated with reference to sport. What exactly is the satisfaction that sport can give us if not the excellent exercise of our vegetative functions? Of course, the excitement of competition or the usefulness of fitness should not be discounted, but they do not, I suggest, constitute the internal, inherent satisfaction or fulfilment of sporting activity.

The appetitive level

Aristotle's positing of an 'appetitive part of the soul' is based on the commonsense phenomenological observation that the human person desires things and strives to attain them. That we have appetites and desires is undeniable. But it is important to recognize that desires are not things that we *have*. They are not mental events which occur in our minds and that we can *own* in some sense. They are certainly not things that happen to us, albeit in the mental domain. They have no separate ontological status. Rather, they are a mode of our being. Our desires are what we are in the appetitive dimension of our being. It is in the nature of the kind of being that we enjoy to be desirous, to be directed upon things that we want and a future that we seek, to be striving for our own selfhood as well as for the objects of our inclination. As the existentialist philosophers have repeated often, we project ourselves into existence.

There is an epistemological dimension to desire. Following Merleau-Ponty, Pellegrino and Thomasma have identified an aspect of our being called a 'lived body' which gives corporeal form to the functions which Kant had attributed to what he called 'the transcendental subject': namely, constructing an intelligible world of appearance.[10] Rather than attribute this function to the mind as dualists in the Cartesian tradition would, phenomenologists attribute it to the body as a presence in the world. The lived body reaches out into the world so as to structure it into a meaningful reality for the subject. This meaning-making or reality-constituting function can never be completely reflected upon by the subject since it precedes all self-consciousness. However, we can know of it that it must be based in a desiring body since, without the appetitive dimension, it would not have the drive to project into the world and exercise its world-making function. This centrality of the appetitive body in the awareness of human subjects constitutes a substantive argument against any form of dualism or compartmentalizing of human persons. Our consciousness of the world is not just dependent upon the operation of our bodies' senses, but also upon the nature of our bodies as desiring organisms.

A different kind of evidence for the desirous aspect of our being is provided by the observation that we have desires and inclinations of which we might not be fully aware. This point is born out by psychoanalysis which identifies desires and drives which can lead us to do and feel things that we are not prepared to acknowledge to ourselves. In these cases we are at odds with ourselves, not just in conflict with parts of us that we can disown. But the kinds of troublesome and hidden desires that psychoanalysis has uncovered are not the only forces that are referred to at this level of our being. I have suggested elsewhere that our concern and sympathy for others and our existential quest for our own existence and integrity are forms of this desiring aspect of our being.[11] We are, at a deep and implicit level, concernful for our own being and for the being of others with whom we are in contact. Caring is part of our nature or an aspect of our souls. Further, in Chapter 8, I argued that the 'inchoate feeling that the living of life is enjoyment and nourishment is the pre-articulated experience of health. Health in this sense is when things go well with us in the conative mode of our subjectivity.' What this

---

[10]   Pellegrino and Thomasma, p. 73

[11]   Stan van Hooft, *Caring: An Essay in the Philosophy of Ethics* (Niwot, Colorado, 1995).

means is that the *telos* of the conative or appetitive aspect of our existence is the feeling of well-being and zest for living that we describe as health. More than the physical well-working of the body, health is the enjoyment of desire itself. These theses point to the richness and depth of that dimension of our being which Aristotle has called 'the appetitive part of the soul'.

The appetitive aspect of our being also allows us to understand emotion and feeling. Insofar as desire generates movement in our being towards cognition, action and reaction, there is a dynamic in our existence the flow of which is experienced as feeling. When this feeling is integrated with cognition, we experience emotions. Such emotions as fear, anger or embarrassment combine a cognitive grasp of the situation in which we find ourselves with an internally sensed urge to movement.[12] Were we not desiring beings, such reactions would not occur in us. Nor would they were we not whole and integrated beings. The cognitive dimension of existence needs to be present for all of this to be possible. Even a wild animal needs to apprehend the danger in its environment in some way in order to express its tendency towards survival by feeling fear and taking flight.

Notice that the desiring aspect of our being is fundamentally teleological. Indeed, it is almost definitive of what teleology means for Aristotle. To be desirous of something is the human or animal way of having a tendency towards a goal. Whether or not the desire is present to consciousness, it constitutes the orientation of the organism towards that which would meet its need or fulfil its tendency. But these would be external goals of the organism. The internal goal of desire or appetite might be understood in a non-intentional sense not as a desire for something outside of the organism such as a child's desire for ice cream, but as a comportment of the organism towards its own fulfilment. In order to distinguish this idea from the commonsense notion of desire where desire is always the intentional desire for some object, I use the technical term 'conation'. In this terminology, the conative aspect of our being – or appetitive part of the soul – is the tendency of the organism to seek its own fulfilment through the excellence of its desires. This fulfilment is not only the excellent pursuit of its desires, but also the having of desires which perfect its being. In this way a person who desires drugs of addiction would not fulfil the internal goal of her being whether or not she obtains what she desires because this is a self-destructive desire to have.

It is this which allows Aristotle to draw the ethical implication that we should desire well, and he understands this not in terms of the external objects of our desire, but in terms of such internal qualities as its intensity (it should not be too great or too little), and whether the desire is worthy of our nature as a human being. Our desires should be an expression of self-fulfilling inclinations and we should not be excessive or deficient in our desires. In a less moralistic tone, we might draw the conclusion that our having desires is part of what constitutes the richness and excitement of our lives. We can enjoy desiring. Moreover, if we situate our existential striving for our own being and our primordial caring for

---

[12]   William James, *The Principles of Psychology* (New York, 1918).

others at this pre-intentional level of our being, then it is clear that the excellent fulfilment of these functions is central to the value of our lives and to the attainment of meaning in our lives. We can return to the example of sport to illustrate this, but this time focus on the competitive aspect. We enjoy competing because we enjoy the self-assertion and self-validation which it brings. Competing in a sporting manner is a self-fulfilling and excellent exercise of the conative aspect of our being.

The deliberative level

The third part of the soul which Aristotle identifies is the deliberative. He thinks of this aspect of our being as distinctive of us as human beings and says that animals do not share in it. He has in mind our ability to think about what we do, to plan our actions, to be strategic in our approach to our needs and to review the effectiveness of what we have done. Rather than being driven by instincts or habits, human beings can be rational and reflective in their approach to the exigencies of life. Now, it is this aspect of our being that tempts us to dualistic ways of thinking. It is this aspect of our being that leads us to posit a 'faculty' called reason or a 'thinking substance' called mind. Aristotle makes no such mistake. He sees deliberation as just as much an aspect or level of our being as the vegetative and appetitive aspects. Deliberation or rational thinking is just one of the functions which whole persons perform and through which they can fulfil themselves in their being.

Admittedly it might be argued that a subject must already exist as a 'lived self' in order to deliberate. We must be self-conscious and be aware of our world, of our place in it and of our plans and intentions. There is a degree of cognitive grasp of ourselves and our situation that is a prerequisite for deliberation. But it would be a mistake to attribute this grasp to the possession on the part of the self of a 'mind'. Rather, as phenomenologists remind us, it is an extension of my lived body and a function of the self-reflective abilities of my bodily being. Once again, this shows that Aristotle could not have been thinking of a metaphysically distinguishable part of us when he spoke of the deliberative part of the soul. Insofar as deliberation requires our bodily presence in a lived world, this function of our being is an aspect of what we are as a whole.

Notice that the deliberative function is also teleological in the two ways that I have identified above. Aristotle says that our deliberation is about the means which we need to attain our goals. It is strategic. In this sense it is directed upon a goal. But it is also teleological in the sense that our doing it well constitutes for us a fulfilment of our being. Insofar as we are rational beings, we enjoy exercising our intellects. Once again, as with the case of sport, it is the non-purposive exercises of these functions that illustrate this. That we play chess and other mind games shows that we gain a satisfaction from the sheer exercise of our deliberative functions whether or not it is directed to some purpose external to us. This internal fulfilment is the inherent teleology of the deliberative aspect of our being.

The deliberative part of our being is inextricably linked to action. For Aristotle, it is distinctive of human beings that we act rationally. We engage in actions and practices which have goals, and our deliberation is our thinking about how those practical goals can be achieved. These goals are, once again, of two kinds. There are the more obvious external goals that are the ends we are pursuing in our actions, and there are the internal goals. These latter are the satisfactions that come from doing the job well. They are internal in the sense that they are experienced by the agent, more or less self-consciously, as feelings of attainment or of enjoyment in the exercise of the task. A craftsman relishing the sheer physical activity of working with his materials would be an example of this, although there are links here also with the conative aspects of our being in that this enjoyment arises from his feeling himself able to overcome difficulties. And there are links with the bodily aspect of our being in that this enjoyment is for him a form of physical well-being in rapport with his environment.

The contemplative level

The fourth part of the soul or aspect of our being which Aristotle identifies is what he calls the 'contemplative part'. He sees this as a further aspect of our reasoning but it is distinguished from the deliberative part in terms of what it is about: that is, in terms of its objects. Whereas deliberative reason is about the means that we need to achieve our goals and about the things we can change in the world by our actions, contemplative reason is about the things we cannot change. What Aristotle has in mind here includes the goals and values that we strive after (which he takes to be given by our human nature), the laws of physical nature that order the way the world works, and the nature and will of the gods. In brief, Aristotle suggests that the contemplative aspect of our being is detached from our active lives and is fulfilled by thinking about eternal and changeless things. Modern examples of such thinking would include theoretical physics and mathematics, philosophy and theology. I think of it as a form of theoretical thinking which has as its external goal the understanding of the universe and of our existence in it, and which has as its internal satisfaction and fulfilment the creation of a sense of wholeness and meaningfulness in our lives. We are interested in such big questions as the origin and nature of the universe, the source and meaning of morality, the existence or non-existence of God, and the significance of beauty and truth in our lives, because thinking about such things (whether or not we obtain answers) is part of what makes our lives meaningful. Moreover, having a theory about such things (whether we acquire it from our cultures or by our own efforts) gives our lives an integrity or structure in which day-to-day events can gain their meaning as part of an overarching whole. It allows us to feel that we are part of a larger story or reality.

The fulfilment of this aspect of our being does not necessarily consist in gaining answers to our theoretical questions which are ultimately true. As Nietzsche has assured us, we need answers to live, but they will always be perspectives of our own devising.[13] Rather, the fulfilment of this aspect of our being consists in contemplating well. This means being honest with ourselves and being consistent. It means not clinging to false hopes or merely comforting theories if they are inconsistent with our other beliefs. It means having faith that is not superstition. And it means being able to affirm life with our most spiritual intellect as well as our deepest emotion.

The mention of the contemplative and appetitive parts of the soul together in that last sentence serves to highlight a point that I think the Western philosophical tradition has neglected. I think it is fair to say that the tradition of Western philosophy has focused on the vegetative and deliberative parts of the soul, has mapped them onto the distinction between body and mind, and has thus produced, along with the error of dualism, the error of neglecting that emotional part of us which desires and that spiritual part of us which thinks about eternal things. And I also suspect that these aspects of our being are more closely related than many have realized.

A new view of suffering

How does all this help us to understand suffering? My hypothesis is that suffering is the opposite of what Aristotle called *eudaimonia* and which his English translators have rendered as 'happiness'. In Aristotle, happiness can be understood as the fulfilment of the *telos* or inherent goals of human existence. Happiness in this sense is achieved at all four levels of our existence. To be healthy, to be competitive, to be just and caring, to be successful in our endeavours, and to have a coherent theory of the world would be to fulfil the internal goals of all the aspects of our being. As the opposite of this, suffering can be understood as the frustration of the *telos* or inherent goals of human existence in its four dimensions. I will spell out what I mean by this with reference to each of the four levels of human being that Aristotle has identified.

Lower-level suffering

The vegetative level of human existence tends to the well-functioning of the body. When this functioning is frustrated we have what the Hastings Center document usefully calls a 'malady':

> The term 'malady' is meant to cover a variety of conditions, in addition to disease, that threaten health. They include impairment, injury, and defect. With this range of conditions in mind it is possible to define 'malady' as that circumstance in which a person is suffering, or at an increased risk of suffering an evil (untimely death, pain,

---

[13]   Friedrich Nietzsche, *Beyond Good and Evil: Prelude to a Philosophy of the Future*, trans. R.J. Hollingdale (Harmondsworth, 1973), Part 1.

disability, loss of freedom or opportunity, or loss of pleasure) in the absence of a distinct external cause.[14]

If we accept that the inherent goal of the vegetative or biological functioning of the person is healthy functioning, then the frustration of that goal which occurs when there is malady is the opposite of health. This is what I understand by suffering.

This usage may seem counter-intuitive if we think of suffering as a process of which the victim is conscious. If we abstract from the fulness of persons and focus just on the workings of their bodies, we delineate an unconscious set of events of the kind that we might describe as diseases, lesions or injuries, and this seems to fall short of the full meaning of the term 'suffering'. But everyday language bears me out. We do speak of a person suffering an injury. In this context it means little more than 'to undergo' or 'to be the passive recipient of'. In this sense the term can point to a bodily malady of which the person is a passive or even unconscious victim. But I want to suggest that there is good reason why the verb 'to suffer' can be used in this minimal sense as well as the richer senses of mental distress and cognitive reaction which Eric Cassell has identified. There is a continuity as we move from the minimal usage to the richer ones which consists in the fact that the structure of our understanding of what is taking place is the same in each usage. In each case the inherent goal or *telos* of an aspect of human existence is being frustrated.

In the minimal usage, the body itself is said to suffer. If we abstract the vegetative function from the wholeness of the person, we can say that the inherent goals of the body are being frustrated when there is malady, and so the body is suffering. Just as the healthy and excellent functioning of the body, as exemplified in sport, is a form of bodily teleological fulfilment or happiness, so the faulty functioning of the body is a form of bodily suffering.

We could best illustrate this with reference to an organism whose only form of existence is the vegetative one: namely, a plant. If a plant were prevented, whether by an attack from parasites, by human agency or by any other cause, from fulfilling its potential, then that plant could be said to be suffering. Admittedly, this may seem like a metaphorical usage. But is it mere metaphor to suggest that an undernourished tree which has its growth stunted is suffering? The reason that this usage is, perhaps, inescapably metaphorical is that plants do not evince conative functions. Insofar as they do not desire anything, we are not apt to describe them as suffering when their putative desires are frustrated. However, on my definition of suffering, where it consists of the frustration of a being's *telos*, the tree could be said to suffer. This may be a revision of our usual ways of speaking which many would find unacceptable. However, from the point of view of such recent trends of thought as deep ecology, it may also be a revision that we should be prepared to consider.

---

[14]   Callahan et al., p. S9

Perhaps the matter would be less contentious if we considered a human example, though here we must be aware that, in focusing on the vegetative aspect of existence, we are abstracting from the wholeness of human being. Take the case of women in Imperial China who had their feet bound. Let us imagine further that, contrary to fact, this process involved no pain or discomfort. Let us also imagine that, as was often the case, the young women to whom this was done welcomed it as a prerequisite for entry into a luxurious life. My suggestion would be that it would still be appropriate to say that these women were suffering, and my reason for saying so is that the fulfilment of their bodies' inherent goals through the normal growth of their feet was being frustrated. I am aware that, in leaving the actual pain associated with this procedure out of account, I am creating an artificial abstraction. But this is always the case when we consider the vegetative aspect of human existence, or the body, by itself.

In my sense, biological suffering obtains even in the absence of pain. There seems a clear case for saying that even if there were no pain involved in the practice, the frustration of internal bodily goals constitutes suffering. This is one reason why we object to such practices as the binding of feet even when its victims do not object to it. It follows that pain, as the hurtful sensation that is often caused by malady, is a phenomenon apart from suffering in my sense. It is connected to suffering only insofar as it causes the frustration of the victim's inherent goals.

It follows from this that we can speak of a decerebrate person, or a person in a permanent vegetative state, as suffering. Clearly such a person is feeling no pain. Nor is he or she aware of the threat to, and diminution of, his or her being. Nevertheless, insofar as this person is a human being, and insofar as we can delineate the *telos* of a human being as including the four sets of functions that Aristotle has identified, we can say that the *telos* of this being is frustrated and therefore that there is suffering. The ethical implications of this view fall outside of the scope of this chapter, as indeed, does the question of whether such a being should be regarded as a person. But one point that I can make here is that this last question is not central to the issue of whether this being is suffering. On my view, it clearly is.

My analysis of the concept of suffering becomes richer as we move to the appetitive or conative aspect of our being. We could begin by illustrating my thesis on this level with reference to an organism which, according to Aristotle, enjoys only the vegetative and appetitive aspects of existence: namely, an animal. There has been much debate in recent times, occasioned by the emergence of animal liberation and more general concerns for the environment, about whether animals can suffer. Although it was denied by Descartes and other classical philosophers, there seems little doubt that animals can feel pain. Most are sentient beings with the kinds of nervous system that allow for the registering of pain. But, given the distinction between pain and suffering, it might be asked whether animals can suffer, especially if we define suffering with reference to higher cognitive or self-conscious functions. My answer to this conundrum is simple. Animals have inherent goals. Depending on their natures, they love to run, fossick, play, hunt or lie basking in the sun. Any circumstance that frustrates these inherent goals causes suffering to the animal. Locking up a hunting dog in a small suburban backyard, or keeping chickens in battery conditions, even if these practices inflict no pain, would constitute suffering for the animals. My analysis of suffering requires no specific mental state of distress or discomfort, although such states may often be present. It requires only that what can be reasonably posited as a *telos* of the organism – that is, its inherent goal – be frustrated by the circumstances in which it finds itself.

Higher-level suffering

The matter is more complex in the case of human beings. Although we are animals, our natures and inherent goals are harder to define. We have seen that the conative mode of our being has many rich dimensions. Accordingly, its teleological description will be rich and the ways in which it can be frustrated will be many. The most obvious way in which the goals of the desiring part of our being can be frustrated is for us to fail to achieve what we desire. Any failure on the part of human beings to get what they want produces disappointment, which is a form of suffering. So much is clear with regard to intentional desire: that is, desire which is conscious of itself as a desire for a specific object. But the appetitive aspect of our existence also includes our innate caring for others and for ourselves, which is expressed in our lives through our specific concerns and commitments. This explains how it is that when we care for others we suffer when they do. Their suffering is a frustration of my wish that they should flourish. This wish is an expression of my own existential comportment towards them as a significant other. Hence their pain or disappointment touches me deeply in my being and frustrates my concern for them. Fellow feeling or sympathy does not require that I feel the pain or disappointment of the other, as some philosophers suggest;[15] it requires only that I feel my own disappointment in experiencing the frustration of my caring for the one I care for.

Pursuing the Aristotelian form of my argument, I could also suggest that we suffer when we do not desire well. In Aristotle's ethical reading of this phrase, this would mean when we desire the wrong things or desire excessively or too little. If I give in to licentiousness (if I may use an old-fashioned term) I might suffer shame or self-loathing. If I fail to feel the excitement or anger that a situation calls for I might similarly feel shame or self-loathing. In my own less moralistic reading of this phrase in which desiring well includes having a zest for life, the failure to achieve the internal goal would consist in depression. This is clearly a form of suffering.

It is perhaps at this point that we might seek to make a connection to the matter of pain. That pain and suffering are so frequently correlated might be due to the fact that pain, especially when it is persistent, can lead to the loss of zest for life. It

---

15   Max Scheler, *On the Nature of Sympathy*, trans. Peter Heath (London, 1954).

can lead to a feeling that the other-than-me (including my own body, which is often experienced in illness as something other-than-me[16]) is inhospitable to my existence. The fear, anxiety and sense of alienation that this produces is a frustration of the conative aspect of my being and thus a state of suffering. Insofar as my body becomes a threat to my being, it is also a threat to my integration as a person. Such integration is a further *telos* that can be ascribed to my existential being, and thus its frustration constitutes a further form of suffering.

The matter becomes clearer as we move to those aspects of our existence that involve self-consciousness. The deliberative functions of our existence structure our purposive agency in the world. Its external goal is success in whatever we seek to achieve. But Aristotle's notion of *eudaimonia* is most clearly illustrated by the satisfaction that comes from a job well done. The relevant satisfaction is not the achievement of the external goal of our project, whether it be the writing of a paper or the ministrations extended to our patients, it is the achievement of the internal goal of doing well what we had to do. The craftsman who enjoys the exercise of his craft irrespective of what happens to its product, or the nurse who gains fulfilment from the way in which she performs her clinical work even when the patient succumbs to inevitable death, is one who attains the form of happiness that Aristotle identifies. (Note that these distinctions are highly artificial. In real life the internal and external goals of our practices cannot be distinguished so sharply. And the satisfaction that arises from the attainment of our external objectives and the fulfilment of our internal goals cannot be sharply distinguished either.) On my analysis, suffering would be the frustration of the internal goals of action. If I would enjoy the activity that I engage in, then I suffer when this enjoyment is absent. Even were I to attain the external goal of my action and achieve what I had set out to achieve, if I did not feel the satisfaction of a job well done, I would suffer.

What would be a scenario that might illustrate this concept? Suppose I were a health care worker in a clinical setting which, because of the pressures of economic rationalism, demanded a high turnaround rate for patients. Imagine further that, measured in accordance with the biomedical model, patients were discharged with their maladies thoroughly cured. In this situation, a health worker might still feel that he was not able to exercise his functions as a health worker fully because of the restrictions of time and the lack of opportunity for caring exchanges with the patients. In this setting the external goals of the practice would be served (though even this is debatable), but the internal goals of the activity would be frustrated. In this case the health worker is in a state of suffering.

It may even be the case that the suffering of the patient is not relieved in this scenario either, even if the malady, and the pain that is caused by it, is. But we will only be able to see this when we return to the question of the relationship between a malady and suffering.

---

[16] Cassell, *The Nature of Suffering*, p. 57.

To return to the analysis of suffering at the deliberative level of our being, we should identify two more kinds of frustration that might occur at this level. First, there is the frustration that arises when our deliberative powers are frustrated. This might occur because the problem is too difficult for us to solve, it might occur because we are being interrupted or distracted, or it might occur because of anxieties, fears or mental disorders which prevent us from focusing on the task. In all these sorts of cases, we could be described as suffering. In these cases the internal goals and satisfactions of deliberative reason are not being attained. Second, there is the frustration that is caused by physical impairment of our powers of activity. If deliberative reason reaches its fulfilment in well-wrought action in the world, then anything that prevents well-wrought action will occasion suffering. Such prevention might arise from tools breaking down, material not being available, or maladies in the agent. In each case, the agent can be said to suffer. The frustration of deliberative agency is a form of suffering.

Of course we must note here that the frustration of an agent's activity is relative to the abilities of the agent. I am not suggesting that any agent who cannot attain the level of achievement of the most talented and gifted would thereby be said to be suffering. Even a person who is less physically or mentally abled than the social norm can form projects and goals commensurate with their abilities and can attain fulfilment by pursuing those goals well, and can suffer frustration when they are prevented from doing so by malady or other problems.

I turn now to the contemplative or integrative dimension of our being. The name of the suffering we undergo at this level of our being might be called 'alienation'. More technically, we should call this 'disintegration' since the internal goal of this dimension of our being is the integration of our lives in the light of a meaning-giving theory of what the world and our existence in it amounts to. If our lives are meaningless to us, we suffer anomie. We feel that there is no overarching purpose to our existence. If we feel that there is no truth or goodness to be attained or respected in life, we suffer cynicism in that we feel that nothing deserves our commitment or loyalty. If we feel that our lives have no cohesion, that we are subject to the vagaries of fate, or that none of our hopes can come to realization, we suffer from hopelessness. If we feel that we are subject to conflicting pressures, that the valid demands upon us cannot all be met, that the moral requirements in our lives are incompatible, then we suffer the disintegration of our being. We cannot attain integrity, and our desired self-image and our perceived reality are conflicted. If we hold views about the healing power of crystals or about visitations from aliens, if we believe in miracles, and if we also believe in the laws of physical science, we suffer confusion and intellectual incoherence. All of these states exemplify frustrations of the contemplative side of our being and are thus forms of suffering. Like other cases, they are forms of suffering of which the victim may not be aware. A person may be happily benighted, but insofar as the full and coherent integration of their being is not attained, the *telos* of the contemplative aspect of their being is frustrated. They are suffering intellectually or spiritually.

In the clinical setting the most frequent example of this form of suffering is the patient who cannot accept their malady, who has no answer to the perennial question, 'Why me?' This suffering is not caused by the malady or the pain that it may bring. It is caused by the lack of integration of what the patient is experiencing with their theory about what makes their life meaningful. The experience of their malady is destroying the narrative unity of their life, leaving it with no meaning.

My first thesis, then, is that suffering is to be understood as the frustration of the tendency towards fulfilment of the four levels of our existence that Aristotle has identified. Having developed this holistic and inclusive concept of suffering, let us see how it can be applied to the central concepts used in the Hastings Center document and in the literature on health care more generally.

Malady

I have argued that we can suffer in a variety of ways. For example, the biological or vegetative level of human existence tends to the health of the body. Malady is the frustration of this functioning. Malady is the form of suffering constituted by the frustration of the internal goals of the biological or vegetative aspect of our being. Malady is vegetative or biological suffering. It is literally true that we suffer disease.

This point presents an immediate challenge to dualism. Persons can be said to be suffering in this physical way even when they are not aware of it. It follows from this that suffering is not a function of consciousness, or a mental epiphenomenon which supervenes on malady. The malady by itself constitutes suffering. My second thesis, then, is that malady is an objective form of suffering.

It is worth noting that this notion of an objective form of suffering applies to organisms that are not persons or of which the status as persons might be in question. It follows, for example, that animals can suffer whether or not they are capable of self-awareness. It also follows that foetuses and neonates can suffer, and that comatose patients can suffer. The bioethical implications of these points will be considerable. If my conception of objective suffering constitutes an expansion of the notion of suffering beyond that which is accepted in ordinary language, I believe these bioethical implications serve to justify such an expansion. The role of philosophical theory is to provide just such ethically challenging revisions of our ordinary language concepts.

But to return to my analysis of malady, if this analysis were to be confined to the bodily level of our existence, I would fail to acknowledge the wholeness of our being. Even though my analysis is focused on the physiological level, malady can frustrate our existence at all levels. At the conative or appetitive level of our being, malady constitutes suffering in that it frustrates our enjoyment of our desires and alters our sense of relationship with the world and with our own bodies. We no longer feel at home in the world and in our own body. Even the things that we normally enjoy doing such as listening to music or conversing with friends lose their lustre when we are ill. The world seems to have a pall cast over it and our relationship to it is vitiated. If the inherent goal of this aspect of our being is an implicit form of enjoyment and rapport with the world, then malady destroys this relationship. In healthy life, our bodily existence is taken for granted and our functional relationships with the world constitute an innate level of enjoyment to which we do not consciously allude. Drew Leder has called this 'the absent body'.[17] When malady strikes, this pre-conscious harmony in our being is altered and our bodily existence becomes a centre of attention and concern. This is a frustration of an inherent tendency of our being which can lead even to a threat to our sense of self. It is through this pre-conscious sense of enjoyment of existence, as I argued in Chapter 8, that we gain a sense of the power and vigour of our own being so as to enable us to experience our own agency and autonomy in the world. It is from the basis of this sense of ourselves as agents that we venture out into the world, take on projects, establish relationships, and form our identities as persons. This existential project of self-making has its roots in the sense of being at home in the world and the vigour which is given us by our health. When malady strikes, this basis is threatened and our sense of security in our own identity is in jeopardy. It may be that this is what Cassell means when he says that suffering involves a sense of threat to our sense of integrity.

Moreover, at the conative level of our existence, our seeking to form relationships with others is as basic an existential concern as is our project of self-making.[18] It is just as basic in our inner most being to seek to form and maintain a rapport with significant others as it is to create and maintain our own identity. But when malady strikes, the balance between caring for others and our self-project is altered. At such times we normally become overly concerned and preoccupied with our selves and our states of illness. Our relationships with others can be maintained with extra effort and commitment, but our primary inclination will be to attend to our own being. In this way too, the interpersonal dimension of our being will be frustrated by malady, whether this malady is episodic or chronic. Insofar as our relationships with others are constitutive of our identity, so malady will be a pre-intentional threat to that identity. As Cassell has suggested, this is constitutive of suffering. My account differs from his, however, in that it requires no conscious awareness on the part of the victim. It is enough that the inherent tendency of our being to sociability is actually frustrated by the malady. Suffering is an objectively present condition of the person.

In the deliberative dimension of our existence, malady leads to suffering in that it prevents many of our actions from being fulfilling for us, or even from being embarked upon. There are at least two ways in which this is so. First, there is the failure of our actions to achieve their external goal. It may well be that our malady prevents our projects from achieving success. And this will clearly lead to the sort

---

17 Drew Leder, *The Absent Body* (Chicago, Illinois, 1990).
18 van Hooft, Chapter 4.

of disappointment which constitutes suffering. But this form of suffering is not central to my analysis. It can be avoided by taking on only tasks of which we know ourselves to be capable despite our malady. After all, should we be foolish enough to try to fly through the air without special equipment, we would fail. This would disappoint us. But it would not be valid to describe such disappointment as suffering. Rather, it is a case of foolishness because it involves taking on what we know we cannot achieve. As in life generally, our deliberation does not need to be frustrated if it takes our malady into account and if we take on only tasks which are achievable within our reduced powers. Nevertheless, taking on a limited range of tasks will be a limitation imposed on our being by our malady and this is a further way in which our practical and deliberative being can be frustrated. This limitation of the range of projects we can take on constitutes a diminution of our being and is thus constitutive of suffering. But even more importantly, the sense of enjoyment in work and activity that comes easily to the healthy person and which Aristotle describes as the internal goal of doing a task well will often be frustrated by malady in ways that constitute suffering. Even when our capacity is not affected, being ill will often reduce our enjoyment of our work.

At the contemplative or integrative level of our existence, suffering arises from frustrations of the spirit that maladies can bring. A failure to answer the perennial question of the sick person – namely, 'Why me?' – can lead to suffering, as can a sense of injustice or meaninglessness attaching to the malady. It will be constitutive of suffering if victims of malady cannot absorb what is happening to them into a broader conception of their lives or into some overarching meaning. There will be a number of examples of this. The first is the diagnosis itself. Knowing what the malady is, knowing what the disease is that is causing the symptoms or knowing what the source of the pain is are all ways of relating the malady to a broader story or theory. One source of suffering in those afflicted with malady is not knowing what the problem is. It is the fear of an unknown future or threat which frequently constitutes suffering. Patients will often express relief and will stop suffering in this way when they are given the diagnosis of their illness,[19] especially, but not exclusively, when the diagnosis turns out to disclose a non-serious malady. In cases where the malady is serious, the tendency of the contemplative part of our souls will be to understand it as ordained by providence or fate, as a punishment for sin, as a sacrifice with salvific power, or as meaningful in some other way. In each case the meaning that the malady is given arises from a belief in transcendent or ultimately important realities greater than the individual. The tendency of the contemplative part of the soul in the face of malady is to create a faith powerful enough to overcome the despair and fear which the malady would bring with it. Suffering at this level is the frustration of this tendency.

We must also consider the internal, existential goal of the integration of our lives which I map onto Aristotle's model as the tendency to achieve the wholeness of the four aspects of our being and of our relationships with others. In a healthy

---

[19] Cassell, *The Nature of Suffering*, Chapter 7.

person this goal is usually achieved pre-intentionally and without further thought. A healthy person's very embodiment is the expression of their interests and commitments. We feel the vigour of health insofar as we enjoy happy relationships with others, feel at home in the world, and are engaged in tasks that hold reasonable promise of success and which have a meaning in our larger conception of life. Anything that frustrates the tendency to create this wholeness in our lives will constitute suffering. Malady clearly causes such frustration. As already pointed out, malady brings the body into the foreground in our lives in a way that undermines this wholeness. The body is absent, as it were, in an integral life and its foregrounding by malady destroys integrity. As Cassell has pointed out, the body comes to be seen as an alien thing or even as an enemy in the life of a person who is ill.[20] A sick person frequently feels at odds with himself in that his body will not co-operate with his projects. He can lose self-control or find that his body will not obey his will. Moreover, chronically ill persons often seek to withdraw from the world and break off their relationships with others because of the shame and embarrassment which their illness brings them in the social world.[21] These events are not only frustrations of the inherent tendency to sociability which is part of the appetitive part of our being, they also destroy the integration of our being and is thereby constitutive of suffering in a further way.

I argued above that, 'just as all the lights mingle in our analogy of the sphere, so the suffering of malady suffuses our whole being'. Nevertheless, I would now suggest that malady is primarily a form of suffering that can be analysed in terms of the vegetative part of the soul in Aristotle's model of the human person. Even as it affects and suffuses our whole being, it is located in the biological functioning of the body.

Pain

In a similar way, pain is a form of suffering that can be analysed primarily in terms of the appetitive part of the soul. Pain is an unpleasant sensation of the body. I leave aside such metaphorical usages as 'the pain of bereavement' or 'being pained by an insult' for which the term 'suffering' is more apt. I understand pain as a physical sensation. Even when physicians can find no bodily cause, the sensation is still experienced as located somewhere in the body. While there are many qualitative differences and differences of intensity between pains, they all have in common that they are hurtful and unpleasant to some degree. For this reason they are the opposite of sensual pleasure and should be analysed primarily as frustrations of our inherent desire for pleasure and comfort. As such, they are a species of suffering focused in the appetitive aspect of our being.

My third thesis is that pain is a form of suffering rather than a phenomenon distinct from it. By this I mean that pain is to be counted as suffering because it is a

---

20   Ibid., p. 57.
21   Ibid., p. 54.

case of the frustration of the inherent appetitive goals of the person who is its victim. It is not the case that pain causes or gives rise to suffering because it is unpleasant, as if the pain and the suffering were two distinguishable phenomena. Rather, the unpleasantness of the sensation of pain constitutes a frustration of the inherent tendencies of our being, especially the tendency of the appetitive dimension of our being to secure pleasure and the satisfaction of desire. As such, pain just is this suffering. As with malady, pain can constitute suffering in a variety of ways through frustrating a variety of the tendencies of our being. The most obvious way in which it does this is by being unpleasant and hurtful. The appetitive aspect of our being is directly and immediately frustrated by this experience. It is pre-eminently in this way that pain is a form of suffering.

Now, this would seem to counter the point made by the Hastings Center paper and by Cassell that pain and suffering are distinct. As I have noted, they argue that there can be pain from which the victim does not suffer, as when people ignore their toothaches and get on with their lives, and that there can be suffering without pain, as when people fear illnesses when they are not diseased. I can accommodate these points by distinguishing the various kinds of suffering associated with the different aspects of our being identified by Aristotle. Pain constitutes suffering at the appetitive level of our being, but, like malady, it can also occasion suffering at the other levels. But it constitutes suffering in these other aspects of our being in a way that is more contingent and in a way that the victim can overcome. If the person in pain can cope with their pain in such a way that most of the internal goals of their being are not frustrated, then pain will not constitute suffering at the other levels of their being. If the body still works well despite the pain (and pain has positive functions within the workings of the body), then there need be no biological suffering. Phantom limb phenomena would be striking examples of this. If most of the person's desires are still real and attainable and if she feels at one with the world and with others despite the pain, then she will undergo but little conative suffering. If the person in pain can get on with the job and achieve satisfaction in performing activities well and thinking clearly, then there need be no suffering at the deliberative level of his practical life. If the person in pain has an understanding of ultimate things that allows her to understand her pain as part of the scheme of things (and having a medical diagnosis may serve this purpose just as well as having a theory about God's providence), then she might not suffer at the spiritual dimension of her existence. And if the pain is not such as to destroy the unity of a person's life and the integration of the aspects of his being, then again it will not constitute suffering of this kind. The overarching being of the victim can absorb the particular suffering of pain into a life stance which is not one of suffering.

But this way of putting it seems to separate pain from suffering once again. It makes pain the core phenomenon, while suffering is its psychological effect. It suggests that pain can occur without giving rise to suffering. Surely a person who is coping with pain is suffering nevertheless? I would argue that pain is a form of suffering, albeit one that is more focused upon the vegetative and conative aspects of our being. Pain is usually a symptom of malady. Insofar as malady is a frustration of the internal goals of the body and is therefore by definition a form of suffering, pain is usually associated with bodily suffering. This suggests that, far from being a secondary psychological effect of malady, suffering is the fundamental condition, while pain is the sensation of suffering or the epiphenomenal manifestation of suffering. On my analysis, bodily suffering is the silent dysfunction of the body, while pain is the contingently present manifestation of that dysfunction to its conscious or sentient victim. The key point here is that the suffering is in the body just as objectively as the pain is. It is not a conscious or cognitive reaction on the part of the victim. If we were to be tempted to dualistic thinking here, we would say that the pain is the mental state accompanying the purely bodily suffering rather than assert the more usual view that suffering is the psychological state rising from bodily pain. But both locutions are misleading. Just as the bodily dimension of existence should not be abstracted from our being, so bodily suffering should not be detached from the other forms of suffering that the victim may undergo. The suffering of an ill person has a unitary structure. While the pain is the victim's sensation of her bodily malady and, as such, belongs more exclusively to the first two dimensions of our being that Aristotle has identified, suffering suffuses the whole being of the person, both as bodily dysfunction and as frustration of our existential being. In these ways we could say of a person in pain who is coping with that pain that she was not suffering even though her pain is inherently a form of suffering. Objectively, she is suffering because she is in pain, but subjectively, she is not because she is coping with that pain. In this way I can explicate the distinction between pain and suffering made by the Hastings Center paper and by Cassell, but also posit an essential unity between them in the conative or appetitive dimension of our being.

The sick role

The sick role is also a frustration of our being and, as such, it constitutes a form of suffering. In this case the frustration occurs primarily at the practical or deliberative dimensions of our being. Our practical lives are disrupted and, with the sanction of others, we adopt the role of a sick person. This is a strategy for coping with the frustration of the inherent goals of our lives as practical people and the suffering which is constituted by this frustration. The sick role is a suffering role in which the focus of analysis falls on the deliberative and practical aspect of our being. Further kinds of suffering occur, as I have already noted, when sick persons cannot give their malady, pain or debilitation a meaning, or integrate it into their lives.

Spiritual suffering

From what has been said above, it will be clear that my Aristotelian framework allows me to distinguish, within the whole of a person's existence, a form of suffering which relates to the contemplative or integrative aspect of a person's being. Whether we call this form of suffering 'spiritual' or 'existential', the central idea is that it is constituted by a frustration of the tendency of persons to seek integration and meaningfulness in their lives. If I cannot integrate my malady, pain or disability into my existence by seeing it as part of a meaningful narrative of my life or by relating it to a reality greater than myself, I will suffer from psychological distress. It is at this level of our existence that religion can often provide comfort, but in our secular age other sources of relief and equanimity must be sought and developed. I will explore this matter further in Chapter 12. It is enough to note for the moment that this form of suffering often takes the form of the experience of a meaninglessness attaching to malady, or a disintegration of our lives in the face of it.

In this way, spiritual suffering might be related to clinical depression. If such depression is caused neurologically, then we would have a case of malady manifesting itself in the contemplative aspect of our being. If it is not so caused, but is a purely existential or psychological condition, then the suffering would be analysed as focused more fully in the contemplative aspect of our being. The forms of suffering that are associated with mental illness constitute a separate problem which lies beyond the scope of this chapter.

The goals of medicine

We have now seen that my Aristotelian conception of the person allows us to identify a number of forms of suffering corresponding to the 'parts of our soul' only some of which the victim may be aware of. This solves the problem of dualism in the Hastings Center paper. Rather than seeing suffering as a psychological reaction to pain or malady, pain or malady are themselves forms of suffering. And they also constitute further forms of suffering in the deliberative, contemplative and integrative aspects of our being. But although we can use Aristotle's model to distinguish these forms analytically, the light globes in a sphere analogy should remind us that, wherever it is focused, suffering suffuses our whole being.

So what is the role of medicine in relation to suffering? It is clear that it should cure maladies, relieve pain and rehabilitate the sick to the extent that it is able. In this it focuses upon the bodily existence of patients. However, the Hastings Center document along with Cassell and other commentators are right to suggest that medicine should not ignore further aspects of human existence. The question is just how these further aspects should be given their due regard.

In accordance with the third goal above, medicine should seek 'the cure and care of those with a malady'. In so doing it would remove suffering at at least the first three dimensions of our being and usually the fourth. Helping a person in such a way that the fulfilment of the internal goals of their being is not frustrated, whatever that may involve in a particular case, is what a health worker does by attending to the needs of the body. But in doing so the health worker is in effect relieving suffering. This means that the doctor does not have to do anything beyond that. Curing malady just is relieving suffering. Similarly, if pain is understood as suffering in the appetitive dimension of our being, then the relief and palliation of pain already is the relief of suffering. Relieving pain relieves the phenomenal form of suffering which belongs to the bodily and appetitive dimensions of our being. Further, if the sick role is understood as suffering at the deliberative level of our being, then curing the malady and removing the need for adopting the sick role will relieve suffering. A doctor does not need the skills of a psychologist or social anthropologist in order to relieve suffering. She needs only to be a good physician.

My objective concept of suffering also justifies the first goal of medicine identified by the Hastings Center discussions: namely, that of preventing malady. In my analysis, people who are experiencing health-threatening conditions such as lack of education, poverty, unhygienic living conditions, addictions of various kinds, poor diet, dangerous working conditions, and so forth are actually suffering even though they may not be aware of it or feel their lives or integrity threatened. The tendencies of their being are actually being frustrated and in this sense they are suffering. The call to relieve suffering thus translates into a call to alter social and material conditions of life so as to enhance health.

Whether suffering at the spiritual dimensions of our being can be relieved by curing malady, relieving pain, rehabilitating the sick or preventing disease and injury is a contingent matter. Certainly malady and pain will be the most immediate occasion for appetitive, deliberative and even contemplative forms of suffering, and their removal will relieve suffering. But the issue is whether the spiritual suffering of the patient, occasioned by the malady or pain, can be relieved by the physician even while the malady or pain continues. It doesn't help to say that these forms of suffering will disappear when the malady or pain is relieved. The challenge is to explore whether the physician might do anything to relieve them as part of the process of health care even while malady and pain persist. It is here that the Hastings Center paper is wise to suggest that a patient's inability to get on with their lives or to make sense of their affliction is a problem which can be approached only with the greatest diffidence by a physician.

My theses do not imply a return to the biomedical model. I am not arguing that the kind of medical practice which has been rightly criticized in recent times for being mechanistic and insensitive to the human dimension of the patient should be endorsed. What I am arguing is that the professional focus of medicine and other health professions should be upon the biological and conative levels of human existence. Effecting cure or palliation at these levels will reduce suffering. The kinds of suffering that occur at the deliberative and contemplative levels of human existence and that are implicated in breakdowns of the integration of aspects of human living are not within the scope of the healing arts as a part of its explicit project.

But they are within the scope of the healing arts as a potential for problems. Insensitivity to suffering at these levels would add to that suffering. It is part of the traditional Hippocratic calling of doctors that they must not cause suffering. The principle of non-maleficence demands the same. The recognition of suffering at the higher levels of human existence that I have identified does not raise for health workers the responsibility to relieve suffering at these levels. Rather, it raises the responsibility to not add to suffering at these levels. The curative regimens that doctors institute should disrupt the practical lives and relationships of patients as little as possible. If hospitalization is required, there should be minimum disruption to the forms of life of the patient and to his ability to maintain relationships with others. The meanings that patients give to their lives should not be threatened by the curative process. Hospitalization should not involve an institutional context of which the belief system is at odds with that of the patient. The doctor–patient relationship should be fully interpersonal and rich, rather than objectifying, routinized and bureaucratized. All of the failings of the current biomedical regimen have the potential to add to the suffering of patients in the non-bodily dimensions of their being. It is because of this that the doctor should take note of them and avoid them. But it will not be possible for a doctor to relieve all of the patient's suffering. When all is said and done, a malady, especially in the form of chronic illness, is a tragedy that cannot be made good. It can only be ameliorated. Whatever medicine may achieve in the way of the cure of malady, the relief of pain, the rehabilitation of the sick, the prevention of disease and injury and the avoidance of spiritual suffering arising from its procedures, suffering can remain a problem at the integrative level of our being. I will return to this level of our existence in Chapter 12.

Chapter 11

Pain and Communication

We take it for granted that clinicians have a duty to relieve pain. We do not consider it questionable to take an aspirin when we have a headache and, in the case of others, we accept that we should seek to relieve pain when we are asked by the sufferer to do so. And yet, when it comes to others, we sometimes do adopt differing attitudes. It is not uncommon for patients in various clinical settings to receive inadequate palliation for pain. For example, according to a recent newspaper report, internal hospital research has shown that for cancer sufferers in palliative care at the Peter MacCallum Cancer Institute in Australia, 17 per cent of prescribed doses of morphine and 35 per cent of doses of paracetamol were not administered.[1] Very frequently, pain-relieving drugs tend to be administered in time-regulated and parsimonious amounts irrespective of the expressed wishes of patients, or even of doctors. Patients who complain or seek more frequent relief are sometimes deemed soft, self-seeking or trouble-making. Pain relief is considered a scientific and objective discipline administered by experts on the basis of objective regimens rather than that of patient needs. Perhaps one of the causes for this approach is that pain is thought of as not directly communicable. As a result, clinicians must use an objectifying, diagnostic form of judgement in relation to it and the treatments that they prescribe are based only upon such judgement rather than upon the communication of pain on the part of the patient.

In this chapter, I raise the question of the extent to which pain is communicable and of the form in which it might be communicable. I then suggest that there are ethical implications arising from the analysis which I offer.

Pain defined

Pain is defined as 'an unpleasant sensory and emotional experience associated with actual or potential tissue damage, or described in terms of such damage'.[2] What this definition highlights is first the unpleasantness of pain. It goes without saying

---

[1] Victoria Button, 'Cancer patients not given drugs', *The Age* (23 November 1999), p. 8.

[2] H. Merskey and N. Bogduk, *Classification of Chronic Pain: Descriptions of Chronic Pain Syndromes and Definitions of Pain Terms*, second edn (Seattle, Washington State, 1994).

that, standardly, pain is something we would rather be without. Our bodies react with withdrawal reflexes and with flinches and cries when we are subjected to it. 'That hurts!' is a cry for help or an appeal for the cessation of the hurtful event. The second most obvious point that this definition highlights is that pain is an experience. It makes no sense to say that a person is in pain but that he does not feel it. A person may suffer an injury or a malady of a kind that typically causes pain but, unless they feel it, they are not in pain. Third, this definition points to the body. Pain is an experience that is felt in the body and, indeed, usually in specific organs or regions of the body. Even though there are cases such as those of phantom limbs or of psychogenesis, where pain is felt in the absence of any bodily lesion, pain is always felt *as if* it were located in a specifiable portion of the body.

This point is important in that it allows us to distinguish pain from other forms of suffering. The grief that we might feel at the loss of a loved one or at some other kind of disappointment, the fear that we might feel at the thought that we might be suffering from a disease, or the depression that we might feel at the thought that our illness has rendered our projects meaningless, are sometimes described as pain, but they do not fall under the official definition. They are emotions and forms of suffering, but they do not have that essential reference to the body which the definition of pain points to. Nor do they have that phenomenological quality of physical hurt which is definitive of pain. This is not to deny that such forms of emotional or spiritual distress may be accompanied by, or cause, visceral forms of discomfort, but such a bodily state should be thought of as pain separately from the grief, fear or depression that may be causing it. The emotion mentioned in the definition is the feeling of aversion and distress which colours the sensory experience. It is an inseparable quality of the experience rather than an element which is added to it.

There is a vast range of kinds of pain which differ as to type, intensity, frequency, recurringness, location and other phenomenological qualities. Some pains are so mild that we hardly suffer because of them, in the sense that we feel but little distress and undergo but little disruption to our lives. Other pains are so intense as to cause deep suffering. The most appalling pains of all are those intense and chronic pains that seem to admit of no relief and of which, sometimes, the aetiology cannot be clearly identified. Whether a person suffers because of their pain is a function of a range of factors, and not just of the nature of the pain itself. One person may be more susceptible than another to reacting badly to pain, and some societies will be more permissive than others in allowing victims of pain to adopt a suffering stance towards it.

Our definition also speaks of pain as a sensory experience. 'Sensory' here does not mean that we see our pain or hear it. We do not even feel it in the way that we feel the surface of an object that we are touching. Pain is not an object of the senses. Rather, calling pain 'sensory' means that the pain is actually felt and experienced in the body rather than in thought. Pain is not an idea. It is not spiritual. It is an immediate and insistent, physical experience of hurt. It is a felt condition of my body, or a part of it.

Normally most parts of my body are, as it were, absent from my attention.[3] Internal organs like the heart, lungs or liver do their life-preserving work without calling attention to themselves in any way. Even where we are able to be aware of them indirectly, as in the case of our own heart and lungs, our attention is normally upon the things in the world with which we are actively engaged. Similarly, those parts of our body which we regularly use and can apprehend, such as our legs and hands, are absent from our attention as we use them. Our agency flows through them, as it were, and focuses upon the things in the world with which we are dealing. Let any part of our body be in pain, however, and our attention is likely to be drawn to it. Rather than an anonymous aspect of our agency in the world, that part of our body will now be an object of our concern. While we may be able, like an active person with a toothache, to get past this concern and focus on the tasks at hand, pain brings a part of our body into explicit awareness. We are aware that this part of our body now exists in a new way. It is no longer hidden on our side of the divide between self and world, but becomes part of our world as a problem for us to deal with. Just as the senses give us objects in the world for us to apprehend, so pain makes parts of our body into objects as the locus of hurt. It is in this sense that pain is sensory.

And pain is, lastly, an emotional experience because of our negative reaction to it. It hurts and we want to be rid of it. There may be circumstances when we do not want to be rid of it, whether because we have adopted a policy of extreme asceticism or because we are masochistic, but it is still essential for what we want to achieve in such cases that the experience be unpleasant. Again, we might have a pain which is not so distressing and which we are too busy to worry about. But even then there is some unpleasantness and some small degree of negativity in our attitude towards it. Cases of intense and meaningless pain such as are often encountered in clinical situations will elicit powerful negative emotions and distress. Even if we had a theory about pain which allowed us to accept it intellectually, as when we call to mind the evolutionary advantage of being able to feel pain, or understand pain to be a warning of something gone wrong in the body,[4] or when we consider pain to be an acceptable part of God's plan for humanity,[5] we still feel it in its immediacy as unpleasant. To overcome this feeling and to accept it or even feel blessed because of it requires that I objectify the pain to some degree. It requires that I ask what the merits of pain as such, or of a pain such as mine, might be. It requires that I place a little distance between myself and my pain so as to frame it in an intellectual construct. But to the degree that the pain is mine in an immediate and felt way, it cannot but be unpleasant and unwelcome. My body recoils from it. Its very nature is to be an attack upon, or a disturbance of, my bodily equanimity. Pain is a hurtful mode of subjectivity: a way of being which

---

3   Drew Leder, *The Absent Body* (Chicago, Illinois, 1990).

4   Thomas S. Szasz, *Pain and Pleasure: A Study of Bodily Feelings*, second expanded edn (New York, 1975), p. 83.

5   C.S. Lewis, *The Problem of Pain* (London, 1940).

is distorted, tortured and distressed. In itself and as an experience, pain cannot but be of negative value. Notice that I am not arguing that pain is a value-neutral physical condition and that it is the suffering which it may cause that is unpleasant. This would be to separate pain from suffering in a dualistic manner. Pain is a form of suffering. It is inherently unpleasant.

The privacy of pain

Like other forms of suffering, pain leads its bearers to powerlessness, alienation, loss of control, *anomie*, and the withdrawal of the self into itself. Relief and comfort will therefore comprise not only alleviation of the pain, but also the empowerment of the patient, their enlivenment, their re-engagement with the world, and the re-establishing of communication and rapport with others. Clinicians will seek to achieve all of these goals. But this chapter focuses just on the last of these because there are some understandings of pain that seem to suggest that this is hardly possible.

As a mode of subjectivity, pain is intensely private. As a mode of subjectivity, my pain is radically my own. There exists no objectification of it that would allow another to share my pain. It is this feature of pain which sets up a difficulty for a clinician's approach to it. Clinicians respond to what, in a clinical situation, calls out for a response. If pain were as intensely private as I have just suggested, therefore, how can it be an operative and salient feature of a clinical situation for a clinician to respond to? The idea that pain is intensely private and non-communicable would seem to suggest that nothing can be done to overcome the isolation that severe pain forces upon its sufferers and that there is nothing communicable for a responsible clinician to respond to with caring. So let us look more closely at the notion that pain is private.

An observation frequently made about pain is that it is incommunicable. These sentences from Virginia Woolf are often quoted:

> English which can express the thoughts of Hamlet and the tragedy of Lear has no words for the shiver or the headache. ... The merest schoolgirl when she falls in love has Shakespeare or Keats to speak her mind for her, but let a sufferer try to describe a pain in his head to a doctor and language at once runs dry.[6]

It is suggested that the words that we do use to describe pain – words like throbbing, piercing, persistent, stabbing, and so forth – are clumsy at best. They are metaphors and do not carry literal meaning. I may have a stabbing pain without actually being stabbed. It is also said that such descriptions are not as helpful towards the clear delineation of symptoms and the making of diagnoses than are the visible or otherwise detectable lesions found in the body. After she notes that

---

[6]   Norman Autton, *Pain: An Exploration* (London, 1986), p. 2.

pain is frequently described with metaphors, the claim that pain is essentially incommunicable is expressed by Irena Madjar in this way: 'Thus, because bodily pain resists objectification in language, it is marked by a strong element of *unshareability*. In other words, pain silences and actively destroys language.'[7]

This seems to me to overstate the case. First, there is nothing unusual about experiences having to be described in metaphors. Try describing the beauty of a sunset without using them. That we need metaphors here does not imply that the experience is radically private, incommunicable or unshareable. Second, all experience is inherently unshareable in some sense. It is in the nature of experience, being subjective, that it is the experience only of the experiencer. As such it is not shareable. It cannot be another's experience. You cannot make another feel a pain by talking about it. But this is both obvious and uninteresting. I am not prevented by this unshareability from communicating the experience to another in a variety of ways. Reading the paper over breakfast is an unshareable experience in this sense but I can certainly communicate aspects of it to you by commenting on the stories I have read, by getting you to read them, or by saying that I found it very interesting to be reading them. Similarly, the experience that I have when I enjoy a beautiful sunset is unshareable, but I can communicate much of it to another through language even if to do so effectively I might have to become rather poetic or metaphorical.

Is it any different with pain? As a subjective experience, it is as unshareable as any subjective experience. But Majdar's own table of pain descriptors (burning, stinging, searing and so on) shows that communication about it is possible. Virginia Woolf may be right in suggesting that our repertoire of words is relatively poor for communicating pain, but this just shows why we need a range of metaphors. Indeed, we often use them quite successfully. It is noteworthy that attempts have been made to systematize the descriptors of pain into a more coherent symptomology. The McGill Pain Questionnaire developed by Melzack and Torgerson[8] explored the connotations, relationships, contrasts and similarities between the metaphors used in describing pain and their relation to actual maladies. It drew up numerical scales and tables. The result is a more systematic and reliable set of interpretations of such pain descriptors which allows clinicians a more assured access into the conditions that patients are suffering. This is not to deny that pain words are highly relative to the context and emotional state of the sufferer. Despite the refined diagnostic tool that the McGill Pain Questionnaire provides, there can be no simple lexicon of words for describing pain. The metaphors that patients use must be heard in their contexts and with their contrasts, and clinicians must here, as in other cases, be sensitive to the particularities of the case before them.

---

[7] Irena Madjar, 'The body in health, illness and pain', in Jocalyn Lawler (ed.), *The Body in Nursing* (Melbourne, 1997), p. 53–73.

[8] Marion V. Smith 'Talking about pain', in B. Carter (ed.), *Perspectives on Pain: Mapping the Territory* (London, 1998), p. 39.

What might it mean to say that pain can destroy language? Elaine Scarry has argued this point with reference to such extreme situations as torture and war.[9] We might refer also to cases of extreme, chronic and unbearable pain which clinicians attempt to alleviate in the clinical setting. In such cases, sufferers often find themselves unable to speak. Not only might their distress physically prevent them from speaking but, were they able to speak, nothing that they would say would be adequate to the severity of what they were experiencing. The moans and cries to which such victims are reduced by extreme pain are not cases of language. In a strict sense, this is true. But it does not follow that such aural gestures are not communicative. Even a flinch is communicative. It is difficult to imagine a more eloquent expression of pain and a more effective communication of its cruelty than a cry of distress. That language is unable to convey this verbally does not mean that it cannot be conveyed at all.

It is interesting to note that many sufferers of chronic pain cease to evince not only expressive bodily gestures such as cries, but even direct bodily expressions such as dilated eyes or increased heart rate. The objective signs of pain seem to be repressed.[10] The only evidence for pain in such patients is what they say and the ethical difficulty that they present is that of whether the clinician should give credence to what they say in the absence of any such objective signs. Perhaps it is this problem that gives rise to the documented aberrations in clinical practice where clinicians are apt to regard their patients as faking the severity of their pain and thus to give too little pain relief.

There are a number of philosophical reasons for the difficulties that attend the communication of pain. The first of these is that pain is not 'intentional'. What this technical philosophical term means is that it is not *about* anything and does not refer to anything aside from itself. Other subjective states of persons are not like this. When I am angry, I am angry about something. When I feel fear, there is an object or an imagined object that I am afraid of. While there may be some mood-like states which seem not to have an object in this way, they are nevertheless manifest by the way that objects in the world or in thought present themselves to me. If I am depressed without being depressed about anything in particular, my world and my thoughts take on a colourless hue and events lack excitement or interest. In this way even an objectless state like depression manifests itself in the way that the world appears to me when I am in that state. But pain does not refer to the world in this way. Not only does it make no sense to speak of a pain as being about anything, but also pain need not colour the world in any way. If anything, it distracts from the world. I do not see objects in the world in a pained way, and my pain does not refer me through it to objects or other things. What my pain does is draw attention to itself. It comes to preoccupy me in direct proportion to its severity. It is not a way of apprehending the world, but a mute and brutal presence

[9]   Elaine Scarry, *The Body in Pain: The Making and Unmaking of the World* (New York, 1985).
[10]   Edward Shipton, *Pain: Acute and Chronic* (London, 1999).

that pushes all other subjective states, and the world itself, to the periphery of my attention. The consequence of this for our problem is that pain becomes hard to describe. I can describe my anger by saying what it was that annoyed me. I can describe my fear by saying what I was afraid of. But I cannot describe my pain in this way. I can refer to that part of my body in which the pain is located, of course, but this is not identifying an intentional object of pain so much as its locus. The ways in which I can describe my pain in language (as opposed to expressing it in gestures) is certainly limited by this feature.

Another technical argument, and one offered by Scarry,[11] is that pain defeats language because the primary function of language is to refer to objects. When I say 'hat' in an appropriate context, I can be taken to be referring to a hat, whether a particular hat present in that context, or the more general idea of a hat. What makes communication possible in such a context is the presence in the world of hats, such that my words can refer to one or more of such hats. It is then suggested that pain is not an object in the world in this way and so is not an object that words can refer to. Now, if this argument were sound, then it would not be possible to speak about any of our inner, subjective states. What am I referring to when I say that I am happy or that Mary is happy? Without going into the technicalities of linguistic philosophy, it might be enough to say that even in the absence of worldly objects to refer to, language requires objective criteria for the ascription of such terms. I can call Mary happy on the basis of seeing how she behaves. If she were crying at the time, my description can be deemed to be wrong. Similarly, I can call myself happy when I notice myself behaving in certain ways as well as experiencing certain feelings. It is the burden of Wittgenstein's so-called 'private language argument' that I cannot attribute inner states to myself solely on the basis of my own experience of those states. My own experience does not tell me what such terms mean in the public domain. I must be able to apply the public criteria for ascribing a subjective state to myself in just the way that I have learnt to ascribe them to others. I cannot have learnt what the word 'happy' means just by noting my own internal states. How do I know that the state I am experiencing is the state that our language designates as 'happiness'? By seeing that my expressions of that state are similar to the expressions that others evince when they are standardly described as happy.

And so it is with pain. Certainly the experience is irreducibly subjective. My pain is radically my own. But how do I learn to call it pain? I do so by noting that the way in which the term 'pain' is used in the public domain is in order to describe a person who is grimacing, holding his mouth and making a dental appointment, or a person who has suffered an injury to his leg and is hobbling to a surgery for treatment. When such persons say they are in pain, they are not only expressing their inner state, they are also, in effect, teaching me what the word 'pain' means. I will then be able to use the term to describe my own inner states when I suffer such or similar injuries, engage in similar behaviours and experience

---

[11] Scarry, p. 5

hurtful sensations. And having learnt it, I can use the term to describe similar inner states of mine which arise in differing contexts. In this way language can refer to pain, even though pain is not an object in the world. This is not to deny, however, that things are more difficult when we come to describe the qualities of pain. There are few external or objective criteria for describing a pain as 'throbbing' or 'piercing'. The meaningfulness of these terms arises from their being metaphors. We know what it is for an item to throb or to be pierced. These words do have an external reference in their non-metaphorical usages. And we can go on to imagine what it might feel like for our bodies to throb or to be pierced. What a victim of pain is saying is that a pain feels like that. Provided we can imagine what throbbing or piercing might feel like in our own bodies, we can understand what they are saying to us.

But this whole argument is premised on the thought that the primary function of language is to refer to objects, whether these objects are things in the world or inner subjective states of people. But a further function of language is to express ourselves in an intersubjective world. More simply put, it is simply to chat. We spend a lot of our time in idle conversation. If we were to reflect on the amount of time we spend talking in a typical day, we might find a surprisingly high proportion is non-pragmatic or apparently purposeless communication. The real purpose of such exchanges is not to convey information about the world so as to complete some task or other, but to establish and maintain intersubjectivity. It is an expression of sociability and of our need for community. Perhaps the thought that pain destroys language means that it destroys such sociability.

One effect of pain that is relevant here is that pain isolates. Pain presses its victims back from the world into a preoccupation with the state of their bodies, and in so doing it isolates persons from the world and from others. Despite what I have been saying about the communicability of pain, it remains true that it moves the boundary between subjectivity and the world inwards. Healthy and pain-free persons are able to transcend themselves into the world and project their subjectivity in such a way as to invest the world with meaning. Moreover, such persons are able to relate to others by reaching out to them in an encounter in which they lose themselves to a degree in the reality of the other and of the relationship. But persons in pain withdraw into themselves. For them, in proportion to the severity of their pain, their world reduces to their own isolated reality. The world ceases to engage such persons. They are not able to forget themselves and be fully in the world. They are not able to throw themselves into relationships with those around them and partake of the common subjectivity characteristic of social existence. Their pain crowds out all other interests and commitments. Their attention is focused upon themselves. They are obsessed with the states of their own bodies. It is not just that their experience is their own or that it is unshareable. All subjective states are like that. It is not that they do not have the words to express or describe their pain as others have argued. It is that they are not able to escape the prison of self-involvement which their pain has created around them. There is no reality for them but their own suffering. There is no subjectivity present to them but the nagging and searing insistence of their own tortured and isolated subjectivity.

For the clinician to open up a communicative channel to such a self-absorbed subjectivity requires a form of rapport which is different from that established by everyday language. The objective and intersubjective world which language establishes and refers to is no longer available to the patient in severe pain. Thus a new form of intersubjectivity needs to be established: namely, one grounded in empathy.

Empathy

Empathy as a form of intersubjectivity is already known to us from everyday experience. Imagine yourself engaged in conversation with another person. It may be about a practical matter or project upon which you are both engaged, or it may just be idle chat through which social relationships are maintained and enriched. There is communication here and it is mediated by language. But now suppose that, in the course of the conversation, your eyes meet those of the other and you suddenly become aware of a new depth of rapport between you. Sometimes such a moment can be embarrassing. At other times it may have a sexual component. When it is not appropriate to the socially structured nature of the relationship, it can cause problems. But at other times, it can be a moment of unique joy and encounter with the other.

Emmanuel Levinas has theorized such moments by suggesting that in them we come into contact with the mystery of another's subjectivity. Whereas our apprehension of things in the world and our talk about them is always mediated by concepts through which we understand them, and whereas those concepts are part of our own linguistic and conceptual repertoire through which we make sense of, and appropriate, the world, the mystery and infinity of the other cannot be grasped in this way. The other person is always 'Other' in the radical sense that he or she cannot be appropriated by me in my understanding or perception. I cannot understand another person in the way that I can understand a motorcar, for example. In the case of a motorcar, even without much mechanical knowledge, I can completely grasp what it is, what it is for, and how it stands in relation to me. I can put it into the category in which it belongs. I cannot do this with another person. Even a person whom I know well (indeed, especially a person whom I know well) will always be beyond my intellectual, emotional or conceptual grasp. The Other is infinite and ungraspable.

It follows from this, for Levinas, that the way in which I approach another person, my comportment and attitude towards them, is ethical in nature from the very first. It always places an ethical demand upon me. If I do classify them and put them into a pre-defined category, and if I do relate to them just and only as structured by that classification, then I act unethically. If I relate to an employee just as a functional item in my enterprise, or if I relate to my patient just as a problem to be solved, then my comportment is unethical. Kant had already said as much when he said that we should not use people as means to our own ends, but Levinas deepens the point by showing that it is not just a matter of what we do, but also a matter of how we perceive the other. More positively, the ethically proper comportment that I ought to adopt toward the Other is that of letting their mystery be. I must not appropriate or classify. I must leave space. I must be open to encounter. I must be prepared to be surprised. I must be generous in my comportment, accepting in my attitude and caring in my approach.

The point that I wish to draw from this is that, despite my arguments showing that pain is more communicable than many have claimed, there is still something important being expressed in the claim that pain is radically private and unshareable. Like so many other identity-constituting features of subjectivity, pain is a mystery to the one who observes it from the outside. It is part of the infinite and ungraspable nature of the 'Other'. For a clinician, as for anyone, observing another person is a case of trying to do the impossible. It is a case of trying to grasp and understand Otherness or infinity. Just as I cannot fully understand the love that you feel, the beauty that you experience or the fear that you undergo, so I cannot grasp your pain. The theoretical reason for this is that, to me, your pain is not a phenomenon. It is not a percept. It is a modality of your subjectivity. It is a condition of your mystery, of your otherness and of your infinity. While you can convey much of it to me by the things you say, the metaphors you use or the bodily or verbal gestures that you evince, it remains *your* pain. At the deepest levels of encounter, I cannot grasp it or classify it. Even if I compartmentalize it as part of a diagnosis or treatment regimen, I cannot take possession of it or make it mine. I must respect it as yours. The irony of the argument is that pain is indeed mysterious. Just as the subjectivity of the other is mysterious, so that modality of their subjectivity which we call pain is mysterious.

Pain as an ethical challenge

But more, I must accept pain as an ethical challenge. The ethical challenge of encountering the other as the Other is that of letting the other be and of establishing intersubjective rapport. More specifically, in the case of pain, the ethical challenge is to reopen the patient's world so as to break open the isolation into which their pain has forced them. In the clinical context, empathy or compassion is the form that this challenge takes. Communication of and about pain must therefore be possible. But this is not just communication of factual and pragmatic information. It is not just answers to questions like 'Where does it hurt?' or 'What does it feel like?' It is the establishment of intersubjectivity, an encounter between two selves. The pain of the other, which tends to their self-enclosure, must be made into an opening through which the care of the clinician flows through to the patient. The clinician must bring to this encounter a mode of apprehension which does not objectify the other or their pain.

Levinas' analysis of the other relates to the nature of both parties in an intersubjective encounter. Not only does it imply that the clinician, in encountering the person in pain, must not objectify or classify that person, it also implies that the person of the other, the person in pain in the clinical case, is a different kind of entity from that which can be appropriated in a knowing and assimilating gaze. The first significance of the point that the other is a mystery or an infinity is that it cannot be grasped epistemologically so that our response must be non-grasping and therefore ethical. But the point is not only that the other may not be appropriated or used as a means. It is also that the other *appeals* to me in an ethical manner. The other calls out to me for help. Many things in the world appeal to me, of course. If I see a fancy sports car, it may strike me as a thing of beauty and of power. It may strike me as desirable. Or it may strike me as something objectionable in a world of poverty and exploitation. But in each of these cases it is my mode of apprehension of the object that dictates how it will appeal to me. In each case, and especially in the case where I desire the object, the way the object appeals to me will be a function of the way I appropriate it into my world. In the case where it strikes me as desirable, it will be because I am one who desires to possess the object.

But another person is not to be assimilated or possessed in that way. The otherness of the other dictates not only that I should not appropriate it or that I cannot, it also constitutes a primordial, ethical appeal to me. As I look into the eyes of another, I feel a call upon my being. As Levinas puts it: 'In expression the being that imposes itself does not limit but promotes my freedom, by arousing my goodness.'[12] It is as if the other reaches out to me in the expression of their pain. Their depth and mystery, their infinity, is a space that draws me into it. Their needs and desires, whether or not they are articulated to me, become like a magnet to my being. I am drawn into their Otherness. The encounter between us is structured not only by my ethical refusal to appropriate the other into my world, but also by the lure of the mystery of the other which draws me out of myself into the infinity of the other so as to elicit my ethical response. The other is a call to me to become engaged with that other.

Of course, it is perfectly appropriate that the forms and structures of everyday life place an overlay of reserve over this intersubjective magnetism. We cannot, in our routine situations, answer this call to personal rapport fully. The business of everyday life could not go on if we succumbed to the lure of the other in every context. This is why it is considered bad etiquette to gaze too deeply into the faces of others and why we resent what we call intrusions into our personal space. Nevertheless, the potential for deep rapport is always there and various degrees of friendship and communication that the structures of social and private life permit to us should be such as to allow such deep rapport with significant others.

---

[12] Emmanuel Levinas, *Totality and Infinity: An Essay on Exteriority,* trans. Alphonso Lingis (Pittsburgh, Pennsylvania, 1969), p. 200.

In professional settings such as health care there is a special need to negotiate the right degree of rapport with patients. On the one hand, a patient is a client with whom the clinician's relationship is mediated by the forms of the professional setting. As is well known, there are risks here of objectification and routinization. On the other hand, the patient is a human being with all the depth, mystery, and infinity that Levinas has described. More to the point, the patient is suffering. Specifically in this chapter, the patient is envisaged as being in pain. This condition adds urgency and immediacy to the ethical call that the other places upon the clinician. Not only is the other an infinity that calls out to me for my response, but the other's pain and need is an intensification and focusing of this appeal. The other calls out to me from their need. And I hear the other from out of my general ethical stance of letting the other be and my more specific and professional ethical comportment of caring and professional attention.

It will be the eyes of the other that most eloquently send out this appeal. But, in the clinical setting, it will also be their bodily state. The cries and groans, the flinches, the writhings and the bodily contortions that express pain will all be gestures of appeal. They are all modes of supplication. They are not just symptoms of malady. They are not just indicators of where and how palliative interventions should take place. They are also personally expressive gestures that open up the interpersonal space into which the clinician enters as rescuer. Moreover, the patients' reports of their own pain, whether formalized into a symptomology or not, will be more than useful diagnostic information. They will be appeals for help that arise from the deepest need of the other and appeal to the deepest ethical levels of the clinician. However it is expressed and whether or not it causes suffering in milder cases, pain is a direct appeal from the depths of the otherness of the patient to the depths of the humanity of the clinician.

Contrary to the often repeated contention that pain is silent, private, incommunicable and destructive of language, therefore, I would contend that pain is an eloquent amplification of the intersubjective rapport which human beings naturally establish between themselves. Pain not only causes its sufferers to become self-preoccupied but it also leads them to seek help from others. Pain amplifies and intensifies the interpersonal appeal that exists between people who engage in genuine encounter. It amplifies it because the need of the other is greater and more immediate and because the comportment of the clinician is one of caring and benevolent attention. It intensifies it because, along with the lure of mystery and infinity which each person presents to another in encounter, pain highlights the vulnerability and finitude of each one of us. It is from this finitude that we reach out to each other and it is because of this finitude that we embrace one another in rapport.

Chapter 12

The Meanings of Suffering

Suffering is one of the most profound and disturbing of human experiences. The word 'suffering' has a resonance which relates to our sense of life's meaning and of threats that are posed to our hopes of happiness. It does not refer just to maladies, pains and difficulties with which we can and should cope. It involves crises and threats to our existence which constitute a degradation or alienation of our being.[1] It is the spiritual dimension of our existence or the 'contemplative' aspect of our being, to use Aristotle's term, not only the bodily aspects of our selves, which is implicated in suffering. Suffering is a spiritual phenomenon, an event that strikes at the faith we can have in life. The meaning of suffering in our lives can therefore be contested at the level of discourse at which cultural meanings and visions of human life are negotiated.

In evaluating its role, the central question that suffering raises is whether it is a good thing or a bad thing. This may seem an odd question to pose when it seems so obvious that, by its very nature, suffering is an evil. However, given the ineliminability of suffering from our lives, a central project of human thought is to make it bearable or acceptable, and one of the most common ways of doing this is to show it to be good in some way. If suffering were seen as a positive event or force in our lives, then we would be better able to endure it. Accordingly, our cultural tradition contains many attempts to make suffering positive.[2] On the other hand, there are those who think such attempts a species of bad faith and who argue that, if we are to be authentic in the face of it, suffering must always be considered negative. This chapter explores a few attempts in the Western tradition to give suffering meaning and then asks whether it is possible to conceive of an authentic acceptance of suffering as something inherently negative, destructive and adverse to human happiness.

---

[1]   Eric J. Cassell, *The Nature of Suffering and the Goals of Medicine* (New York, 1991).

[2]   For a fuller treatment of these ideas in the context of health care, see Rodney L. Taylor and Jean Watson (eds), *They Shall Not Hurt: Human Suffering and Human Caring* (Boulder, Colorado, 1989).

Ancient conceptions: Suffering and the world

From the very earliest of times in the West, suffering has been associated with the concept of justice. What the spiritual or contemplative functions of our thinking seek is a coherent and totalizing world view in which everything has its place and nothing is a disturbance to the way things should be. Within such a divinely decreed cosmos ruled by fate or destiny, suffering would result either from a violation of the supernatural order on the part of human beings or from a divine response to such a violation.

Perhaps the most primaeval and naïve reaction to suffering is to think of it as punishment. Cultures and religions around the world abound with examples of the belief that suffering is a punishment exacted by the gods.[3] But this is already an anthropomorphic rendering of a more primitive idea: namely, that, despite its ubiquity, suffering is something that should not happen. It is something that is inherently negative. It is a departure from how things should be. But why? Clearly, it is contrary to what the victim or victims of the suffering would want. But it would be *hubris* to suppose that the mere wishes of individuals could establish the axiological status of suffering. The value status of everything, including suffering, must arise from an order of reality greater than that of puny human individuals or peoples. It must arise from the gods. Suffering must be seen as part of the divine order, and the most obvious explanation in a universe that contains gods who have emotions and desires like human beings is that suffering is sent by the gods to punish human beings for deeds that displease the gods. In this way suffering becomes part of the divine order despite its apparent evil and acquires an explanation which shows that it is, after all, to be borne with equanimity.

The genius of ancient Greek thought was to have transcended the anthropomorphic gods and replaced them with more abstract concepts. The concept of justice acquired a content similar to that of destiny; it alluded to the cosmic order itself. The one fragment of the thinking of Anaximander which has come down to us expresses the matter thus:

> Things perish into those things out of which they have their birth, according to that which is ordained; for they give reparation to one another and pay the penalty of their injustice according to the disposition of time.[4]

Two crucial elements comprise this thought. First, there is the notion of change as a constant flow into and out of existence in accordance with an overarching destiny (an idea that, secularized further, became the concept of causal determinism).

---

[3]   Loretta Kopelman, 'The Punishment Concept of Disease', in Christine Pierce and Donald VanDeVeer (eds), *Aids: Ethics and Public Policy* (Belmont, California, 1988), pp. 49–55. Kopelman argues that the punishment concept is irrational.

[4]   Quoted in F.M. Cornford, *From Religion to Philosophy: A Study in the Origins of Western Speculation* (New York, 1957), p. 8.

Second, there is the somewhat more complex idea that such change is somehow an offence to the divine order and that reparation therefore has to be made for the very contingency of the existence of things. Change is an offence to the eternal and changeless scheme of justice, where justice involves that fated order in which everything is as it should be. In contrast to this divine order, changeable reality is an offence that calls for reparation. The penalty that needs to be paid is suffering. In this way a conceptual association is expressed and forged between suffering, existence in this world and punishment. Suffering in this world was inevitable, negative and necessary. But it was ordained by the supernatural order, and therefore ultimately positive in its meaning.

Plato developed this contrast between two worlds; one of divinely constituted perfection and the other of worldly change and corruption, into a secular metaphysical system. Martha Nussbaum has argued that Plato's metaphysical system was a response to the fragility, danger and sorrow of worldly existence.[5] In the face of these afflictions, the contemplative mind created a realm of perfection from which to draw consolation. On the eve of his death, Plato's hero Socrates welcomes his fate on the ground that it will take him out of this world of suffering, change and obfuscation and into a realm where clarity and light will guarantee his knowledge of the Forms of Beauty, Truth and Goodness. Although there is not a direct link here between suffering and punishment, there is an association between suffering and a lesser form of existence: namely, existence in a world of variability, corruption and epistemological uncertainty.

Christianity: Suffering as reparation

The idea that suffering is an inevitable and inescapable aspect of worldly existence but that it can be escaped by a form of self-transcendence or an elevation to a higher mode of existence can be found in many of the great world religions including Hinduism, Buddhism and Christianity. In the West, the predominant way of giving suffering meaning is still derived from Christianity. For a Christian, human beings are tainted with original sin.[6] This is another transformation of the notion that worldly existence is less than perfect, and even corrupt, but in this version, the primordial condition of humanity requires reparation. As a cultural outgrowth of a religious tradition in which ritual blood sacrifice was used to appease God and seek His favour, and in which guilt for sin was washed away in sacrificial blood, suffering came to be seen as a price that had to be paid for sin. And so heinous was the original crime of humanity that nothing less than the

---

[5]   Martha C. Nussbaum, *The Fragility of Goodness: Luck and Ethics in Greek Tragedy and Philosophy* (New York, 1986).

[6]   Elaine Pagels, *Adam, Eve and the Serpent* (London, 1988). Pagels argues that this idea owes more to Saint Augustine (who had absorbed Plato very thoroughly) than to the biblical texts.

suffering of a God was required to achieve reparation for it. Christ's suffering on the cross thus becomes a paradigm case of positive suffering. It was this sacrifice that saved humankind from sin, and every Christian is called upon to participate in it by dedicating their own suffering to this salvific task or by declaring their faith in its achievement. Thus the Christian believes that salvation is achieved through suffering, whether his or her own or that of Christ.

This account can become more complicated. At least one writer in the Christian tradition, Stanley Hauerwas, has recently argued that Christians should not in any simplistic way align their suffering with that represented by the cross. According to Hauerwas, only suffering accepted for some moral reason is Christlike. Hauerwas argues that suffering is an intrinsic part of our moral lives. No human life could be complete without accepting suffering as part of its moral project. Just as we should be prepared to accept death for some overwhelmingly noble cause, so we should be prepared to accept suffering in proportion to the value at issue. Even in mundane contexts our moral self-project or our autonomy involves being able to give up things that we want. As Hauerwas puts it:

> Suffering is not morally significant only because things happen to us that we cannot avoid, but because the demand of morality cannot be satisfied without asking the self to submit to limits imposed by morality itself. In this sense, without allowing ourselves and others to suffer we could not be human or humane.[7]

This insightful observation about human life recasts the meaning of suffering by turning it into sacrifice. Suffering for a cause, even merely giving up something we want for the sake of something worthier, frustrates our desires and might for that reason be thought of as suffering. Insofar as these experiences are freely accepted for the sake of some good, however, they are actually cases of sacrifice. That is, we accept some frustration, pain or negative experience for the sake of something better or worthier.

However the relation between the Christian's suffering and the suffering of Christ is understood in detail, the outlines of the Christian theory of suffering are clear. At the contemplative level of our being, where we establish the meaningfulness of our lives by relating it to a larger story, reality or cosmic theory, Christians relate their suffering to the story of Christ so as to give it meaning. In this way Christians feel that they can contribute their suffering to the salvific plan of God. Suffering loses its *prima facie* negative character for the victim by being given a transcendent, positive meaning. The Christian concept of divine providence, which is present in other religions also, works in a similar way, by suggesting that all the unfortunate things which occur in the world have a larger

---

[7]   Stanley Hauerwas, 'Reflections on Suffering, Death, and Medicine', in his *Suffering Presence: Theological Reflections on Medicine, the Mentally Handicapped, and the Church* (Notre Dame, Indiana, 1986), pp. 23–38, p. 25. I am grateful to Mark Hanson of the Hastings Center for bringing this issue to my attention.

purpose and will ultimately tend to the good, as guaranteed by God. This too is a theory which belongs to the meaning-seeking or contemplative aspect of our existence. It too allows us to understand suffering and misfortune as meaningful; in this case by situating it within a divine, providential plan.

The key point about an *authentic* acceptance of suffering, however, is that suffering is *not* made meaningful. It is inherently negative. What is crucial in the Christian theories is that suffering is experienced as negative – it really is suffering – but that when this suffering is given meaning within the larger story, it becomes something positive. Suffering will be negative in that it hinders the fulfilment of the biological aims of the body, negative in that it involves pain or other frustrations of our desires and needs, and negative in that it frustrates our practical projects and our pursuit of everyday goals. Yet it becomes positive by virtue of the meaning-giving aspect of our existence. Our bodies might suffer maladies, we might suffer pain, our zest for life might be lost, our relationships shattered, our projects failures, our suffering real, and yet we can think of it as for the ultimate good. And in this way the meaningfulness and integration of our existence can be preserved and even enhanced despite the trauma that we experience. It is among the highest triumphs of human existence that it can achieve the overcoming and transformation of suffering in this way.

Yet even within the Christian tradition, these ways of turning suffering into something positive have been questioned. In a rich and complex argument, Simone Weil has stressed the irreducibly negative character of suffering even when conceived from a theological perspective. Weil argues that some suffering amounts to what she calls 'affliction': a form of suffering which damages the selfhood and crushes the spirit of its victim. Whereas everyday pain or suffering are troubles that we can cope with and in the face of which we can bless God for the challenges He sends us, affliction cannot but lead to despair. Whether because of the intensity or the interminable duration of the agony, the victim of affliction is reduced to being a *thing* completely determined by the blind forces of causality. Such suffering is a form of humiliation and of absolute degradation. To endure it is to be a slave to the pain and anguish that the victim undergoes. Moreover, by focusing the victim's attention exclusively on their own distress, it constitutes the victim as totally alienated in relation to others and to Otherness. Affliction leads to total separation from hope, from society and from God.

And yet, Weil goes on to say, it is precisely in this total abnegation that the victim participates in the affliction of Christ. Christ also suffered abandonment by God. The following passages give the flavour of Weil's thinking:

Men struck down by affliction are at the foot of the Cross, almost at the greatest possible distance from God.

As for us men, our misery gives us the infinitely precious privilege of sharing in this distance placed between the Son and his Father.

If the tree of life, and not simply the divine seed, is already formed in a man's soul at the time when extreme affliction strikes him, then he is nailed to the same cross as Christ.[8]

The key to Weil's thinking in these quotations is the notion of distance. Weil argues that the incarnation both establishes and bridges the distance between God and creation, but without thereby alleviating the meaninglessness and alienation of creation. The Cross of Christ therefore represents the reality of the abandonment and hopelessness of the human condition arising from its distance from God. Affliction is a state which we must all accept, just as Christ did, because it is inevitable within our created condition.

And yet Weil does not deduce from these insights that affliction has a positive meaning. She rejects utterly any doctrine of providence. Creation really is meaningless and purposeless and our place in it really is subject to the utter degradation of affliction. The perennial cry of every afflicted person, 'Why?', was uttered by Christ himself and received no answer. We must simply accept that the love of God sets up this distance between creation (including the incarnate Christ) and Himself. It is because of this distance that affliction (as well as other more positive mysteries such as beauty) occurs. Our quest for meaning yields only silence, and in this silence is the space for love and faith: 'God's secret word of love can be nothing else but silence.'[9]

Suffering in a secular age

The Jewish philosopher Emmanuel Levinas also firmly rejects the possibility that suffering has any providential meaning. Reflecting on the Holocaust, Levinas concedes that suffering of such magnitude and such uselessness cannot be absorbed into a justifying theological narrative. God was silent in Auschwitz, and remains so. And yet there is a non-theological meaning that can be ascribed to suffering if our view of our own suffering might be different from our view of the suffering of others. Indeed, it must be different. To say of the suffering of another that it is justified by having a meaning or a purpose is to denigrate the other by making him a means to some purpose. It is an immoral gesture which refuses to see the suffering for what it is: useless. Our response to the suffering of the other must be compassion, not explanation. Indeed, Levinas argues that suffering is a unique possibility for overcoming the isolation that we all experience as atomistic individuals in a narcissistic society. Even in our own experience, suffering cannot be absorbed into the world that we constitute for ourselves as our own. It is always strange and foreign. Whereas it is the existential nature of our being to be active in relation to the world, in the face of suffering we are passive. As a result, suffering

---

8   Simone Weil, 'The Love of God and Affliction', in George A. Panichas (ed.), *The Simone Weil Reader* (New York, 1977), pp. 444, 446 and 453.

9   Ibid., p. 467.

is always an alienation of our being. It destroys our self-possession and our enjoyment of life.

This allows us to be open to the suffering of the other through compassion. Rather than being enclosed in the solipsism of self-concern with the presence of the other experienced as a mere rational posit unable to touch our being in its intimacy, our encounter with the suffering of another calls upon our responsibility and awakens us to the real presence of the other in his or her need. In this way the negativity and meaninglessness of suffering, rather than being wiped out in a theodicy, provides the basis of real contact with others. It creates the interpersonal space in which ethics can occur. As Levinas puts it, 'For pure suffering, which is intrinsically meaningless and condemned to itself without exit, a beyond takes shape in the inter-human.'[10] My helping the other is a recognition of that person's being, and a recognition no mere theoretical thought could accomplish. Suffering, therefore, has a meaning in the interhuman world that preserves its inherent negativity, and, as such, it grounds ethics.

Are such ways of giving meaning to suffering still available in a postmodern secular age? What meaning is available for people without religious or even humanistic faith? A schematic answer can be found in the ancient Stoic philosophers and in Nietzsche, who in different ways embraced a tragic sense of life. They held that there is no plan, no purpose and no meaning to existence arising from reality itself. The cosmos does not run in accordance with a divine plan or inherent goal. There is no overarching fate or justice. The world is just a vast dynamic system of change and becoming. Everything becomes what it is and changes in systems of mutual interaction and effect. Human beings are subject to 'the slings and arrows of outrageous fortune'. Whatever happens is caused by blind and purposeless processes. It is appropriate to do what we can to protect ourselves from bad luck and evil, but if we become victims we can only accept what has happened as inevitable. There is no transcendent meaning to be given to it.

Nonetheless, to accept suffering as the result of blind fate, or even to love fate, as Nietzsche would put it, is to give meaning to our suffering. To see suffering this way is still to exercise the contemplative and meaning-giving side of our existence, since to adopt such a view is still to insert our suffering into a larger theory of reality. It gives suffering the meaning of tragedy even while it says that suffering is meaningless. And so the tragic view of life is a real alternative among the various ways that the contemplative aspect of our being gives meaning to suffering.

The Stoic philosophers encapsulated their view in saying that we should live life 'in agreement with nature'.[11] By this they variously meant that we should live in accordance with human virtue or with natural law. To be moral was all. This in

---

[10]   Emmanuel Levinas, 'Useless Suffering', in R. Bernasconi and D. Wood (eds), *The Provocation of Levinas: Rethinking the Other* (London, 1988), p. 159.

[11]   Diogenes Laertius, SVF I, 179a (I, 552), taken from the compendium 'Early Stoic Ethics', edited by J.L. Saunders, in *Greek and Roman Philosophy After Aristotle* (New York, 1966).

turn meant that we should seek good things, shun bad things and be indifferent to things that are indifferent. Among the indifferent things is health, since it can be used for good or bad actions and so is in itself morally neutral.[12] Good things are those that make us morally good, and bad things are those that make us morally bad, but of itself, health does neither. And so it is with the opposite of health. As Seneca put it: 'That which is evil does harm; that which does harm makes a man worse. But pain and poverty do not make a man worse; therefore, they are not evils.'[13] Epictetus offers similar advice in paragraphs 8 and 9 of his *Manual*:

> Ask not that events should happen as you will, but let your will be that events should happen as they do, and you shall have peace.
> Sickness is a hindrance to the body, but not to the will, unless the will consent. Lameness is a hindrance to the leg, but not to the will. Say this to yourself at each event that happens, for you shall find that though it hinders something else it will not hinder you.[14]

Epictetus' thought is, first, that those people who accept everything that befalls them in the physical world will live with equanimity, and second, that illness, lameness and other forms of suffering are physical events: they affect the body but not the will or moral being of a person. Provided this moral being is kept intact, the person will experience inner freedom and peace. Acceptance of fate, along with a focus on our inner existence, are the guarantees of a peaceful mode of being.

In this conception, suffering is something towards which the victim should remain indifferent. It is neither good nor bad. It is to be given no meaning. The contemplative dimension of our being should not trouble itself with it and should look beyond it towards an eternal and changeless nature conceived as moral and transcendent. We can see the influence of Plato's Socrates on this view. The tragic view of life, as articulated by the Stoics, leads to a life that secures our moral being and integrity by withdrawing from our worldly existence. But it is not likely to be useful to us today. While we may view it with admiration, its emphasis on withdrawal from life as lived ensures that it will not have much appeal to our modern sensibilities.

---

[12] An anonymous reviewer of this journal article has pointed out that the Stoics did differentiate amongst the indifferent things. Some could be preferred.: 'According to this doctrine, some ultimately indifferent things, including health, are nevertheless preferable to their opposites and are therefore legitimate objects of pursuit so long as one keeps in mind their ultimate status as indifferent to true human fulfilment, which consists in moral worth alone.'

[13] Diogenes Laertius, SVF III, in Saunders, p. 166.

[14] 'The Manual of Epictetus', paragraphs 8 and 9, in Saunders, p. 135.

Pain within a life project

Although he owes much to the Stoic philosophers, Nietzsche presents us with another suggestion as to how a positive meaning might be given to suffering. He develops it in this typically rhetorical and eloquent passage:

> You want if possible – and there is no madder 'if possible' – *to abolish* suffering; and we? – it really does seem that we would rather increase it and make it worse than it has ever been! Wellbeing as you understand it – that is no goal, that seems to us an *end*! A state which soon renders man ludicrous and contemptible – which makes it *desirable* that he should perish! The discipline of suffering, of *great* suffering – do you not know that it is *this* discipline alone which has created every elevation of mankind hitherto? That tension of the soul in misfortune which cultivates its strength, its terror at the sight of great destruction, its inventiveness and bravery in undergoing, enduring, interpreting, exploiting misfortune, and whatever of depth, mystery, mask, spirit, cunning and greatness has been bestowed upon it – has it not been bestowed through suffering, through the discipline of great suffering?[15]

Nietzsche praised suffering as the means whereby a higher order of humanity will evolve, and strongly disparaged pleasure and comfort as goals of human life. He hated utilitarianism, thinking it a doctrine that gave moral worth to the satisfaction of desire for its own sake. Rather, he admired what he saw as the overcoming of our human natures by way of effort and striving. He admired commitment, dedication and the willingness to put up with hardship and pain in the pursuit of a noble goal and, in particular, in the fulfilment of our existential quest for self-affirmation and self-assertion. He saw this quest as leading to a newer and better kind of human being. But this being who would overcome mere humanity would not emerge if we focused only on comfort and the avoidance of suffering. The avoidance of pain and amelioration of suffering were forces of decadence which led to the softening of the human spirit and a loss of focus upon the task of self-overcoming, which was essential to human advancement. Suffering was the crucible in which a higher form of humanity could be forged.

Nietzsche's view is attractive. It is implicitly accepted by nations that define their identity through the suffering and sacrifice of its founding fathers or its war heroes,[16] as Australia does with its annual celebration of a major military defeat on Anzac Day. In at least one respect, too, Nietzsche's view is similar to the view of some Christians since it embraces suffering as a sacrifice for a higher goal. Indeed, Nietzsche's view might seem noble were it not for his further view about pity. Nietzsche thought that pity belittles the person who feels it as well as the person

---

[15] Friedrich Nietzsche, *Beyond Good and Evil*, trans. R.J. Hollingdale (Harmondsworth, 1973), paragraph 225. (Emphases in the original.)

[16] For a thorough exploration of this issue, see Joseph A. Amato, *Victims and Values: A History and a Theory of Suffering* (New York, 1990).

who is its object. It belittles the person who feels it because it shows that that person fails to appreciate the positive power of suffering, and it belittles the object of pity because it represents that person as failing to bear suffering courageously. Pity goes hand in hand with the desire for comfort, thought Nietzsche, and should be repudiated on that account. But if the rejection of pity constitutes a rejection of compassion, then Nietzsche's view should itself be repudiated. So understood, Nietzsche comes to seem callous and uncaring.

Whether or not we reject Nietzsche's ideas, however, his position is important for understanding how we confront suffering. Even if abhorrent, it expresses the attitudes to suffering that many people in our culture have. It is yet another theory, created by the contemplative aspect of our being, of how suffering might be made more meaningful. In this theory there is a story of how humanity reaches its highest types and of how suffering is necessary for this to be achieved. Interestingly, Nietzsche himself would not dispute this framing of his account; he would react to it with irony. It was his view that humanity tells itself a variety of stories in order to make life livable, and that his own story is just one of these. None of these creations of contemplative reason could be taken as ultimately true, including Nietzsche's own.

The reason that Nietzsche's view and its self-deprecating irony finds a ready response in contemporary postmodern thinking is that such thinking rejects meaning-giving accounts which depend on overarching theories of providence or human progress. In postmodern thinking there is little scope for contemplative reason. However, the existential quest for meaning that used to be expressed in the theoretical aspect of our being is still in us. In a postmodern culture it is exercised in the 'integrative' aspect of our being,[17] the aspect in which we engage in the pre-conscious task of combining the various dimensions of our lives together so as to constitute our wholeness and identity. This can be achieved by faith or commitment. Just as a sports coach urges commitment upon us so that our whole being becomes focused upon the task of winning a match, so Nietzsche might be seen as urging us to live in a committed way. Which ideals and hopes we are committed to does not much matter; they would all be meaning-giving stories anyway. But the key point is that we achieve the integration of our being by infusing every aspect of our existence, including the bodily, with the enthusiasm for, and commitment to, those of our goals that define our identity. Both our zest for living and our practical tasks would in this way become, along with our very biological being, an expression of our commitment. Our highest ideals would shape the way we live. Our bodies would be infused and enlivened by our commitments, not just as their vehicle, but as their very expression, for we feel more alive when we are engaged upon an absorbing task. In this way we overcome the all-too-human desire for comfort and security and extend ourselves both physically and spiritually towards the goal of self-overcoming. Our pain, effort and

---

[17]   For a wide-ranging discussion, see Zygmunt Bauman, *Life in Fragments: Essays in Postmodern Morality* (Oxford, 1995).

struggle would then not be meaningless suffering since it would not frustrate our whole being. While there might be pain and hardship, our commitment and drive for becoming would shape all of them into a single life project. Our pain and hardship would validate our identity.

Whether this way of thinking would allow us to embrace the suffering that is inflicted by disease or accident, the suffering which is not part of our life's plan, is perhaps still doubtful. Useless suffering in the face of which we are passive might continue to be meaningless in terms of our life's goals. Or it might be embraced as the test of our mettle: the ultimate ordeal through which our existential faith and commitment might be tested. Whether one is a Christian who sees suffering as part of God's salvific plan for humanity, a humanist who thinks that suffering grounds the possibility of ethics through compassion, a Stoic who maintains an indifference towards suffering as something morally irrelevant, or a Nietzschean who holds that suffering ennobles the human spirit and makes possible human advancement and personal self-validation, the perennial and inescapable question of the one who suffers is: 'Why me?' But rather than seek an answer to that question, we should ask, in the spirit of Nietzsche, why we want an answer to it. The challenge of postmodern authenticity is to sever the link between suffering and justice. It is to accept the blindness of fate and the inevitability of bad luck. It is to refuse the false consolations of theodicies or metaphysical theories that make suffering positive. Suffering is to be borne. There is nothing more to it.

The only question remaining about this way of thinking would be whether it could give rise to compassion for the suffering of others. That is, if we reject the ancient and Christian attempts to accept suffering, are we left with a self-assertive Nietzschean position which rejects pity, or can we incorporate some part of Levinas' humanistic insight? The latter seems possible. Insofar as suffering is borne, it opens us to the suffering of others. Indeed, attempts to make suffering seem good blind us to the reality of our and of others' suffering by allowing us to accept it as something that ought to happen or that ought to be accepted. Cruelty and insensitivity lie down this path. The tragic bearing of suffering, on the other hand, awakens us to its reality. If neither the gods, the cosmos, providence nor a faith in human progress rob suffering of its negativity, then we are left just with the brute fact that we and others suffer. And in this there is community. Our own suffering awakens us to what the other is going through and thus creates in us the compassion through which relieving actions can be motivated. In this community of suffering, a meaning might yet be found for our own suffering. Perhaps all the meaning that suffering can have is that it teaches us to care for others.

Bibliography

Agich, George J., 'Professionalism and Ethics in Health Care', *Journal of Medicine and Philosophy*, 5/3 (1980): 186–99.

Allmark, P., 'Can there be an ethics of care?', *Journal of Medical Ethics*, 21/1 (1995): 19–24.

Amato, Joseph A., *Victims and Values: A History and a Theory of Suffering* (New York: Greenwood Press, 1990).

Anscombe, G.E.M., 'Modern Moral Philosophy', *Philosophy: The Journal of the Royal Institute of Philosophy*, 33 (1958): 1–19.

Aristotle, *Nicomachean Ethics*, in Richard McKeon (ed.), *The Basic Works of Aristotle* (New York: Random House, 1941), pp. 935–1126.

Audi, R., *Moral Knowledge and Ethical Character* (New York: Oxford University Press, 1997).

Autton, Norman, *Pain: An Exploration* (London: Darton, Longman and Todd, 1986).

Barondess, Jeremiah A., 'Disease and Illness – a Crucial Distinction', *The American Journal of Medicine*, 66 (1979): 375–6.

Bauman, Zygmunt, *Life in Fragments: Essays in Postmodern Morality* (Oxford: Blackwell, 1995).

Beauchamp, Tom L., 'What's So Special About the Virtues?', in Joram Graf Haber (ed.), *Doing and Being: Selected Readings in Moral Philosophy* (New York: Macmillan, 1993), pp. 212–20.

———— and Childress, J.F., *Principles of Biomedical Ethics,* 4th edn, (New York: Oxford University Press, 1994).

Bedau, H.A., *Making Mortal Choices: Three Exercises in Moral Casuistry* (New York and Oxford: Oxford University Press, 1997).

Blattner, Barbara, *Holistic Nursing* (Englewood Cliffs, New Jersey: Prentice-Hall, 1981).

Blum, Lawrence A., 'Compassion', in A.O. Rorty (ed.), *Explaining Emotions* (Berkeley, California: University of California Press, 1980), pp. 507–18

————, *Moral Perception and Particularity* (Cambridge: Cambridge University Press, 1994).

Boele, Dries, 'The "Benefits" of a Socratic Dialogue. Or: Which Results Can We Promise?', *Inquiry: Critical Thinking Across the Disciplines*, XVII/3 (1997): 48–69.

Boorse, Christopher, 'On the Distinction between Disease and Illness', in Arthur L. Caplan, H. Tristram Engelhardt Jr and James J. McCartney (eds), *Concepts of Health and Disease: Interdisciplinary Perspectives* (Reading, Massachusetts: Addison-Wesley, 1981), pp. 545–60.

Boykin A. and Schoenhofer S., *Nursing as Caring: A Model for Transforming Practice* (New York: National League for Nursing Press, 1993).

Buber, Martin, *I and Thou*, new translation with a prologue by W. Kaufmann (Edinburgh: T. & T. Clark, 1970).

Button, Victoria, 'Cancer patients not given drugs', *The Age*, 23 November (1999): 8.

Callahan, Daniel et al., 'The Goals of Medicine: Setting New Priorities' *Hastings Center Report*, 26/6 (1996): S9–S13.

Calnan, Michael, *Health and Illness: The Lay Perspective* (London: Tavistock, 1987).

Campbell, E.J.M., Scadding, J.G. and Roberts, R.S., 'The Concept of Disease', *British Medical Journal*, 29 September (1979): 757–62.

Carper, B.A., 'The Ethics of Caring', *Advances in Nursing Sciences*, 1/3 (1979): 11–20.

Cassell, Eric J., *The Nature of Suffering and the Goals of Medicine* (New York: Oxford University Press, 1991).

———, 'The Nature of Suffering: Physical, Psychological, Social, and Spiritual Aspects', in Patricia L. Starck and John P. McGovern (eds), *The Hidden Dimension of Illness: Human Suffering* (New York: National League for Nursing Press, 1992), pp. 1–10.

Cates, D.F. and Lauritzen, P. (eds), *Medicine and the Ethics of Care* (Washington, DC: Georgetown University Press, 2001).

Cocking, D. and Oakley, J., *Virtue Ethics and Professional Roles* (Cambridge, Cambridge University Press, 2001).

Cooper, David E., *The Measure of Things: Humanism, Humility, and Mystery* (Oxford: Oxford University Press, 2002).

Cornford, F.M., *From Religion to Philosophy: A Study in the Origins of Western Speculation* (New York: Harper Torchbooks, 1957).

Coulter, Harris L., *Divided Legacy: A History of the Schism in Medical Thought*, 3 vols (Washington, DC: Wehawken Book Company, 1977).

Dancy, Jonathan, *Moral Reasons* (Oxford: Blackwell, 1993).

Davidson, Donald, *Essays on Actions and Events* (Oxford: Oxford University Press, 1980).

Dewey, John, *Art as Experience*, first published in 1934 (New York: Paragon Books, 1979).

Dordoni, Paolo and van Hooft, Stan, 'Socratic Dialogue and Medical Ethics', in Patricia Shipley and Heidi Mason (eds), *Ethics and Socratic Dialogue in Civil Society* (Münster: Lit Verlag, 2004), pp. 205–12.

Dossey, Larry, *Beyond Illness: Discovering the Experience of Health* (Boston, Massachusetts: Shambhala Publications, 1984).

Dubos, René, *Mirage of Health: Utopias, Progress and Biological Change* (New York: Harper and Row, 1959).

——, *Man, Medicine and Environment* (Harmondsworth: Penguin Books, 1970).

Engel, George L., 'The Need for a New Medical Model: A Challenge for Biomedicine', in Arthur L. Caplan, H. Tristram Engelhardt Jr and James J. McCartney (eds), *Concepts of Health and Disease: Interdisciplinary Perspectives* (Reading, Massachusetts: Addison-Wesley, 1981), pp. 589–607.

Evans, J.H., 'A Sociological Account of the Growth of Principlism', *Hastings Center Report*, 30/5 (2000): 31–8.

Fabrega, Horacio, Jr, 'The Scientific Usefulness of the Idea of Illness', in Arthur L. Caplan, H. Tristram Engelhardt Jr, and James J. McCartney (eds), *Concepts of Health and Disease: Interdisciplinary Perspectives* (Reading, Massachusetts: Addison-Wesley, 1981), pp. 131–42.

Fitzgerald, L. and van Hooft, S., 'A Socratic Dialogue on the Question: What is Love in Nursing', *Nursing Ethics*, 7/6 (2000): 481–91.

Flanagan, O., *Varieties of Moral Personality* (Cambridge, Massachusetts: Harvard University Press, 1991).

Flew, Anthony, *Crime or Disease?* (New York: Oxford University Press, 1973).

Foucault, Michel, *The Birth of the Clinic: An Archaeology of Medical Perception*, trans. A.M. Sheridan Smith (London: Tavistock Publications, 1973).

Frankfurt, Harry, 'The Importance of what we care about', *Synthese*, 53/2 (1982): 257–72.

Fulford, K.W.M., *Moral Theory and Medical Practice* (Cambridge: Cambridge University Press, 1989).

Fuller, Benjamin F., *Physician or Magician: The Myths and Realities of Patient Care* (New York: McGraw-Hill, 1978).

Gastmans, C., Dierckx de Casterle, B. and Schotsmans, P., 'Nursing Considered as Moral Practice: A Philosophical-ethical Interpretation of Nursing', *Kennedy Institute of Ethics Journal*, 8/1 (1998): 43–69.

Gilligan, Carol, *In a Different Voice: Psychological Theory and Women's Development* (Cambridge, Massachusetts: Harvard University Press, 1982).

Gillon, Raanan, 'On Sickness and on Health', *British Medical Journal*, 292/1 (1986): 318–20.

——, *Philosophical Medical Ethics* (Chichester: John Wiley, 1986).

Griffin, A.P., 'A Philosophical Analysis of Caring in Nursing', *Journal of Advanced Nursing*, 8/4 (1983): 289–95.

Griffin, J., 'Virtue Ethics and Environs', *Social Philosophy and Policy*, 15/1 (1998): 56–70.

Gustafson, Winnifred, 'Motivational and Historical Aspects of Care and Nursing', in Madeleine M. Leininger (ed.), *Care: The Essence of Nursing and Health* (Thorofare, New Jersey: Slack, 1984), pp. 61–74.

Haber, J.G. (ed.), *Doing and Being: Selected Readings in Moral Philosophy* (New York: Macmillan, 1993).

Habermas, Jürgen, *Knowledge and Human Interests*, trans. J.J. Shapiro (London: Heinemann, 1972).

Hafen, Brent Q., Karren, Keith J., Frandsen, Kathryn J. and Lee Smith, N., *Mind/Body Health: The Effects of Attitudes, Emotions and Relationships* (Boston, Massachusetts: Allyn and Bacon, 1996).

Hammer, Leon, *Dragon Rises, Red Bird Flies: Psychology, Energy and Chinese Medicine* (New York: Station Hill Press, 1990).

Hare, R.M., *Moral Thinking: Its Levels, Method and Point* (Oxford: Oxford University Press, 1981).

Harré, Rom, *Social Being: A Theory for Social Psychology* (Oxford: Blackwell, 1979).

Hauerwas, Stanley, 'Reflections on Suffering, Death, and Medicine', in Stanley Hauerwas, *Suffering Presence: Theological Reflections on Medicine, the Mentally Handicapped, and the Church* (Notre Dame, Indiana: University of Notre Dame Press, 1986), pp. 23–38.

Heidegger, Martin, *Being and Time*, trans. John Macquarie and Edward Robinson (Oxford: Blackwell, 1962).

Helman, Cecil G., 'Disease versus Illness in General Practice', *Journal of the Royal College of General Practitioners*, 31 (1981): 548–52.

Humber, James and Almeder, Robert (eds), *What is Disease?*, Biomedical Ethics Reviews Series (Totowa, New Jersey: The Humana Press, 1997).

James, William, *The Principles of Psychology*, authorized edn, first published in 1918, unabridged (New York: Dover Publications, 1950).

Johns, C. and Freshwater D. (eds), *Transforming Nursing Through Reflective Practice* (Oxford: Blackwell Science, 1998).

Jourard, Sidney, *The Transparent Self* (Princeton, New Jersey: Van Nostrand, 1964).

Kant, Immanuel, *Religion within the Limits of Reason Alone*, trans. Theodore M Greene and Hoyt H. Hudson (New York: Harper and Row, 1934).

Kass, Leon, 'Regarding the end of Medicine and the Pursuit of Health', in Arthur L. Caplan, H. Tristram Engelhardt Jr and James J. McCartney (eds), *Concepts of Health and Disease: Interdisciplinary Perspectives* (Reading, Massachusetts: Addison-Wesley, 1981), pp. 9–18.

King, Lester S., 'What is Disease?', in Arthur L. Caplan, H. Tristram Engelhardt Jr and James J. McCartney (eds), *Concepts of Health and Disease: Interdisciplinary Perspectives* (Reading, Massachusetts: Addison-Wesley, 1981), pp. 107–18.

Kluge, Eike-Henner W., 'Nursing, Vocation or Profession', *Canadian Nurse*, 78/2 (1982): 34–6.

Komesaroff, P.A., 'From bioethics to microethics: ethical debate and clinical medicine', in P.A. Komesaroff (ed.), *Troubled Bodies: Critical Perspectives on Postmodernism, Medical Ethics, and the Body* (Melbourne: Melbourne University Press, 1995), pp. 62–86.

Kopelman, Loretta, 'The Punishment Concept of Disease', in Christine Pierce and Donald Van De Veer (eds), *Aids: Ethics and Public Policy* (Belmont California: Wadsworth, 1988), pp. 49–55.

Kovesi, Julius, *Moral Notions* (London: Routledge and Kegan Paul, 1967).

Kuhse, H., *Caring: Nurses, Women and Ethics* (Oxford: Blackwell, 1997).

Lear, J., *Love and its Place in Nature: A Philosophical Interpretation of Freudian Psychoanalysis* (New York: Farrar, Straus and Giroux, 1990).

Leder, Drew, *The Absent Body* (Chicago, Illinois: The University of Chicago Press, 1990).

Leininger, Madeleine (ed.), *Care: The Essence of Nursing and Health* (Thorofare, New Jersey: Charles B. Slack, 1984).

Levin, David Michael, *The Body's Recollection of Being: Phenomenological Psychology and the Deconstruction of Nihilism* (London: Routledge and Kegan Paul, 1985).

—— and Solomon, George F., 'The discursive formation of the body in the history of medicine', *Journal of Medicine and Philosophy*, 15 (1990): 515–37.

Levinas, Emmanuel, *Totality and Infinity: An Essay on Exteriority*, trans. Alphonso Lingis (Pittsburgh, Pennsylvania: Duquesne University Press, 1969).

——, 'Useless Suffering', in R. Bernasconi and D. Wood (eds), *The Provocation of Levinas: Rethinking the Other* (London: Routledge, 1988), pp. 159–67.

——, 'Ethics as First Philosophy', in Seán Hand (ed.), *The Levinas Reader* (Oxford: Basil Blackwell, 1989), pp. 75–87.

Lewis, C.S., *The Problem of Pain* (London: Collins, 1940).

Lewis, G., 'Some Studies of Social Causes of and Cultural Response to Disease', in C.G.N. Mascie-Taylor (ed.), *The Anthropology of Disease* (Oxford: Oxford University Press, 1993), pp. 73–124.

Louden, Robert B., 'On Some Vices of Virtue Ethics', in Joram Graf Haber (ed.), *Doing and Being: Selected Readings in Moral Philosophy* (New York: Macmillan, 1993), pp. 191–214.

Lyddon, William J., 'Emerging Views of Health: A Challenge to Rationalist Doctrines of Medical Thought', *The Journal of Mind and Behavior*, 8/3 (1987): 365–94.

MacIntyre, Alasdair, *After Virtue: A Study in Moral Theory* (London: Duckworth, 1981).

——, 'To whom is the Nurse Responsible?, in Howard Murphy and Catherine Hunter (eds), *Ethical Problems in the Nurse Patient Relationship*, (Boston, Massachusetts: Allyn and Bacon, 1983).

Mackenzie, Norah, *The Professional Ethic and the Hospital Service* (London: The English Universities Press, 1971).

MacLean, Anne, *The Elimination of Morality: Reflections on Utilitarianism and Bioethics* (London and New York: Routledge, 1993).

Madjar, Irena, 'The body in health, illness and pain', in Jocalyn Lawler (ed.), *The Body in Nursing* (Melbourne: Churchill Livingstone, 1997), pp. 53–73.

Marcel, G., *The Philosophy of Existence*, trans. R.F. Grabow (ed.) (Philadelphia, Pennsylvania: The University of Pennsylvania Press, 1971).

Margolis, Joseph, 'The Concept of Disease', in Arthur L. Caplan, H. Tristram Engelhardt Jr and James J. McCartney (eds), *Concepts of Health and Disease: Interdisciplinary Perspectives* (Reading, Massachusetts: Addison-Wesley, 1981), pp. 561–77.

Maslow, Abraham H., 'Health as Transcendence of Environment', *Journal of Humanistic Psychology*, 1 (1961): 1–7.

Mayeroff, M., *On Caring* (New York: Harper and Row, 1971).

Mead, George Herbert, *Mind, Self and Society from the Standpoint of a Social Behaviorist* (Chicago, Illinois: University of Chicago Press, 1934).

Mechanic, David, 'The Concept of Illness Behaviour', in Arthur L. Caplan, H. Tristram Engelhardt Jr James J. McCartney (eds), *Concepts of Health and Disease: Interdisciplinary Perspectives* (Reading, Massachusetts: Addison-Wesley, 1981), pp. 485–92.

Merleau-Ponty, Maurice, *The Phenomenology of Perception,* trans. Colin Smith (London: Routledge and Kegan Paul, 1962).

Merskey, H. and Bogduk. N., *Classification of Chronic Pain: Descriptions of Chronic Pain Syndromes and Definitions of Pain Terms,* 2nd edn (Seattle, Washington State: International Association for the Study of Pain Press, 1994).

Mill, John Stuart, 'Utilitarianism', in Alan Ryan (ed.), *John Stuart Mill and Jeremy Bentham: Utilitarianism and Other Essays* (London: Penguin Books, 1987), pp. 272–338.

Nagel, Thomas, 'Sexual Perversion', in Alan Soble (ed.), *The Philosophy of Sex: Contemporary Readings* (Totowa, New Jersey: Rowman and Littlefield, 1980), pp. 76–88.

———, *The View from Nowhere* (New York: Oxford University Press, 1986).

Nelson, L., *Socratic Method and Critical Philosophy* (New Haven, Connecticutt: Yale University Press, 1940).

Newman, Margaret A., *Health as Expanding Consciousness* (St Louis, Missouri: C.V. Mosby, 1986).

Nietzsche, Friedrich Wilhelm, *The Will to Power*, trans. W. Kaufmann and R.J. Hollingdale (New York: Vintage Books, 1968).

———, *Beyond Good and Evil: Prelude to a Philosophy of the Future,* trans. R.J. Hollingdale (Harmondsworth: Penguin Books, 1973).

Nokes, Peter, *The Professional Task in Welfare Practice* (London: Routledge and Kegan Paul, 1967).

Nussbaum, Martha C., *The Fragility of Goodness: Luck and Ethics in Greek Tragedy and Philosophy* (New York: Cambridge University Press, 1986).

Oakley, Ann, *Telling the Truth about Jerusalem* (Oxford: Basil Blackwell, 1986).

Oakley, J., 'Varieties of Virtue Ethics', *Ratio* (New Series), IX/2 (1996): 128–53.

Pagels, Elaine, *Adam, Eve and the Serpent* (London: Weidenfeld and Nicolson, 1988).

Parsons, Talcott, 'Definitions of Health and Illness in the Light of American Values and Social Structures', in Arthur L. Caplan, H. Tristram Engelhardt Jr and James J. McCartney (eds), *Concepts of Health and Disease: Interdisciplinary Perspectives* (Reading, Massachusetts: Addison-Wesley, 1981), pp. 57–81.

Pellegrino, Edmund D. and Thomasma, David C., *A Philosophical Basis of Medical Practice: Toward a Philosophy and Ethics of the Healing Professions* (New York: Oxford University Press, 1981).

———, 'Towards a Virtue-Based Normative Ethics for the Health Professions.' *Kennedy Institute of Ethics Journal*, 5/3 (1995): 253–78.

Pincoffs, Edmund L., *Quandaries and Virtues* (Lawrence, Kansas: University Press of Kansas, 1986).

Radley, Alan, *Making Sense of Illness: The Social Psychology of Health and Disease* (London: Sage Publications, 1994).

Rawls, John, 'The Sense of Justice', *Philosophical Review*, 72 (1963): 281–305.

———, *A Theory of Justice* (Oxford: Oxford University Press, 1971).

Reznek, Lawrie, *The Nature of Disease* (London: Routledge and Kegan Paul, 1987).

Riemen, Doris J., 'The Essential Structure of a Caring Interaction: A Phenomenological Study', PhD thesis, Texas Women's University (Ann Arbor, Michigan: University Microfilms International, 1983).

Roach, S.M., 'The Act of Caring as Expressed in a Code of Ethics', *Canadian Nurse*, 78/6 (1982): 30–32.

———, 'The Aim of Philosophical Inquiry in Nursing: Unity or Diversity of Thought?', in: J.F. Kikuchi and H. Simmons (eds), *Philosophical Inquiry in Nursing* (Newbury Park, California: Sage Publications, 1992), pp. 38–44.

Saran, Rene, and Neisser, Barbara (eds), *Inquiring Minds: Socratic Dialogue in Education* (Stoke on Trent: Trentham Books, 2004).

Sartre, Jean-Paul, *Being and Nothingness: A Phenomenological Essay on Ontology*, trans. Hazel E. Barnes (New York: Philosophical Library, 1956).

———, *Sketch for a Theory of the Emotions*, trans. Philip Mairet (London: Methuen, 1962).

Saunders, J.L. (ed.), *Greek and Roman Philosophy After Aristotle* (New York: The Free Press, 1966).

Scarry, Elaine, *The Body in Pain: The Making and Unmaking of the World* (New York: Oxford University Press. 1985).

Scheler, Max, *On the Nature of Sympathy*, trans. Peter Heath (London: Routledge and Kegan Paul, 1954).

Schultz, P.R., 'Clarifying the Concept of "Client" for Health-care Policy Formulation: Ethical Implications', in: J.W. Kenney (ed.), *Philosophical and Theoretical Perspectives for Advanced Nursing Practice* (Sudbury, Massachusetts: Jones and Bartlett, 1996), pp. 133–40.

Sedgwick, Peter, 'Illness – Mental and Otherwise', in Arthur L. Caplan, H. Tristram Engelhardt Jr and James J. McCartney (eds), *Concepts of Health and*

Disease: Interdisciplinary Perspectives (Reading, Massachusetts: Addison-Wesley, 1981), pp. 119–29.

Shipton, Edward A., *Pain: Acute and Chronic* (London: Arnold, 1999).

Singer, Peter, *Practical Ethics* (Cambridge: Cambridge University Press, 1979).

Slote, M., *From Morality to Virtue* (New York: Oxford University Press, 1992).

Smart, J.J.C. and Williams, B., *Utilitarianism For and Against* (Cambridge: Cambridge University Press, 1973).

Smith, Judith A., *The Idea of Health: Implications for the Nursing Professional* (New York: Teachers College Press, 1983).

Smith, Marion V. 'Talking about pain', in Bernadette Carter (ed.), *Perspectives on Pain: Mapping the Territory* (New York: Oxford University Press, 1998), pp. 26–45.

Smith, Peter and Jones, O.R., *The Philosophy of Mind: An Introduction* (Cambridge: Cambridge University Press, 1986).

Solomon, R.C., *A Passion for Justice: Emotions and the Origins of the Social Contract* (Reading, Massachusetts: Addison-Wesley, 1990).

Sontag, Susan, *Illness as Metaphor* (New York: Farrar, Straus and Giroux, 1978).

———, *Aids and its Metaphors* (New York: Farrar, Straus and Giroux, 1989).

Staiano, Kathryn V., *Interpreting Signs of Illness: A Case Study in Medical Semiotics* (Berlin: Mouton de Gruyter, 1986).

Statman, D., 'Introduction to Virtue Ethics', in D. Statman (ed.), *Virtue Ethics: A Critical Reader* (Edinburgh: Edinburgh University Press, 1997), pp. 1–41.

Stocker, M., 'The Schizophrenia of Modern Ethical Theories', *Journal of Philosophy*, LXXIII/14 (1976): 453–66.

Susser, Mervyn, 'Ethical Components in the Definition of Health', in Arthur L.Caplan, H. Tristram Engelhardt Jr and James J. McCartney (eds), *Concepts of Health and Disease: Interdisciplinary Perspectives* (Reading, Massachusetts: Addison-Wesley, 1981), pp. 93–105.

Szasz, Thomas S., *Pain and Pleasure: A Study of Bodily Feelings*, 2nd edn (New York: Basic Books, 1975).

Taylor, Rodney L. and Watson, Jean (eds), *They Shall Not Hurt: Human Suffering and Human Caring* (Boulder, Colorado: Associated University Press, 1989).

Temkin, Owsei, 'The Scientific Approach to Disease: Specific Entity and Individual Sickness', in Arthur L. Caplan, H. Tristram Engelhardt Jr and James J. McCartney (eds) *Concepts of Health and Disease: Interdisciplinary Perspectives* (Reading, Massachusetts: Addison-Wesley, 1981), pp. 247–63.

Tillich, Paul, *The Meaning of Health: Essays in Existentialism, Psychoanalysis, and Religion*, Perry LeFevre (ed.), first published 1946 (Chicago, Illinois: Exploration Press, 1984).

Toombs, Kay, 'The Body in Multiple Sclerosis: A Patient's Perspective', in Drew Leder (ed.), *The Body in Medical Thought and Practice* (Dordrecht: Kluwer Academic Publishers, 1992), pp. 127–37.

Toulmin, S.E., 'The Tyranny of Principles', *Hastings Center Report*, 11/6 (1981): 31–9.

van Hooft, Stan, 'Caring and Professional Commitment', *The Australian Journal of Advanced Nursing*, 4/4 (1987): 29–38.

———, 'Obligation, Character, and Commitment', *Philosophy*, 63 (1988): 345–62.

———, *Caring: An Essay in the Philosophy of Ethics* (Niwot, Colorado: University Press of Colorado, 1995).

———, 'Acting from the Virtue of Caring in Nursing', *Nursing Ethics*, 6/3 (1999): 189–201.

———, 'Kuhse on Caring', *Nursing Inquiry*, 6/2 (1999): 112–22.

———, 'What is Self-Fulfilment? A Report on a Socratic Dialogue', *Practical Philosophy*, 4/1 (2001): 47–54

———, *Life, Death, and Subjectivity: Moral Sources in Bioethics* (Amsterdam and New York: Rodopi, 2004).

———, *Understanding Virtue Ethics* (Chesham: Acumen, 2005).

———, Gillam, L., and Byrnes, M., *Facts and Values: An Introduction to Critical Thinking for Nurses* (Sydney: MacLennan and Petty, 1995).

Veatch, Robert M., 'The Medical Model: Its Nature and Problems', in Arthur L. Caplan, H. Tristram Engelhardt Jr and James J. McCartney (eds), *Concepts of Health and Disease: Interdisciplinary Perspectives* (Reading, Massachusetts: Addison-Wesley, 1981), pp. 523–44.

Watson, Jean, *Nursing: Human Science and Human Care: A Theory of Nursing* (Norwalk, Connecticut: Appleton-Century-Crofts, 1985).

Weil, Simone, 'The Love of God and Affliction', in George A. Panichas (ed.), *The Simone Weil Reader* (New York: David McKay, 1977), pp. 444–53.

White, Alan R., *Attention* (Oxford: Basil Blackwell, 1964).

Williams, Bernard, 'Internal and external reasons', in Bernard Williams (ed.), *Moral Luck* (Cambridge: Cambridge University Press, 1981), pp. 101–13.

———, *Ethics and the Limits of Philosophy* (Glasgow: William Collins, 1985).

Wittgenstein, Ludwig, *Philosophical Investigations*, trans. G.E.M. Anscombe (Oxford: Basil Blackwell, 1963).

World Health Organization, *Official Record No. 2* (New York: World Health Organization, 1946).

Zaner, Richard M., 'Chance and Morality: The Dialysis Phenomenon', in Victor Kestenbaum (ed.), *The Humanity of the Ill: Phenomenological Perspectives* (Knoxville, Tennessee: The University of Tennessee Press, 1982), pp. 38–68.

Index